INTERVENTION OR ABSTENTION

Intervention

The Dilemma

or Abstention:

of American Foreign Policy

Robin Higham, editor

The University Press of Kentucky

ISBN: 0-8131-1317-2

2-6-76

Library of Congress Catalog Card Number: 74-18934

CONTENTS

PREFACE

THE PURPOSE of this volume is to show that intervention or abstention is not merely a military matter, but that it encompasses several facets of a nation's life. More than this, how that intervention or abstention is viewed and how the armed forces as the most visible part of the decision-making process is viewed depends on where the observer is standing. Thus this volume is not devoted solely to martial affairs but is concerned with a number of facets of American interests including both domestic and foreign views. It is notable, as the essay on the Manchurian crisis reveals, that even in such crucial internal discussions, as apparently in more recent ones, there has at times been a failure to take a realistic view of the position and prospects of the armed forces. The lessons of British experience between the two world wars should not be forgotten—that diplomatic positions have no power unless backed by force. But the lesson of the 1971 Bangladesh affair must not be lost sight of either—that a threat of force based upon personal pique, in addition to backing an ally who could not be aided, is a sure way to lose the respect of both friends and opponents.

Robin Higham

EDITOR'S INTRODUCTION

THE FOREIGN POLICY of any power—its intervention, neutrality, or abstention—varies roughly in relation to its economic activity and its military power. Thus political activity abroad in the national interest followed trade in settled areas, as well as in colonial, until America reached the peak of her power in 1945. Thereafter confidence was replaced by fear (reaction rather than action started to determine the nation's destiny) and the activity tended to reverse itself. In the days of self-assurance, diplomacy followed trade and investment when needed, and sometimes, as when Secretary of State Philander C. Knox pushed a consortium for railroad building in the Far East, even propelled it. But since 1945 American diplomacy has had twin thrusts more important and obvious than the promotion and protection of trade and investment. Washington has actively campaigned for a world made over in the American image and has intervened militarily, either through supplying arms or, on a number of occasions, such as in Korea (1950-1953), Lebanon (1958), the Dominican Republic (1965), and in Vietnam in the 1960s, by direct military force.

The measurement of these intrusions has to be both in terms of the area into which armed forces were thrust and in relation to the support for and reaction to these actions at home. The reaction has even been determined by the type of forces employed. The navy has been maintained on station in the Far East and the Mediterranean in full fleet strength both as a shield and a threat, not only to the littoral powers but also against Russia and, later, China. But the navy has almost always enjoyed a sympathetic base at home, especially in its happy recruiting grounds of the isolationist Midwest. The marines caused no great stir when they went ashore in Lebanon (1958), but the use of the army in Dominica (1965) raised all the old liberal resentments at home that have their roots in the attitudes to British redcoats of colonial days.

The measurement of the employment of power, perhaps like the measurement of power itself, is both a contemporary matter and one which historians have to judge in the light of what people conceived the situation to be at the time. Perhaps too often in history, governments have been overly concerned with what the Machiavellian other side was going to do, without seeing the real or nominal opponent as sometimes but a simple victim. In the years since 1945 perhaps the closest this came to reality was when Kennedy confronted Khrushchev over the installation of Russian missiles in Cuba in 1962. To one who was in London in 1938 and in 1962, it was most interesting to hear the British saying, "JFK, who was here during Munich, is doing what Chamberlain should have done in 1938!" The difference is that Kennedy remembered his earlier experience, was confident that he had the power, and was backed by at least one adviser, his brother Robert, who delighted in political confrontations. Thus a Russian attempt at intervention in the Western Hemisphere was dramatically turned into an abstention of which James Monroe would have been proud.

In both the pre- and post-Potsdam eras—that is, before and after World War II—these generalizations about intervention or abstention would have to be modified by the conditions and attitudes in the three traditional areas of American diplomacy: Europe, the Western Hemisphere (really meaning south of the border), and the Far East. And even these traditional divisions have left a third segment of the world a no-man's land which is now being arbitrarily divided into South Asia, Africa, and the Middle East. The Third World was largely an area in which Britain was dominant and into which an ignorant America felt itself compelled to enter to forestall the Communists, and this in the best American crusading spirit. More recently the attitude toward Africa has been influenced by fear of a black mark if the response is favorable to apartheid South Africa, a strategically important point. But in this area the U.S. can hedge its bets by leasing the Cape to South Africa and Rhodesia, while supporting the Portuguese in East and West Africa by supplying arms to its NATO ally. This frees older weapons for use in the colonial war where they are efficient enough. New arms can thus be presumed for use only in Portugal's NATO role.

Undoubtedly American, *yanqui*, attitudes toward intervention or abstention have been influenced by the patterns of our history. In the westward movement since 1783 the whites pushed aggressively ahead, first as hunter and then as settler. Generally they intervened in Indian affairs and usually they used the army and the Indian agents as their attorneys. The French, the Spanish, the Mexicans, and the British were plainly told when they were not welcome. The French sold (1803), the British in 1812-1814 fought a battle of brothers, the Spanish ceded (1819), and the Mexicans were trounced in 1846. These actions allowed unhampered internal expansion, but did not guarantee the general security of the United States.

However, in the course of pursuing manifest destiny, the secretary of state latched onto the proposal of the British foreign secretary. The Monroe Doctrine, the culmination of the struggle for neutrality, assured George Canning that the United States would not interfere in Europe if the Royal Navy would keep Europeans from intervening in the Western Hemisphere, while assuming that the rest of the Canadian border problems, stalemated by the War of 1812, the Peace of Ghent, and the 1818 Rush-Bagot disarmament agreement could be settled by negotiation, as they were in 1842. This left the United States free to exploit the Louisiana purchase and eventually to take Texas, California, and the intervening barrens. For much of the rest of the nineteenth century, especially after 1865, there was enough unexploited space within the country to maintain an open frontier and to keep most dissatisfied citizens occupied on the land or in the industrial revolution. Improvements in health and rising immigration created such a domestic market that foreign trade was not a requirement. Indeed, the Civil War economically marked the end of the eighteenth century in that it finished the great overseas trading firms because their beautiful fast clipper ships were forced to take refuge under foreign flags and not allowed to return after the Confederate raiders were driven from the seven seas. Even by that time, the capital generated by New Englanders—in particular, in overseas trade, which has been thought to have been largely unsupported (though new scholarship may now disprove this) and even, indeed, sometimes actively opposed by southern presidents—had been reinvested in textiles and other manufacturing concerns. The Civil War and the westward movement provided markets and the new capital which, together with very large European investments, went into railroads and ranching to enable the new manufactures to be marketed in the West and the food raised there to be brought back to the urban workers who were forsaking agriculture for urban slums.

While the Civil War engendered some touchy moments diplomatically, there was far less concern in Europe to intervene in a civil war in a backward area such as the South or a developing one like the North than patrio-ethnocentric United States historians think. The Russian fleet came in 1863, for instance, not to help the Union, but to threaten Britain and France at sea in case they should be foolish enough to try to intervene in the Polish province. The Civil War was a turning point. The Union supplied the stimulus to build a railroad across the country and people began to think about Hawaii and other colonial spots. A small trade with the Far East continued as did involvements on occasion in Latin America. But just as the Civil War marked a change in the United States, in the apparent recementing of the Union, so the 1860s also saw a change in the emergence of the Dominion of Canada, the new Japan, and the rise of Germany and the humbling of Austria in Europe, as well as the end to France's Mexican violation of the Monroe Doctrine. However the United States did not react to an 1866 Spanish naval bombardment of Valparaiso. For the next thirty years, the U.S. was busy internally grabbing land or riches or grubbing for gold or subsistence. Few outside of Washington and occasional naval officers cared what the world did until the 1890s when the United States forced Chile to apologize for an attack on drunken seamen from the U.S.S. *Baltimore* and followed this with a strong stance in the Venezuelan incident, the acquisition of Hawaii and Samoa, the Spanish-American War, and the Open Door policy in the Far East. The argument may still rage over whether at this period trade followed the flag or the flag, trade, or whether the real impetus was crusading Anglo-Saxonism and the desire of God's chosen people to spread the true word. Whatever the reasons, the United States emerged as a world-conscious power.

1898-1945

Some of this new globalism can be found in the interests of various people in power from James G. Blaine with his pushy Latin-American policy to the opinionated, but more widely read and educated, Theodore Roosevelt. The latter, in particular, a rough-riding knight, was a man of aristocratic background and adventurous character who delighted in teasing European ambassadors (they sent back reports of his formidable and eccentric nature), who, at the Portsmouth Navy Yard, settled the Russo-Japanese War and brought peace to the Far East, and who followed this by sending the Great White Fleet around the world, and then retired to visit the Kaiser during maneuvers in Germany and attend with delight the funeral of Edward VII of Great Britain. The old Virginia dynasty, whose ultimate expression of foreign policy was the Monroe Doctrine, had worshiped (and suspected) Europe; Teddy was amused by it. America had become ebulliently of age.

Nevertheless, the Monroe Doctrine still held, reinforced in fact by the Roosevelt Corollary which declared the right of the United States to prevent Latin American nations from placing themselves in default to Europeans, who would thus have an excuse to intervene. William Howard Taft made no drastic changes. But Woodrow Wilson was an Anglophile scholar who hoped to play in World War I the role of peacemaker, which Napoleon III had muffed in Europe in 1866, though Wilson's approach would have been a combination of United States aloofness and British procedures. But he was forced to enter the war so as not to endanger the peace; he was helped to do so by German machinations in Mexico, revealed in the Zimmermann telegram (courtesy of British naval intelligence). It is doubtful if he understood the importance of a European balance of power to America as much as he was exercised by concepts of neutrality and maritime rights. Then he adopted British war aims as the famous Fourteen Points, a sort of American party platform to catch international and national votes. Self-determination, making the world safe for American democracy, and Wilson's peacemaking, it can be argued, attempted to restore British power so as to safeguard the Monroe Doctrine, while at the same time extending the Roosevelt Corollary to the European scene. Wilson went to Versailles in the role of the interventionist Savior. But he neglected mundane politics, and the Senate to spite him reverted to abstentionism.

Neither Harding nor Coolidge has been noted for much vision and fortunately the world was quiescent. But Coolidge and Hoover, a much traveled engineer and relief specialist, had wider views, if not interventionist ones. Hoover at least was a realist and followed the Coolidge administration's Dawes Plan with the Young Plan and then a moratorium on reparations and war debts. But what else could he do in a period of worldwide economic disaster? Franklin Delano Roosevelt was somewhat traveled, but essentially a domestic-minded patrician politician in an isolationist country until after the 1940 elections, and even then he moved cautiously, although his policy, after Winston Churchill became prime minister in Britain, was increasingly Anglophile. In the Far East he had to let matters ride as the United States simply did not have much more power to deal with events there than the gunboats, established on the Yangtze in 1920, for the Philippines were so vulnerable that they could not be used as a safe forward base. Moreover, post-1918 isolationism helped by the powerful lead of Republican Charles Evans Hughes in the State Department, forced the navy to accept a reduced fleet rather than a Wilsonian navy second to none and to accede to the Japanese demand that no major naval bases be developed within 1,500 miles of her home islands. To this settlement, which created a battle-ship-building holiday until 1936, was added a guarantee of the territorial integrity of China thus assuring the United States that her navy would be the equal of the major European naval powers and so could protect the Monroe Doctrine in the Atlantic while being stronger than Japan in the Pacific and thus able to maintain the Open Door. The assumption was, of course, in spite of later war plans, that Britain would be an ally. But the lack of secure bases for the Royal Navy and the United States Navy close to Japan meant that neither the League of Nations nor the United States could take action in the Far East to defend China as the Nine-Power Washington pact required them to do. The League took the attitude that Manchuria was really rather outside its area anyway, but Secretary of State Henry L. Stimson in Washington did try to create a world opinion that would support the Japanese liberal civilian government against its army, but to no avail. In spite of Stimson, as Norman Graebner shows, most Americans regarded it with something of the same affection that Chamberlain had in 1938 for "that far distant" place called Czechoslovakia. Whatever his sympathies in the Far East, Roosevelt could do not much more for China under the Neutrality Acts than refuse to recognize her having a war on her hands. It was the best he could do in the way of an open-door policy. In both the colonial area and in Latin America, FDR's policy was one of emancipation and benevolent interference in both his own and other people's outposts of empire with the ultimate hope of being able to wash his hands of both expensive colonies and indigent and corrupt clients. He had enough on his hands at home. There he hit the nail on the head with regard to America domestically when he said "We have nothing to fear but fear itself," for the United States is an introspective nation with a veneer of confidence glossing over a multitude of fears.

It is the American character which does much to explain the nature of U.S. diplomacy, for Americans range from the brash and biblical to the timid, with fundamentally good honest folks in between. When asked to describe an American, college students here give a bewildering list of adjectives. This is a country that talks a great deal and listens some—it gets hypnotized by rhetoric—and all this is reflected in the media and in the Congress, where the natural nervous talkativeness of the politician is accentuated by the biennial elections. It has also taken some time in the world of electronic communications for people on both sides of a border or an ocean to understand the difference between speeches made for domestic and foreign ears. In all these things, from Puritan religion to economic well-being, both overconfidence and fear have played a prominent part.

The turning point in American foreign relations in the shift from abstentionist isolationism to interventionist containment on a worldwide scale paralleled the rise of Nazi Germany, the apparent failure of the League and of the Wilsonian peace, the Jewish persecutions, the expansion of the Japanese at the expense of Henry Luce's friends the Chinese, and the changing nature of the American population. The latter was proportionately less stirred by new immigrants and less divided, less propagandized by the Great Powers, yet through radio, Luce's *Life* and *Time,* and movie-news shorts, were more aware of the world and stiffened by veterans who remembered the First World War as another short and glorious experience (American troops were only in action from July to November 1918). The outbreak of the war in Europe in 1939, if not the Anglo-French spending after the Munich crisis of 1938, stimulated the American economy just struggling through a New Deal mini-depression. Arguments for national defense could thus be used to stimulate war production into which the British and French had already poured millions to build new plants in which their orders could be produced. Though the isolationists and America-Firsters were strong, FDR gradually swung the country into a worldwide campaign. Though he was working up to a war against Hitler's Germany by inserting American forces into the North Atlantic in the hopes of bringing on a congressional demand for war, it was the expansion of the Japanese, already anticipated by some in Washington, which compelled the United States to do an about-face. The 1937 sinking of the gunboat *Panay*, no more than the 1969 seizure of the spy ship *Pueblo*, had brought no violent reaction. However, these relations reached a turning point with FDR's economic moves against the Japanese in oil, scrap, and liquid assets. The attack on Pearl Harbor was an affront that could not be ignored. It made America intervene in the most massive way.

Then the United States not only was involved in direct physical confrontations but also engaged in protective interventionist diplomacy, such as supplying fuel oil to Spain to keep her from allowing the Germans to outflank American landings in North Africa in 1942. More than this, she actively encouraged the cooperation of Latin American nations as a further step of the Good Neighbor policy. The United States led the way in the creation of a truly world organization to replace the Francophile League of Nations. Here FDR proved to be a far better and more tolerant politician than was Woodrow Wilson. He carefully organized a bipartisan delegation to the talks in San Francisco, so that no matter who won the 1944 elections, world peace would continue to be sought. Given the global nature of the war and the rising decolonization inspired and accelerated by Japanese successes, probably no American president could have ignored the role. In fact, it can be argued that the more successful a president is domestically, the more he turns to foreign affairs as a field in which to seek the ultimate accolades. After all, apart from John Quincy Adams and Grover Cleveland, no ex-president of the United States has returned to political office. But, as Donald Mrozek and Kenneth Hagan have suggested, FDR either came to accept or really intended the United Nations to be a device to keep the small nations in line after the major powers had settled matters outside the world organization. And in this he would be true to the authoritarian approach which delights in wielding power while apparently allowing lesser forces to have a say. FDR may not have been thinking of the Congress of Vienna, but rather of Versailles. In 1972, of course, Henry Kissinger, the Austro-American student of Vienna played or was presented as playing the role of Metternich in the Vietnam settlement.

1945-1972

The American's natural love of technology and exuberance at massively decisive power came to its fruition in the development and deployment of the atomic bomb. But that awesome weapon was the product of scientists, thinkers who had moral doubts even before their work proved itself in action. So just at the time the Pentagon was started and Parkinson's law of great buildings set in, self-confident America lost its cool. The battle between the military services for the postwar budget, the hiving off of an independent air force, the creation of a Department of Defense, and the dominance of civilian strategists led to a further extension of the concept of victory through airpower. The result was an interventionist policy based upon the transoceanic reach of the air force and its ability to bring catastrophic destruction to any city on earth. Simultaneously, that old British war dog, Winston Churchill, went to the heart of mid-America and updated his 1918-1919 anti-Bolshevism, anti-Laborism by claiming to see an Iron Curtain descending across Europe. What happened was that doubting Americans and fearsome Englishmen combined to see the Russians as a highly dangerous force supplemented by Communist cells scattered all over the world, but notably in Greece and China. True some of these peoples were bellicose, but equally true that they were either settling traditional local quarrels or were, like the Russians without the bomb, scared. The Soviets were scared because they had experienced the devastation of war and wanted to spend their energies rebuilding and settling internal problems. But the concept of a cold war between the parties on opposite sides of the Iron Curtain suited the politicians on both sides who, as George Orwell predicted in *1984*, always needed an enemy. And what better enemy than one outside, a country which denied access to United States citizens so that most information had to come from "usually reliable sources" via the CIA or occasionally from neutrals. The whole idea fitted well with the American love of crusades, that continuing thread of small-town Puritan intolerance focusing on those who do not believe as they do and of whom they are usually suspicious. It was in this spirit that Truman developed his doctrine of economic aid and General George C. Marshall as secretary of state, his of military support. This involvement against communism—called containment and soon linked to the domino theory—was accelerated by the creation of

NATO, the United Nations intervention in Korea to prevent it from repeating the 1931 Manchurian pattern (possible in 1950 because the United States was in Japan), and followed by the creation of SEATO. Americans were now thoroughly involved in the world, but a world which no longer allowed the creation of a balance of power because it appeared there were just two super powers teetering on a seesaw.

Korea, which P. Wesley Kriebel describes, was doubly shattering to the American ego and confidence. Less than five years after the end of World War II, the opening round of the Korean conflict looked all too like a repeat of the Philippines in 1941-1942. But this time MacArthur was able in short order to stage a brilliant end-run landing and drive north, only to be beaten back by a Chinese invasion. But the real blow came in the refusal of the high command to allow bombing beyond the Yalu and the humiliation of a draw in place of a victory.

Korea also in retrospect should have emphasized that it was possible to have a more subtle debate beneath the nuclear umbrella which involved the not-so-deadly domino theory and interventions and abstentions on a guerrilla warfare scale. Ironically, here the United States has continually ended up, like the middle-aged spinster defending autocratic regimes against national liberation movements. This has made her the hostage of a small nation when she has intervened.

Granted that at the time the U.S. could not be sure that the Russians would not undertake offensive action in the West and that Chiang Kai-shek had been ousted from China, leaving the Maoists in control, it can be accepted that NATO, SEATO, and the Strategic Air Command acted as a deterrent to a third world war. But it can equally be argued with hindsight that neither the Russians nor the Chinese were prepared to undertake expansionist policies unless the opportunity arose. Instead they engaged in offensive-defensive nuisance tactics and the support of nationalist movements in much the same way that the United States had in the nineteenth century, well aware that they were vulnerable to American A-bombs, as threatened by John Foster Dulles's massive retaliation. So what they succeeded in doing was to "outpsych" the American character by playing to a free press which, coupling its revelations to those from official sources, created scares. Minor actions were reported as sensational. New weapons were immediately advanced verbally from the prototypes shown on May Day parades to fully operational swords of Damocles. This spurious overkill spurred on

Congress for twenty years until the crusade ran its natural course in the bog of Vietnam. A new sanity may not have been achieved, but at least a less super-Kahnian posture was exhibited. In 1972 it was hard to tell if Nixon was going to be able to retreat from atomic brinkmanship any more than it was clear that in 1940 FDR could move the country to save Britain. For its part in the early 1970s the American public finally began to realize that if the millennium was not here, at least neither was Hell. Fortunately, new problems such as racial equality and pollution presented themselves into which Americans could channel their worries and energies.

The shape of American foreign policy since Truman can perhaps be explained in part not by externals but rather by the art instead of the science of the historian. Presidents Eisenhower, Kennedy, Johnson, and Nixon all served in the Far East. Eisenhower had had extensive experience in both Europe and the Philippines by the time he became chief executive. Kennedy had been brought up in London in the days of Munich, but had served in the navy in the Pacific. Johnson and Nixon were both veterans of the naval campaigns in the Pacific in the Second World War. This suggests that they viewed the problems in that great basin as most important. Though it could be argued that it guided Eisenhower to end the war in Korea, he was more concerned to quiet both Korea and Indo-China in order to strengthen NATO to face down the Russians in Europe. The Pacific influence did take Kennedy and Johnson along the fatal road of involvement on the Asian continent, but it led Eisenhower's former vice president to attempt to extricate the U.S. from the Vietnam mess while at the same time recognizing that with the death both of Luce and of Joseph McCarthy and his attacks on the State Department that he was free to move with the world and admit Red China to the UN and reestablish the traditional American-Chinese ties in a new Union Pacific. That Nixon could do this can be attributed to his well-cemented relations with his party and his old Red-baiting reputation which made him "safe" in conservative eyes. Not only did Nixon's visit to China follow in the traditions of Wilson, and especially FDR, of visiting other world leaders, but it was also a case of trade following the flag. Not long after the Peking talks wheat deals were completed and the Boeing Company sold 707's to China (perhaps to be copied in due course).

In relations with the Third World, apart from Latin America, the

U.S. was far more circumspect. Aid treaties were developed and nations such as Pakistan and India supplied because it suited an anti-Communist purpose. But when local conflicts pitted American allies against each other, the United States was placed in a serious dilemma as to whom to supply, as William Richter notes. Nixon, because he did not like Indira Gandhi, attempted to supply Pakistan indirectly via Jordan and inserted the nuclear carrier *Enterprise* into the Indian Ocean. Whether the latter move was intended merely as a lifesaver or really as a threat to Indian operations in Bangladesh was not clear; it was plain that it was resented. In other Third World areas, the United States adopted a hands-off attitude, abstaining often because she had neither the bases nor the forces to intrude, or because congressional or other opinion at home seemed to make it politically inadvisable from a domestic point of view. In still other cases, nonintervention came from apathy since friends were involved on both sides. Janice Terry explores a Third World abstentionist case in her study of the Aswan Dam incident; James C. Carey sees another economic case in his look at Chile; and P. Edward Haley analyzes American intervention in force in Latin America in its privileged Monroe Doctrine approach before and after the Good Neighbor policy.

Foreign aid also reflects both the American character and national politics. The United States likes to talk about her Christian generosity, but she is often hypocritical. Aid stimulated the domestic economy, benefited United States shipping companies, and was given on a Carnegie self-help basis. And so after nearly thirty years since Lend-Lease, it was not surprising that aid programs should be in trouble because the public felt by the early 1970s that enough had been done for minorities and the poverty-stricken, even though the average voter has little idea who lived in the United States and who lived outside—it was just that they were known locally!

The problems of intervention or abstention have fallen especially heavily on naval commanders. While the general deterrent air force requirements were for bases in North Africa and Spain as well as in NATO countries and in Okinawa, the fleet has actively operated in two major areas in which the U.S. has long had a commercial interest—off the China coast and in the Mediterranean. In the former the Seventh Fleet, operating at long ranges due to the underway logistics system developed so successfully in the Pacific in World War II, acted as a shield between Formosa (Taiwan) and China, notably in the 1958 protecting of the offshore islands of Quemoy and Matsu. In the latter it has been a peacekeeping (Lebanon 1958) as well as a strategic deterrent force in the Mediterranean. Kenneth J. Hagan notes the origins of this policy in the navy's search for a post-1945 role. The problem of bases is not one that can be ignored, especially when, as Theodore Couloumbis and M'Kean Treadway show in Greece, it involves ignoring liberal attitudes toward the morality of the government concerned. Military necessity in World War II compelled the United States to deal with Franco in Spain and Pétain in France. She has consistently dealt with dictators and generals in Latin America of which the most notorious in recent years was probably Trujillo. But the recent case of the Greek colonels, who seized power in 1967, caused perhaps the most outcry because idealist teaching of Western Civilization coupled with the Byronic connection with Greek Independence in the early nineteenth century and the Jeffersonian heritage of neoclassicism made it seem that the very cradle of democracy was being despoiled. Negotiation of a new bases deal was not hurt, of course, by the fact that the vice president in Washington at the time was of Greek extraction, even though the Greek vote is hardly a consideration in domestic elections. Moreover, Greece was a country into which the United States had been thrust, she felt, by force of circumstances when the Labour Government in Britain in 1947 decided that it could no longer afford to fight communism in Greece. The United States went in both because some Americans thought socialist governments like Clement Attlee's in Britain were soft on communism and because they believed that if they did not, the Russians would take over, and what then would happen to Yugoslav partisan heroes?

Interestingly at the same time the United States forced an unreluctant Britain out of Palestine and created the new state of Israel in an action somewhat reminiscent of Theodore Roosevelt's engineering of the independence of Panama. Dennis Deutsch points out how hard American Jews worked to bring about that result and how it was not so much the public propaganda as private friendship that made it possible. The result has been a client at the end of the Mediterranean, but whether it is the Israelis or the Americans is not always clear. It is plain, however, that Israel has owed part of its survival to money raised in the United States and to its ability to obtain American aircraft. Its military victories and its sturdy independence, which included in 1967 the driving off of the United States naval intelligence ship *Liberty*, have converted the image of the Jew from bearded ghetto loan-shark to the epitome of the American virtues of rugged individual homesteader. Diplomatically the United States find itself in the whole Middle East in a strange relationship where it is in official minds and the press tied to Israel, but where it also has relations with Arab states and citizens. The whole problem is intimately linked to the Palestinian refugees and to the Arab love of politics as a game.

At the time of this writing, the Vietnam peace treaty has been negotiated. That longest and most costly of American misadventures based upon misperceptions has been given an apparent burial. Whether or not a carefully screened, covert, censored operation will continue from Thailand in defense of the domino theory and in Laos and Cambodia remains to be seen. After all, at least in the two pocket states the CIA has long had an active interventionist policy. For two of our authors a treaty would bring especial delight, for it would give them a positive point upon which to end their assessments. Ted Goertzel studies the domestic pressures for withdrawal from the Vietnam conflict, while Donald J. Mrozek evaluates the use of air power in Southeast Asia as an interventionist cudgel.

What has developed in Washington since 1941 is an increasingly complex decision-making bureaucracy deriving in part from the Joint Chiefs of Staff which has often worked well, but which can also allow a perception to become a deception, especially if the president does not either himself or through his immediate staff ask the right questions. In this respect it will be interesting to see how the Kissinger-Bundy-Rostow-Kissinger cycle is rated. Of the complex system that did arise, we can ask certainly why in the Aswan Dam affair Dulles did not say frankly that it was doubtful that Congress would provide the money, a face-saving ploy the Egyptians could have accepted.

The illogic of logic can also emerge from the decision-making process. It seems that the United States has intervened after both World Wars to compel the vanquished to turn commercial with a vengeance and in each case has created a nemesis, Hitlerian Germany and the dynamic Japanese economy, the latter especially making the U.S. reconsider lowered tariffs.

What the reader has before him, then, is a panorama of case studies showing the complexities and contradictions in American foreign policy in the twentieth century. The foreign policy is not clear—it never has been. If anything it has been a blend of opportunism by "God's own people" modified by traditional relationships set almost from the day of Washington's nonentangling Farewell Address as modified also by minority pressure groups, congressional desires, aspirations, fears, and presidential personality, not to mention economic interests and the needs of national defense. From an ivory tower, it looks rather like the work of Tammany Hall without the finesse because it has been run by good people, well motivated, but sometimes lacking in credibility, or by, in revisionist eyes, a self-perpetuating bureaucracy hypnotized by power.

Conclusion

Just as this was being written, I received a call from a student at another university charged with asking me to appear for their ROTC enrichment program. He asked me if I would give a public lecture on "Is the U.S. becoming a second-class power?" His question makes a suitable theme for the end of this introductory essay.

If the history and growth of the United States is viewed in Toynbeean terms, in terms of its intervention or abstention, then there was a long growth which started before Independence and ended in 1945. During this period American governments sought and obtained a means to remain independent. The War of 1812, which for the British was merely a sideshow in the Napoleonic Wars, showed the British that America was not to be reconquered. It was quickly followed not only by the settlement of European-American disputes in the northern part of the western hemisphere but also by the Monroe Doctrine. The latter was a shield for American growth and enabled the country to expand in the English manner with families making the frontier a home. Thus American imperialism in much of the nineteenth century was within the continent. Even during the Civil War only the French had the temerity to violate the Monroe Doctrine and that at a time when Franco-British relations were more harmonious than usual. But once Appomattox had cleared the air, that adventure was liquidated, not so much, however, by a United States threat as by the Mexican guerrillas. Thereafter Americans continued a vigorous expansion until it was clear that there was no frontier. Even so the available land was by no means used up. Indians were forced to move onto reservations, and a last great land rush was held in Oklahoma in 1893; at that time Frederick Jackson Turner predicted an imminent end to the Frontier as an era in American history.

In the meantime, the roots of further American expansion had been sown by traders and naval officers with some help from Washington. In the heyday of the American merchant marine before Southern raiders drove it under foreign flags, merchants, investors, and the navy had been exploring markets, opportunities, and coasts, especially in the Pacific. In the post-Civil War years, a much more limited expansionist program continued. In the 1880s a new steel coast-defense navy was developed and Admiral Alfred Thayer Mahan studied the British victories in the long wars from 1660 to 1815 and laid down the rules for offensive success. These were heeded by his friend Theodore Roosevelt, and America embarked upon a visible and bellicose overseas expansion, starting with the War with Spain of 1898. This was still very much in the Toynbeean concept of growth. And America responded too to the challenge of the First World War, but not to that of peacemaking. But momentum after a period of abstention or withdrawal was regained by Franklin D. Roosevelt's intervention in the Second World War, which can be construed as a Wilsonian interpretation again of the Monroe Doctrine. The 1941-1945 war continued the American victory tradition and left the United States standing as the international power most capable of intervening in anyone's affairs anywhere in the world. Russia was not a naval power and had no long-range air arm and so could not play a strong role outside of Europe and part of Africa, while the British were exhausted in both manpower and resources and could no longer afford the role of world policeman.

Jubilantly the United States took the stand that the goodness of the American democratic-economic system was so self-evident that given a little cash and a bulldozer everyone should be willing to follow the example of a nation of Horatio Algers and Andrew Carnegies. But this simplistic concept was soon shattered by the contrariness of foreigners and by legacies of the late war.

The United States had to take over from the British in Greece to save it from the Communists or the Russians. She had to protect her interests in the Far East from the disruption of the settlement in Korea.

And there the United States found that the best that a peacekeeper could expect to get was not a victory, especially when the public was unwilling to face a land war in Asia against a giant she did not recognize as existing, but a return to the status quo. So intervention remained a stalemate thanks to the Red Chinese, at least to 1972. Panmunjom took on new meaning as a nonnegotiable truce table. Thus the United States was only able to keep the door partly open and she allied herself with an autocrat in South Korea.

Pressure of events caused the joint occupations of Japan and Germany to be terminated as Americans learned the old diplomatic truth that yesterday's enemy may need to be today's friend. Though the United States did severely change ideologies and aspirations, she also slowly learned that some states could be neutral, that just because they were not allies, they were not necessarily enemies, even if they did speak to the other side. By the 1960s old attitudes on many of these matters looked foolish as the United States government found itself supporting Pakistan in alliance with Red China against India, while also trying to talk to India to prevent her from aligning with Russia. In the meantime the Indonesians had already proved that ex-colonial states were not only unlikely to welcome a new master, but were equally capable of dealing with their own autocrats as well.

Not long after the Second World War General MacArthur had said that the defenses of the United States rested on the shores of Asia. By the time John F. Kennedy was elected many of these things were becoming apparent, though how they were seen may have depended upon whether or not the viewer's background intellectually was American or European in orientation.

In Latin America the United States also continued her traditional policy of the Roosevelt Corollary, though increasingly after World War II (and this was another sign that she had passed her peak) she aided and abetted increasingly reactionary regimes. Here as elsewhere she often simplistically failed to distinguish between socialism and communism, just as Harold Stassen in 1948 at the University of New Hampshire was unable to see that the socialist British Labour government of Clement Attlee was not the same as the Communist regime of Joseph Stalin. Socialism was often the logical reform program, yet Americans made moral judgments against such reforms just as Wilson had done so about the backward-looking Huerta in Mexico, and this led the government to make a forward-looking Fidel Castro into an enemy, a mistake that may be long regretted. Dominica in 1965 was another intervention in a pattern of fearful repression that denied democracy.

If America had reached her peak in 1945, she was still on only a slightly declining plane until the fateful decision to ignore MacArthur's words and trespass beyond the shoreline of Asia. Korea may have been necessary to save the United Nations; Vietnam was interference in a civil war which was of no concern to the United States. It came in part from a hysterical misreading of the Chinese character due to murky Lucite glasses which did not allow the U.S. to see Mao and the Reds as part of the mainstream of Chinese development and to recognize that not only was China nonaggressive, but that, in spite of Korea, she was a paper dragon.

Vietnam may correctly lead many to believe that the United States is a declining civilization which has entered upon the stage of militarism that comes before the final recognition that as a state she can only be content when she turns from the macrocosm of the world and lunar probes to the microcosm of the problems at home. In the gloom of 1972, President Nixon could be seen as an extremely calculating political diplomat who recognized that casualties bothered America, but that bombing would satisfy those who refused to abandon the campaign. He was successful in this, while at the same time proving that China was not a devil. His use of air power, on the other hand, was in terms of tonnages devastating, but at the same time economical, since American casualties were minimal. Even the prisoner-of-war issue was turned into a skillful means of assuring continuing involvement because few wanted him to abandon the war until after the promised release of the handful of POW's. In this sense Vietnam typifies the difficulties especially of American diplomacy.

In 1972 many feel that since 1945 the United States has been a *military* intervener. Looking back, the U.S. has been a worldwide presence, but apart from Vietnam and possibly Korea, the rest of her activities have not been out of proportion to her own patterns in the isolationist nineteenth century. In fact her activities have been less than the British in their role as world policeman in the nineteenth century—in the first decades of the twentieth—or even when they pursued an active interventionist policy. Given the enormous power available to the U.S. as the world's leading economic and military power, the judgment of history surely will be that except in Vietnam the U.S. has conducted itself in its traditional pattern, and that with restraint. It has emancipated the Philippines and given statehood to Alaska and Hawaii. It has exported technology and ideology and thus, not by military intervention, sown the seeds of its own microcosm.

The decision to intervene or to abstain, especially militarily, may be a minority one based far more on domestic, emotional, and moral considerations than on calculating realities. Hopefully America will not intervene anymore except as part of a United Nations peacekeeping police force.

At the beginning of 1973 United States foreign policy was still unsettled. The state of flux was due to the failure of the hopeful peace negotiations with North Vietnam which seemed to be trying to apply the concept Willy Brandt was using in Germany and the Koreans were accepting, i.e., one nation, but two states. Air power, because it involved the fewest constituent mothers was unveiled and used to drive the point home to Hanoi that the war should be ended. But as Norman Graebner pointed out in the book *Civil Wars in the Twentieth Century* (Higham, ed., 1972), the United States remained tied to the puppet South Vietnam regime. At the other end of the scale were American relations in Europe where the entrance finally of Britain into the Common Market signified both the end of two special relationships— with the British Commonwealth and with the United States— and the creation of a much stronger European economic bloc. Yet the United States was tied into this by its NATO attachments so that a real part of its diplomacy remained its treaty commitments. In a shrinking world of increasingly complex relationships, it was more and more difficult to act in the simple Washingtonian nonentanglement manner. In both Vietnam and Europe, the United States, as even in the Indian Ocean-South Asian sphere, found itself faced again with the twin dilemmas of intervention or abstention, or even a bit of both at the same time.

THE HISTORICAL SIGNIFICANCE OF
AMERICAN NAVAL INTERVENTION

Kenneth J. Hagan

IT IS A POPULAR belief in the United States that intervention by American military or naval forces in other countries has been a rare occurrence in the last hundred years. Moreover, many Americans believe that intervention was a practice of relatively few presidents, most notably Theodore Roosevelt and Woodrow Wilson, and that the Good Neighbor policy of Herbert Hoover and Franklin D. Roosevelt spelled the end to intervention in Latin America, the geographical area where it was most prevalent. Yet there remain troubling episodes from the very recent past which raise doubts about an American reformation in relations with Latin America and the rest of the world. Of these, the abortive Bay of Pigs invasion and the 1965 landing in the Dominican Republic are the most disturbing. In addition, beyond the western hemisphere elements of the United States Sixth and Seventh fleets intervened in the Mediterranean and far Pacific during the administrations of the last five presidents.

A facile reconciliation of the paradox of benevolent abstention and intermittent intervention is frequently attempted by those historians whom Jerald Combs categorizes as "nationalists" and "realists" in his extremely useful book *Nationalist, Realist, and Radical: Three Views of American Diplomacy* (1972). In general terms, the nationalists say that the foreign policy of the United States is inspired by high moral purpose and works in the best interest of mankind. The realists, who are less saturated with American ideology, contend that a delicate equilibrium must prevail between national goals and the power available to achieve them. Realists concede that at times the leaders of the United States have miscalculated this balance. Together with the nationalists, the realists accept the premise that in the decades since World War II international communism has posed a serious threat to the national security of the United States. Scholars of the two schools therefore defend acts of American intervention as responses to aggression or excuse them as regrettable and probably misguided—but never malevolent—aberrations from the noninterventionist norm.

Arthur M. Schlesinger, Jr., is unquestionably the most persuasive and significant spokesman for the nationalist school. In his chronicle of the Kennedy administration, *A Thousand Days,* Schlesinger describes the Bay of Pigs as a tragic error committed by a well-meaning president who was badly advised. Military leaders and top officials in the Central Intelligence Agency were at best inaccurate in their appraisal of the possibilities for a successful invasion. At worst, they intentionally misled the president in order to win implementation of a scheme to which they had mortgaged their own prestige. What distinguishes this account as particularly nationalistic are the final few paragraphs in which Schlesinger makes it clear that the interpretation he advances was first suggested to him by the principal actor in the drama, John F. Kennedy. Thus a historian offers the American people what amounts to an official interpretation of events under the imprimatur of serious scholarship. This easy acceptance of the executive branch's explanation of its own actions typifies the nationalist school as it grapples with American intervention overseas.

Another salient aspect of the school is the contention that at any given time a president chooses the only course of action available to him, that is, he does not perceive any alternatives. H. Wayne Morgan develops this thesis when discussing the pivotal decision for war with Spain in 1898, an intervention that shaped the course of twentieth-century American history. Why did President William McKinley fail to realize a peaceful settlement to the dispute with Spain, one that would have terminated the Cuban insurrection by ending oppressive Spanish rule without an American war of liberation? Morgan writes: "The real fault in McKinley's diplomacy was not a lack of consistency or courage, but of imagination and alternatives. He sought peace by the only means available, threatening war, and continued [President Grover] Cleveland's policy of pressuring Spain, gambling that she would give way rather than face a war she could only lose. The basic problem was a lack of alternatives to intervention."

Realist historians share some of the brooding sense of historical inevitability that characterizes the writing of the nationalists, but they qualify it with an indeterminable element of governmental and popular willfulness. Thus they do not exclude the possibility that events might have been otherwise. George F. Kennan perhaps best exemplifies these two somewhat contradictory aspects of the realist school when he discusses the Spanish-American War. As for its causes, he regrets the American leaders' failure to apply the touchstone of national security before acting: "Our national security, as we think of it today [1951], was not threatened. But American property interests were damaged; the activities of American filibusterers and arms salesmen, on behalf of the [Cuban] insurgents, caused a lot of trouble to our government. And, above all, American public opinion was deeply shocked by the tales of violence and misery from the island."

Thus, under the pressure of public opinion, the United States government declared war on Spain at a time when "the possibilities of settlement by measures short of war had by no means been exhausted." The goal of a free Cuba was realistic in that its achievement lay within reach of American power; it was sadly unrealistic in that no threat to American national security necessitated its pursuit. Moreover, once the war began and Commodore George Dewey attacked the Spanish fleet in Manila harbor, events assumed a momentum of their own. In Kennan's opinion, Dewey's victory and the United States Army's occupation of Manila "shattered Spanish rule in the [Philippine] islands, made it impossible for us to leave them to Spain, and left us . . . no agreeable alternative but to take them ourselves."

Most radical historians also subscribe to a concept of historical inevitability, but it is totally different from that of the nationalists and realists. It consists of economic determinism with overtones of the broader Marxian analysis of class conflict, specifically the cooptive tenacity of ruling classes. Joyce and Gabriel Kolko articulate the extreme radical interpretation in their book *The Limits of Power* (1972). They contend that any society's goals reflect the economic, strategic, and political needs of its power structure. In the United States that power structure long ago assumed a capitalistic form. Apologists may attribute specific examples of the application of American power to social consensus, but in reality what determines the uses of power are the needs of capitalism. "With time," conclude the Kolkos, "such

structural imperatives and limits appear to take on independent characteristics, so that whether academics or businessmen administer it, the
state invariably responds in nearly identical ways to similar challenges."

In other words, United States policy will be the same whether
formulated by Kennedy's "best and brightest," to use David Halber-
stam's ironic epitaph, or by the more traditional elites who staff the
American foreign, military, and naval services. Radical historians may
disapprove of the twentieth-century "globalism" of the United States,
but since they explain it in terms of the inevitable fruits of a successful
capitalistic system they are unable to provide historical or contemporary alternatives short of dismantling American capitalism, which is
obviously to be done only with revolution.

Radical historians who are less ideological than the Kolkos simply
argue the inevitability of expansion under capitalism. Walter LaFeber,
for example, contends that by March of 1898 President McKinley had
no alternative. "Although he did not want war, he did want what only a
war could provide: The disappearance of the terrible uncertainty in
American political and economic life, and a solid basis from which to
resume the building of the new American commercial empire." To be
sure of ample markets abroad, and thereby to insure domestic peace
and prosperity, the United States would have to expand overseas by
means of military and naval force.

At present, then, the state of the American diplomatic historian's art
suggests divergent tendencies which will perplex students for some time
to come. Ultimate resolution of the differences dividing nationalists,
realists, and radicals will only be possible after a cooling of tempers
made quick and volatile by the war in Indochina, the longest and most
costly intervention in American history. In the meantime, it can be very
profitable to examine certain facets of the phenomenon of American
naval intervention overseas with several substantive and historiographi-
cal questions in mind. First, to what extent is it demonstrable that
there has in fact been a consistent tradition of United States naval
intervention over the last hundred years? Second, if such a tradition
does exist, what have been the motivating factors behind it? Finally,
what does a tradition of intervention suggest about the eventual outcome of the debate between nationalists, realists, and radicals?

Historians have repeatedly observed that President Theodore Roosevelt intervened dramatically in Central America and the Caribbean. He

encouraged revolution in Panama, and in 1904 he proclaimed a sweeping United States hegemony: "Chronic wrongdoing . . . may in America, as elsewhere, ultimately require intervention by some civilized nation, and in the Western Hemisphere the adherence of the United States to the Monroe Doctrine may force the United States, however reluctantly, in flagrant cases of such wrongdoing or impotence, to the exercise of an international police power."

The means by which Roosevelt would police the western hemisphere was the United States Navy, an institution he had fostered for many years. In his support of that institution may be found a marked consistency between American intervention in the nineteenth and twentieth centuries and a tentative answer to the questions posed above.

In the mid-1880s Theodore Roosevelt published *The Naval War of 1812,* a book that soon won critical acclaim in American naval circles. As a result he was invited to Newport, Rhode Island, to speak at the newly founded Naval War College. There he made the acquaintance of the school's president, Alfred Thayer Mahan, who was delivering the lectures he would soon publish as *The Influence of Seapower upon History.* Historically, Roosevelt and Mahan are well known for their emphasis on a big-navy policy and a strategy of offensive war at sea, as contrasted with the rather innocuous coastal defense and commerce raiding strategies dating back to Thomas Jefferson and an earlier America.

As a careful historian and observer of world affairs, Mahan had noted the unfortunate tendency of European nations to war with one another in an unending struggle for political, economic, and military preponderance. He admonished his countrymen to stop deluding themselves that the United States was immune to such conflict, and he outlined a strategy of offensive naval warfare with which to meet the inevitable challenges of European powers. He would carry war to the fleets and coasts of enemies rather than passively waiting to repulse their attack on American coasts, warships, and merchant vessels.

Mahanian strategy still guides United States naval planning for war with major powers, and thus it is universally studied and praised by American navalists. But there existed in the 1880s another doctrine which was never as formally articulated as Mahan's and yet remains extremely important to naval strategists. Concerned with intervention, this other body of thought was vividly reflected in the phrasing of

Roosevelt's 1904 "Corollary" to the Monroe Doctrine. And today it shapes American naval policy toward less powerful nations.

When Roosevelt wrote in 1904 that "chronic wrongdoing" might require "intervention by some civilized nation," he was using terms frequently on the lips of nineteenth-century American naval officers who conceptually divided the world into "civilized" and "semi-civilized" segments. Great Britain, the United States, and western Europe represented the highest civilization. China and much of the East were semi-civilized, as was Latin America. Other parts of the world, notably Africa, appeared to nineteenth-century American naval officers as perhaps barbarous and certainly no more than semi-civilized. This comfortable, ethnocentric view of the world served as the rationale for the global operations of the United States Navy through the late 1800s. In the minds of naval officers it helped to justify a constant showing of the American flag and a fairly frequent threatening of force by United States warships in all areas of the world beyond Europe.

Mahan was a typical naval officer in his conceptualization of the world. His writings brightly mirror the Darwinistic determinism permeating American intellectual circles in the 1880s and 1890s. His premise was that the Anglo-Saxon "race" was superior to all others. Among the Anglo-Saxons, the Americans stood at the pinnacle of evolutionary maturity. Mahan held it inevitable that Anglo-Saxon civilization would spread around the globe, and one vehicle of that expansion was naval power. The process was already well begun by the mid-1880s, but Mahan observed pockets of resistance by semi-civilized and barbarous peoples. He predicted more opposition by the benighted in the future and urged the civilized nations to use force to extend their power if necessary. Certain natural attributes of the Anglo-Saxons, especially the British and Americans, presaged ultimate success in this struggle. Among these were energetic populations, dynamic governments, and favorable geographic locations.

Evidence that the United States, Britain, and western Europe were superior could be found in any of several indexes, but the one most fascinating to naval officers was the symbiotic combination of industrial production and exportation of manufactured products. And as the nineteenth century drew to a close, this index of greatness became a worrisome indicator because American navalists increasingly subscribed to the conviction held by men like Secretary of State William M. Evarts

(1877-1881) that unless the United States increased its exports it could not be certain of reasonably full employment at home. Without an employed labor force, unrest and revolution would threaten the United States. The depression and labor violence of the 1870s had been omens; exportation of goods was not only desirable, it was essential to national survival.

Commodore Robert Wilson Shufeldt was one of the more thoughtful officers of his time, and in 1878 he explained the interrelationship of overseas commercial expansion and domestic American vitality to Congress: "At least one-third of our mechanical and agricultural products are now in excess of our own wants, and we must *export* these products or *deport* the people who are creating them. *It is a question of starving millions* [of Americans] ."

Shufeldt was not the only officer to sense that the 1870s posed both challenge and opportunity to a navy that had languished with meager appropriations and a confused sense of purpose since the Civil War. In 1873 naval leaders founded the United States Naval Institute as the beginning of an aggressive campaign of argument and debate designed to convince the public and Congress of the need to modernize the navy. They continued the effort into the 1880s and 1890s. One result was the construction of the "new navy" of steam, steel, and rifled cannon. A side effect was the refinement and expression of strategic theory, both in the pages of the Naval Institute *Proceedings* and after 1884 in the classrooms of the Naval War College.

The founder of the war college, Rear Admiral Stephen B. Luce, was an articulate representative of the naval mind of the 1870s and 1880s. It was he who invited Mahan to the college and encouraged his work. Luce also wrote a great deal, and in July 1889 he published an article in the *North American Review* advocating an offensive battleship strategy for the United States Navy. Some historians contend that Luce's article was a catalyst for Secretary of the Navy Benjamin F. Tracy, whose annual report for 1889 was the first official American announcement that henceforth war would be offensive in conduct, while remaining always defensive in purpose. Thus, according to Tracy, it was imperative to "have a fleet of battle-ships that will beat off the enemy's fleet on its approach, for it is not to be tolerated that the United States, with its population, its revenue, and its trade, is to submit to attack upon the threshold of its harbors."

While Luce was prodding Mahan and Tracy to speculate about war in the modern age, he was also thinking seriously about the navy in times of peace. His own study of naval history convinced him that whenever the United States was not at war the navy's preeminent function was protecting commerce. In fact, he thought that Americans, as the quintessence of the "Anglo-Saxon race," possessed "an hereditary genius for the maritime affairs." Writing at the close of the 1880s, he expected to see soon "a gradual revival of American merchant shipping, the relegation of our foreign trade to American bottoms, and a return to our former naval policy." Before the Civil War, he comprehensively observed, "Our 'white-winged' commerce spread over the most distant seas, and thither our war-ships followed to give it moral and material support, whether the trader itself at sea, the merchant in a distant land, or our representative accredited to foreign governments." Cruisers could provide some of this global protection of American commercial interests, but battleships were also essential if the protection were to be complete.

The naval literature of the 1870s and 1880s contains ample evidence that Luce was representative of his generation. Robert W. Shufeldt's explanation of the naval-commercial thesis in 1878 was more blunt than Luce's exposition, but otherwise there was no difference: "In the pursuit of new channels the trader seeks not only the unfrequented paths upon the ocean, but the unfrequented ports of the world. He needs the constant protection of the flag and the gun. He deals with barbarous tribes—with men who appreciate only the argument of physical force. The old paths of commerce are well known, but as manufactures increase, new markets must be found and new roads opened. The man-of-war precedes the merchantman and impresses rude peoples with the sense of the power of the flag which covers the one and the other."

A few months later Shufeldt began a two-year cruise around the world in search of new markets for American manufactured goods, especially cheap cotton cloth. His flagship, the U.S.S. *Ticonderoga,* carried him along the coasts of Africa, into the Persian Gulf, across the broad expanse of the Indian Ocean, through the Strait of Malacca, up the China coast, and finally to Japan. At every port, Shufeldt investigated the opportunities for increasing American exports. Acting under instructions from William M. Evarts, secretary of state, Shufeldt also appraised the ability of consular representatives, nominated candidates for vacant consulships, and urged the improvement and expansion of the consular service as a whole.

While Shufeldt scouted for markets, younger naval officers propagandized incessantly for a vigorous merchant marine and a larger, modern navy. Lieutenant Frederick Collins wrote in the Naval Institute *Proceedings* of 1879 that a recognition of the intimacy of commerce and the navy "should impel any nation discovering its commerce on the wane to redoubled efforts to maintain an efficient navy as one of the most important aids to its resuscitation." Then, whether the nation was belligerent, neutral, or at peace the navy could succor its trade.

Lieutenant John C. Soley drew the contrast between this policy and the strategy of commerce raiding which had characterized American naval operations during past wars. "If we look upon the vessels of our Navy as 'commerce destroyers,' we make a grievous mistake." There must be some warships "whose mission is to 'sink, burn, and destroy,' ... but let the main duty of the Navy be that [of] 'commerce protector,' a duty nobler in every sense of the word and one that more exactly fulfills the ideal of every true hearted sailor."

The decades before Mahan, like those after him, gave naval officers many opportunities to act as guardians of American commerce and property abroad. In 1878 Rear Admiral C. R. Perry Rodgers assumed command of the Pacific Squadron. One of his first acts was to confer for several days with the leading merchants of San Francisco to determine the ports his ships should visit in order best to protect American investments and trade on the west coast of Central and South America. The grateful managers of the Pacific Mail Steamship Company thanked Rodgers and unwittingly revealed the extent to which businessmen shared the naval officers' assessment of the interrelationship between the navy and commerce: "Since the date of your making known to us your intention of visiting all these ports, we have felt a degree of reliance which we had not heretofore known. Great good, and only good, can result therefrom. Officers of those governments who are inclined to treat us with justice and courtesy, will be strengthened in that disposition; while those who may have found gratification in conduct of an opposite kind, will readily discern the advantage of changing their policy." The managers of the Pacific Mail Steamship Company had spelled out the argument for intervention as clearly as anyone could, and the navy acted accordingly throughout the 1880s.

At mid-decade, when a revolution on the isthmus of Panama interrupted railroad communication between the Pacific and Atlantic oceans, Secretary of the Navy William C. Whitney intervened in great strength. He sent most of the ships of the North Atlantic and Pacific squadrons to the isthmus with a total force of over 2,000 men. The landings that followed constituted the largest amphibious operation by the United States Navy between the Mexican and Spanish American wars. Within hours of the major landing the transit of the isthmus was reopened, and the revolution against Colombia was effectively crushed. Only then, after being faced with a fait accompli, did Bogotá request United States aid.

Whitney later concluded that because of this intervention American "commercial and other interests in Central America" had been strengthened, "and an additional guarantee of security" had been given "to the mercantile enterprise of Americans in this quarter." The expedition did not reflect any concern for abstractions such as the Monroe Doctrine or legal niceties such as Colombian sovereignty. It quite simply underscored the navy's determination to support American enterprise overseas. As Whitney and his host of uniformed subordinates believed, "It is largely for the purpose of protecting the mercantile marine and for assisting its healthy development that the Navy exists."

On the China coast in the 1880s the navy acted in a similar manner, although on a smaller scale. The Asiatic Squadron numbered only about six ships, some of which were so unseaworthy that they ventured from harbor only at considerable risk to the safety of the crews. As a result, the navy cooperated with the European squadrons in the Far East more assiduously than elsewhere. In 1884 and 1885 the policy of cooperation was put to its fullest test as France wrested control of Indochina from China. All along the China coast American consuls and naval officers were worried that resentful Chinese mobs, urged on by governmental officials who saw a rare chance to strike back at foreigners, would attack French citizens in retribution for the victories of the French army. In the process, the pent-up anger of decades might well be directed against all westerners. Canton was especially volatile, and early in the conflict the American Asiatic Squadron sent its best warships to that city.

The first American naval vessel to reach Canton was the *Palos,* a small side-wheeler, commanded by Lieutenant Commander George D.

B. Glidden. Upon arrival Glidden immediately organized a landing party, conferred with the resident American consul, and then convened a meeting of the commanding officers of the assembled western gunboats. Designed to coordinate the response to Chinese rioting, this naval conference set a precedent for higher authorities. Soon thereafter the commander of the American squadron met with his British counterpart to draw up plans for joint landings in Shanghai should the populace riot against westerners. The pattern thus set lasted well beyond the duration of the Sino-French war, and it received formal endorsement from both London and Washington.

The policy of intervention just outlined, together with its rationale of protecting and expanding commerce, was the dominant feature of American naval operations during most of the nineteenth century. It has never been comprehensively examined, but James A. Field, Jr., recently documented one important facet in his ambitious *America and the Mediterranean World, 1776-1882* (1969). Field significantly ends his study with the British bombardment of Alexandria, Egypt, in 1882. By that action, and by the diplomacy that followed, Great Britain and other expanding European powers converted the Mediterranean from a highway for overseas commerce into a closed lake.

The obstacle of closing markets was one that American naval officers increasingly encountered during the 1880s. Shufeldt had sensed it, and those who followed him in the Indian Ocean reported that markets gradually were being denied to Americans through establishment of European protectorates. In the 1890s the inexorable momentum of European imperialism threatened China, where pessimistic Americans worried about the shutting of a commercial "open door" that had beckoned merchants and sailors for a century.

The European imperialistic explosion of the 1890s created profound apprehension in the United States of an end to American economic growth and prosperity. Coincidentally, technological innovation was transforming the United States Navy from a collection of wooden sailing vessels into a modern steel fleet driven by steam. These developments forced a new conclusion to the naval-commercial argument. Henceforth, said American navalists, it would be necessary to establish coaling stations and colonies overseas in order to insure access to markets.

The acquisition of colonies by the United States at the turn of the century therefore added a political element to the commercial interests which the navy was committed to protect. Nonetheless, for at least the first four decades of the twentieth century the commercial thesis retained prominence in the propaganda of American navalists. Peter Karsten has traced this theme in the final pages of his book *The Naval Aristocracy* (1972). He observes that many organizations have stressed the interrelationship of a strong navy, healthy foreign trade, and vigorous American economic health. Foremost among these is the Navy League, which is ably seconded by naval officers testifying before congressional committees. Rear Admiral Mark Bristol voiced the traditional appeal to the Senate Foreign Relations Committee in 1923: "When foreign markets close to us American prosperity ends." A decade later, in the middle of the Great Depression, American naval officers were hailing the legendary China market as the secret of American economic revival. In 1935 Rear Admiral Yates Stirling echoed Shufeldt and the officers of the 1880s when he declared, "The course of economic empire evidently lies to the westward." Expansionistic Japan had to be thwarted if the door for American exports were to be kept open in China and throughout the Far East.

Karsten notes "a subtle change" in the arguments of American navalists beginning with the late 1930s. For the first time in the twentieth century real concern was expressed about naval defense of the American homeland. He believes that the attack on Pearl Harbor, creation of a massive American navy during World War II, and postwar development of nuclear naval weapons systems permitted the argument for physical defense of the United States and its possessions to displace the earlier commercial thesis as a rationale for large naval appropriations. Karsten concludes, "The Navy's role in the protection of trade, foreign investment, and the merchant marine are no longer very useful tenets in the ideology of navalism, but are now subordinate to the more ingenuous argument that a navy is essential if the United States is to control the seven seas at all times, for whatever reason." In other words, he believes that the fundamental concern of navalists is an ever-expanding naval establishment and that supporting arguments are introduced, modified, and discarded in a coldly pragmatic way.

But Karsten may be premature in his obituary. Recent articles in the Naval Institute *Proceedings* continue to emphasize the interrelationship of the navy, commerce, and American economic vitality. In October

1972 Vice Admiral Stansfield Turner, the president of the Naval War College, buttressed his case for a "maritime strategy" with the contention that a strong fleet of attack aircraft carriers offers one great advantage: "By thus providing an improved capability to protect our sea lanes, it would guard our access to raw materials and commerce and impart to our allies a higher level of confidence in our ability to come to their aid." The post-World War II emphasis on political alliances, decidedly a departure from earlier American political tradition, is evident in Turner's terse summary. But his concern for raw materials and commerce is no more than a restatement of the nineteenth-century American naval thesis that foreign trade is essential to the prosperity of the United States.

The only new element in the attitude of navalists writing since World War II is an entrancement with the technology of weapons systems to the virtual exclusion of other topics. Since 1945 this preoccupation with sophisticated gadgetry has drained the energies of the navy's best minds. Little thought has been given to reformulation of geopolitical theory or reexamination of the relative merits of either the commercial thesis or what Karsten identified as the homeland defense argument.

In the closing days of World War II the American naval establishment became virtually mesmerized by the brilliance of its technological and operational accomplishments. The pages of the Naval Institute *Proceedings* for the months immediately after the war contain numerous articles depicting the attack aircraft carrier and the amphibious assault force as the peculiarly American contributions to weapons systems technology emanating from that war. Marines such as Colonel R. D. Heinl emphasized the amphibious element, contending that the "United States has emerged as the dominant amphibious power among the contestants." Naval officers such as Fleet Admiral Chester W. Nimitz, who was commander-in-chief of the Pacific Fleet in August 1945, eulogized carriers. Nimitz believed that Japan had been defeated by an American "sea power spearheaded by our carrier-borne air raids and by the excellent work of our submarines." The carriers and the submarines "made possible the bringing forward of troops—soldiers and marines. . . . It was that sea power that made possible the use of the atomic bomb by seizing bases from which the planes could carry it." Secretary of the Navy James Forrestal echoed Nimitz and labeled the carrier task force "a unique creation of the United States."

In 1947 civil war in Greece and Soviet pressure on Turkey, combined with the deterioration of British strength in the area, led Forrestal to establish the United States Sixth Fleet as a permanent American presence in the Mediterranean. The attack carrier was—and probably is—the backbone of that fleet, just as it has been the principal weapons system of the Seventh Fleet, the Pacific counterpart. But amphibious elements are an integral part of both fleets, and they have seen action in "limited" conflicts such as Korea and Vietnam as well as in interventions such as that in Lebanon under President Eisenhower.

The main combatant function of attack carriers in terms of number of sorties flown since World War II has been "close air support" or "tactical air cover" of American ground forces participating in limited wars or acts of intervention. But Congress has forced navalists to justify carriers on the basis of mobility and hence invulnerability as nuclear weapons systems. At first, in the 1950s, the other major contender for appropriations was the United States Air Force, with its manned heavy bombers and Strategic Air Command. More recently, however, the naval establishment has been its own stiffest competition. The article by Vice Admiral Turner cited above is devoted to proving the need for attack aircraft carriers and supporting amphibious assault forces. In the immediately preceding issue of the Naval Institute *Proceedings* (September 1972) there is an equally passionate defense of submarines by Vice Admiral J. T. Hayward, a former president of the Naval War College. Hayward considers the nuclear submarine the most modern weapons system, one virtually indetectable by an enemy and hence invulnerable. Both officers would agree that a "maritime strategy" is preferable to reliance upon the air force or army, but they cannot agree about the most desirable technological composition of the United States Navy.

Preoccupation with technology has caused the geopolitical rationale for employment of weapons systems to slip into the background, a retreat facilitated by the overwhelming American naval supremacy during most of the period since World War II. Little thought has been paid to the strategic implications of limited war and naval intervention. Vice Admiral Turner, for example, envisions the scenario of an Arab-Israeli war in which the Soviet Union would attack Israel's principal immediate source of foreign military support, the United States Sixth Fleet. In such a case, he believes, "there would be limitations or inhibitions on how extensive a force the Soviets would commit." In other words, the American threat of intervention in local wars could lead to a Soviet preemptive attack on United States forces, but that attack would be limited geographically and in total megatonnage unleashed.

Such a forecast badly misreads Soviet intentions. It very vividly documents the absence of profound contemporary American naval theory regarding the impact limited wars and American naval intervention may have upon the relations of the superpowers. It suggests a startling lack of familiarity with Soviet writing. For example, Rear Admiral K. A. Stalbo, one of the leading Soviet naval theorists, has written in *Morskoi sbornik.* [Naval Digest], the Russian equivalent of the Naval Institute *Proceedings,* that a "limited" Soviet-American war such as that postulated by Vice Admiral Turner is impossible. Any exchange between Soviet and American nuclear forces, be they attack carriers, nuclear missile carrying cruisers, or submarines, must entail immediate escalation to total nuclear war between the superpowers.

Stalbo, of course, represents primarily the naval elite of his country, for which he is a propagandist. He is determined, just as are his American counterparts, to make the strongest case possible for the largest, most modern navy equipped with the latest and most expensive nuclear weapons systems. Nonetheless, the tendency of American navalists to advocate strategies on the basis of technological competence and with scant regard to expressed Soviet predictions about the nature of their response is highly dangerous to say the least.

Intervention is one of the strategies most often proposed. Naval strategists have used it in the post-World War II period almost as a reflex when they perceived threats to American overseas trade or a danger of hostile Communist expansion. In the latter case justification for intervention is a contemporary expression of the historic homeland defense argument. The other justification, the commercial argument, is also as old as the United States Navy. It received perhaps its fullest expression during the 1880s when American navalists who were determined to rebuild their navy mounted a most effective propaganda campaign.

The endurance of the commercial rationale is very significant to the interpretation of the history of American foreign relations. It suggests in unmistakable terms that Jerald Combs's radical historians have correctly assessed the importance of overseas economic expansion to at least one important portion of the policy-making elite in the United States. Those historians who are aware of the longevity of this naval-commercial rationale for American naval policy, including intervention abroad during times of "peace," will be the ones least surprised if the United States Navy continues to intervene in places where a clear and present danger to American national security cannot conclusively be demonstrated.

SUGGESTIONS FOR FURTHER RESEARCH

The entire naval-diplomatic history of the period before the Civil War is unwritten. Field's *America and the Mediterranean* is a model for one area. But what about the rest of the world? Consular and naval records in the National Archives are rich with unexamined reports and correspondence. The historians who finally use these will place the "scientific" explorations and sensational episodes of gunboat diplomacy during the nineteenth century in an entirely new and coherent perspective.

Certain aspects of the navy's internal history ought to be chronicled. The controversy between line and staff officers is only partially delineated in Karsten's *Naval Aristocracy*. A thorough history of the Office of Naval Intelligence should now be feasible, given the declassification of archives in Washington. It would say a great deal about American naval diplomacy in the twentieth century. Creation of the Office of the Chief of Naval Operations and its impact on naval policy also would be a worthwhile study.

Technology's impact on naval strategy at any given time is fraught with implications for the present and future, but little has been written on the subject. For example, there is no published history of the development of amphibious warfare, although Richard West has left an unfinished manuscript.

Finally, many biographies remain unwritten, probably most notably ones describing the lives of William D. Leahy and William "Bull" Halsey.

BIBLIOGRAPHIC NOTE

Two comprehensive bibliographies are in print. The reader should first consult Robert C. Albion, *Naval and Maritime History: An Annotated Bibliography* (1972). The Division of Naval History of the Navy Department recently revised its *United States Naval History: A Bibliography* (1972).

Peter Karsten has applied sociological analysis to the naval officer corps in a book that also discusses the nature of overseas intervention. See *The Naval Aristocracy: The Golden Age of Annapolis and the Emergence of Modern American Navalism* (1972). Provocative interpretations of naval theory appear in two books by Walter Millis, *American Military Thought* (1968) and *Arms and Men: A Study of American Military History* (1956).

The standard survey for American naval history prior to World War I is Harold and Margaret Sprout, *The Rise of American Naval Power: 1776-1918* (1946). For the period from the Civil War to about World War II there are three useful histories of the navy. George T. Davis is the author of *A Navy Second to None: The Development of Modern American Naval Policy* (1940). A naval officer, Dudley W. Knox, wrote *A History of the United States Navy* (1948), which should be used along with Donald W. Mitchell, *History of the American Navy from 1883 to Pearl Harbor* (1946).

Two works chronicle the nineteenth-century history of American naval intervention and diplomacy. The most extensive list of landings is in Milton Offutt, *The Protection of American Citizens Abroad by the Armed Forces of the United States,* in Johns Hopkins University Studies in Historical and Political Science, vol. 46, 1928. Charles O. Paullin gives several examples of naval diplomacy in *Diplomatic Negotiations of American Naval Officers, 1778-1883* (1912).

James Cable, *Gunboat Diplomacy* (New York: Praeger, 1971), establishes an interesting typology of naval intervention and has a useful chronology for the twentieth century. Gunboat diplomacy is set within a broader theoretical context by Alexander L. George, David K. Hall, and William E. Simmons in *The Limits of Coercive Diplomacy: Laos, Cuba, Vietnam* (Boston: Little, Brown, 1971).

Mahan is both author and subject of many works. He set forth the ideas that would dominate twentieth-century American naval theory regarding major wars in *The Influence of Sea Power upon History, 1660-1783* (1890). His determination to achieve American hegemony in the Caribbean and much of the Pacific is most succinctly expressed in *The Interest of America in Sea Power, Present and Future* (1897).

The best biography of Mahan is written by another naval officer, William D. Puleston, *Mahan: The Life and Work of Captain Alfred Thayer Mahan, U.S.N.* (1939). A critique of Mahan's ideas is the purpose of William E. Livezey, *Mahan on Sea Power* (1947).

Lance C. Buhl has written a thorough study of all aspects of naval history immediately after the Civil War entitled "The Smooth Water Navy: American Naval Policy and Politics, 1865-1876" (Ph.D. diss., Harvard University, 1968). Robert Seager II was the first to examine American naval theory prior to Mahan, and his article is now a basic reference work. See "Ten Years before Mahan: The Unofficial Case for the New Navy, 1880-1890," *Mississippi Valley Historical Review* 50 (1953). An operational history of the "old navy" in its last days is Kenneth J. Hagan, *American Gunboat Diplomacy and the Old Navy, 1877-1889* (1973). James A. Field, Jr., also discusses operations of the wooden navy in *America and the Mediterranean World, 1776-1882* (1969).

The period of transition and the strategic implications of the new technology are treated in Ronald H. Spector, " 'Professors of War': The Naval War College and the Modern American Navy" (Ph.D. diss., Yale University, 1967). B. Franklin Cooling has reexamined the wellsprings of an offensive American naval strategy in *Benjamin Franklin Tracy: Father of the American Fighting Navy* (1973), a revision of the traditional analysis of Walter R. Herrick, Jr., *The American Naval Revolution* (1966). Important essays on naval theory appear in John A. S. Grenville and George B. Young, *Politics, Strategy, and American Diplomacy: Studies in Foreign Policy, 1873-1917* (1966).

The impact of Mahan's ideas on the naval mind of the early twentieth century has now been carefully analyzed by Richard D. Challener, *Admirals, Generals, and American Foreign Policy, 1898-1914* (1973). William R. Braisted's *The United States Navy in the Pacific, 1897-1909* (1958) is the classic account of operations during that period. All aspects of the changes brought by World War I on American naval policy can now be traced in three works, Harold and Margaret Sprout, *Toward a New Order of Sea Power, 1918-1921* (1941), Thomas H. Buckley, *The United States and the Washington Conference, 1921-1922* (1970), and William R. Braisted, *The United States Navy in the Pacific, 1909-1922* (1971).

Inter-war radical criticism of the navy is typified by Charles A. Beard, *The Navy: Defense or Portent?* (1932). Two recent scholars are friendly critics: Gerald E. Wheeler, *Prelude to Pearl Harbor: The United States Navy and the Far East, 1921-1931* (1963), and Raymond G. O'Connor, *Perilous Equilibrium: The United States and the London*

Naval Conference of 1930 (1962). O'Connor has also collected a series of essays on the international implications of the use of naval power in *Force and Diplomacy: Essays Military and Diplomatic* (1971).

The conception of a naval policy to guide the United States after World War II is ably explained in two works by Vincent Davis, *Postwar Defense Policy and the United States Navy, 1943-1946* (1966) and *The Admirals Lobby* (1967). The implications inherent in the use of naval power in the modern world has been suggested in Jonathan T. Howe, *Multicrises: Sea Power and Global Politics in the Missile Age* (1971).

None of the above secondary works are adequate substitutes for close examination of the primary sources, and there are two journals which amply reveal naval opinion at any given time: the United States Naval Institute *Proceedings* (1874-   ) and the *Naval War College Review* (1948-   ).

COMPARATIVE INTERVENTION: MEXICO
IN 1914 & DOMINICA IN 1965

P. Edward Haley

Introduction

Even as they have been led by American security interests and domestic opinion to renounce intervention in principle, in exchange for hemispheric solidarity first against fascism and then communism, American statesmen have simultaneously accepted intervention in practice. Examples of the renunciation of intervention dot the inter-American diplomatic record, beginning in this century with Woodrow Wilson's speech at Mobile, Alabama, in October 1913 in which he repudiated additional American conquests in the hemisphere. They include Franklin Roosevelt's acceptance of nonintervention at Montevideo. They are enshrined in the Rio Treaty and dominate the litany of the Organization of American States.

Examples of United States intervention in Central America and the Caribbean are as numerous and far more notorious. In this century they begin with the war against Spain and the liberation of Cuba. They include the creation of the Panama Canal in 1903, the occupation of Nicaragua, Haiti, and the Dominican Republic during the next decade, the Mexican involvement from 1914 to 1924, and, after a hiatus during the 1930s and 1940s, reach the present time with the interventions in Guatemala, Cuba, and the Dominican Republic.[1] In the twentieth century, down to and including the present decade, the United States has intervened more often and more extensively in the Caribbean area than anywhere else in the world. My purpose in this essay is to study two Caribbean interventions: Mexico (1914) and the Dominican Republic (1965).

The Pattern of American Intervention

Previous research, notably that of William A. Williams and Robert W. Tucker, as well as my own study of American intervention in Mexico, suggests that a pattern marks American response to foreign revolution. The characteristic American response, first revealed in Mexico, is marked neither by the defense of self-determination nor by the search for oppression and exploitation. Rather, for the past half-century, when actively involved in world politics, the United States has sought a liberal democratic alternative to social revolution. This might be termed a search for alternatives to civil war. This response has accompanied, and often served as an instrument of, the expansion of American power, commerce, and culture throughout the world. Before and after any American military engagement, the United States government attempts to impose the following "conditions" on the revolutionary factions by promises of aid and recognition, demonstrations and threats of force, and, sometimes, force itself: 1) A cease-fire: a halt to civil war and revolutionary violence, to be followed by 2) negotiations between the factions: these differences can only be settled around a conference table, and the good offices of the United States are available, to be followed by 3) the establishment of an interim government: a coalition drawn from the warring factions, if necessary, or a man or group outside of politics, to be followed by 4) free elections: international supervision is available, to be followed by 5) the establishment of a government that will, in probable order of importance: a) be friendly to the United States, at a minimum not join forces with an enemy, preferably adopt a pro-U.S. stand; b) maintain an open economy, at a minimum permit foreign investment and local private enterprise, preferably follow a capitalist pattern of development; and c) maintain a reasonably just and decent society, at a minimum avoid stirring revolutionary discontent, preferably deploy the full panoply of constitutional, democratic, civil rights.

This is, so to speak, the spider's parlor. All nations caught in revolution hear these delights described by willing American statesmen;

[1] The definition of intervention employed in this essay is that of K. J. Holsti: "activities undertaken to influence the political and social processes of another country, usually without the consent of the legitimate (e.g., commonly recognized) government: 1) diplomatic interference; 2) clandestine political action; 3) demonstration of force; 4) subversion; 5) guerrilla (unconventional) warfare; and 6) military intervention.

those governments that fall into the web of American intervention learn of them firsthand.

The Mexican Case. From the beginning of his administration Woodrow Wilson opposed the continuation in power of the military dictator Victoriano Huerta who was responsible for the overthrow and murder of his predecessor, Francisco Madero, the constitutional Mexican president. Wilson's interventions in the Mexican revolution before, during, and after the occupation of Veracruz in 1914 correspond to the pattern of American response already described. His objectives were to eliminate Huerta, to end revolution in Mexico, and to drive the Mexican Revolution into liberal, constitutional, democratic channels. Wilson saw no conflict of principle between capitalism and social justice. He threw the great weight of his nation against both civil war in Mexico and the profound economic change outlined, for example, in the Querétaro constitution. Wilson failed to control the Mexican revolution primarily because of the courage and resourcefulness of the Constitutionalists, the triumphant revolutionary faction, who rejected and defeated his constant meddling at every turn. Wilson's understanding of the need for great change in Mexico tempered his willingness to compel obedience from the revolutionaries, even as it intensified his opposition to Huerta. Finally, the steady movement of the United States toward world war limited Wilson's freedom of action in Mexico and forced him to turn most of his and his nation's attention and resources toward the situation in Europe and Asia.

At each important stage in Mexican-American relations, the same pattern of American response appeared. Wilson's special agent, John Lind, was ordered to press Huerta to accept a cease-fire, a countrywide armistice, early and free elections, and the noncandidacy of Huerta himself. When Huerta refused these terms, Wilson isolated him from European support and threatened to assist the revolutionaries. Huerta managed to hold on, and Wilson fulfilled his threat. In November 1913 Secretary of State William Jennings Bryan told Lind the president was prepared to break diplomatic relations, to allow arms to go to the revolutionaries, to blockade Mexico's ports, and to use the army, in that order. On January 15, 1914, Wilson ordered the secretary of state to allow 10,000 Krag-Jorgenson rifles to "slip through" American customs into Constitutionalist hands.

Even with this aid, no solution was in sight in April. Wilson was ready to act and had been ready since the previous November. When Mexican officials arrested and then released a few American sailors in Tampico, Wilson had the pretext he needed to justify the use of force. When Huerta refused to allow a Mexican salute to the American flag as part of an elaborate official apology for the incident, Wilson moved. On April 20 he asked Congress to approve the use of the armed forces to compel Huerta to render a suitable apology. Before the Senate could act, Wilson ordered American marines to seize the customs houses and wharf at Veracruz in order to forestall the arrival of a new shipment of arms to Huerta on the German steamer *Ypiranga*. The next day, April 22, the marines occupied the entire city in order to suppress the sniping by the Mexicans who had resisted the intervention.

Several observations follow from this account of the intervention of 1914. First, the decision to occupy Veracruz represented not an isolated act but the most violent phase of a long period of intervention in the Mexican revolution. Although he sympathized with the Constitutionalists and understood the causes of the revolution, Wilson next began to press the revolutionaries to accept the familiar conditions: an end to the bloodshed, a provisional regime, free elections, and a return to constitutional democratic government. Because Wilson's objectives were defined in this way, there could be no end to American intervention after Huerta fell. Wilson was willing to use force in Mexico to overthrow a dictator but not to destroy a revolutionary movement that he knew to represent the chance of the Mexican people for justice and a decent life.

The Dominican Case. The American intervention in the Dominican Republic conforms to the general pattern already suggested. The dispatch of more than 25,000 American troops to an extremely small country allowed President Johnson to crush the Dominican revolutionary movement. Wilson had to be content simply to goad the flanks of the movement in Mexico, a far larger and more populous nation. Even so, American goals in both interventions were strikingly similar: ceasefire, negotiations between the factions leading to the establishment of a provisional government, to be followed by free elections and the early return to constitutional democratic rule in a nation whose economy remained fundamentally capitalist. These similarities throw an interesting light on the role of anticommunism in prompting American intervention, and their implications are considered in the next section and in the conclusion.

The Dominican intervention resembled the Mexican in another way. In both cases the decision to land troops represented only a violent and military phase of a most extensive diplomatic, economic, and political intervention in the internal affairs of the two countries, and intervention that preceded the intrusion of American soldiers and continued long after their departure. Deep meddling in the Dominican Republic began in the last year of the Eisenhower administration when the United States supported the decision of the Organization of American States (OAS) to levy economic sanctions against the Trujillo government. A number of well-informed students of the Dominican Republic, Selden Rodman and Howard Wiarda, for example, believe that the Kennedy administration took this opportunity much further and conspired with and aided the Dominicans who assassinated Trujillo in May 1961.

Regardless of the truth of this, the Kennedy administration's decision to make the Dominican Republic a showcase of the Alliance for Progress loosed a waterfall of American money on the little country and pushed at least one American ambassador, John Bartlow Martin, into the actual workings of that country's government. So great was Martin's involvement that he seemed to function as a member of the Consejo (Council) that followed the American-aided overthrow of the last members of the Trujillo family. For Juan Bosch, Martin's role resembled the advisory role he had played with Adlai Stevenson and John Kennedy during their presidential campaigns, an altogether anomalous capacity for a foreign ambassador.

The figures and timing of American foreign assistance to the Dominican Republic support these observations. According to the *Statistical Abstract of the United States,* published by the United States Department of Commerce, no net foreign assistance, military or economic, flowed to the Dominican Republic during the period July 1945 to December 1956. In fact, according to the *Abstract,* from 1945 to the end of 1956 there was a net minus of less than $500,000. From 1957 to 1961 aid in annual amounts of less than $500,000 flowed to the Dominican Republic, for a net total at the end of 1961 of $1 million. In the next year alone, after Trujillo's death, some $22 million in aid went to the Republic, with more than $5 million in military aid. From 1962 to 1964, total military assistance doubled, to reach $12.1 million. By 1970 the total military aid had more than doubled again, reaching $24.8 million. Meanwhile, economic aid also increased enormously. In the ten years from 1961 to 1970 the United States committed some $375 million of economic aid to the Dominican Republic. The peak years of American aid were 1965 to 1967, when economic and military aid together reached figures of $79 million, $54 million, and $60 million. Total aid from 1961 to 1970 was $399 million.

In an account of his eighteen months as ambassador and his role in the intervention of 1965, Martin gave $5 million instead of $1 million as the total for American aid for the period 1945-1961. He also reported that during his tenure as ambassador, from March 1962 until September 1963, the United States made available to the Dominicans a total of $84 million. This obligated sum, which does not include military aid, consisted of $56.1 million from the United States Agency for International Development (including $22 million in refunded sugar premiums), $17.9 million of PL - 480 food, $3.4 million from the United States Export-Import Bank, and $6.5 million from a "Social Progress Trust Fund." About three-quarters of this sum, or $50.4 million, was spent. Interestingly, Martin observed that Juan Bosch received only $22 million in refunded sugar quotas, which had been arranged by the conservative regime that preceded Bosch. The flow of American money, then, followed an uneven and highly selective pattern: little for Trujillo, enormous amounts to the middle- and upper-class Councils of State before and after Bosch, as well as to the post-1965 presidency of Joaquin Balaguer, and next-to-nothing for Juan Bosch. The cost of the United States intervention in 1965 was $150 million.

These figures, although impressive, fail to reveal the extraordinary scope and intimate nature of American political intervention they permitted and facilitated. The best primer on this subject is Martin's account, *Overtaken by Events.* While ambassador, Martin became a crucial part of the Dominican political system. He acted as the flywheel of a violent, steamy engine. He spun around and around endlessly, and his momentum, given weight by the power of his own country, carried the Dominicans into and through free elections and seven months of constitutional government. He failed to stop the coup that overthrew Juan Bosch in September 1963 largely, one concludes from his memoir, for two reasons: even if Bosch had asked him, which he did not, Martin was unwilling to intervene as freely in the operation of the constitutional government as he had in the workings of the self-appointed regime that followed Trujillo's downfall, and Martin came to believe Bosch was a weak man and a failure. Ironically, it was the extraordinary American participation that had made possible democracy and the election of Juan Bosch. When Martin's constant surveillance and deft regulation were removed, an explosion would surely follow. His restraint contributed to Bosch's downfall in a military coup. Apparently Martin's successor, W. Tapley Bennett, took an even more restrained, limited, and traditional view of the role of American ambassador to the Dominican Republic. The explosion came on April 24, 1965.

Excellent accounts of the intervention already exist, notably those of Tad Szulc, Marcel Niedergang, Theodore Draper, José Antonio Moreno, and Jerome Slater. In public, the United States Government gave three reasons for American intervention: to protect the lives of Americans, to stop a Communist takeover, and to assure for Dominicans the right of self-determination. The testimony of eyewitness observers, notably Szulc, verified the wisdom of evacuating foreigners. That testimony also showed that the evacuation could have been accomplished without massive American intervention. It follows that the Johnson administration used the genuine need for evacuation as a cover story to justify full-scale armed action. The cover was needed for at least two reasons: to provide the constitutional basis for an immediate unilateral executive decision to intervene against the revolution, and to win widespread popular support for the undertaking.

José Moreno and Howard Wiarda have argued persuasively that communism was of negligible importance in Santo Domingo before and during the revolution there. That is of use in assessing the validity of official American political reporting and in judging the long-term consequences of American policy and action. Regardless of the actual strength of communism in the revolution, there is every reason to conclude that American policy makers thought it likely that allowing the revolution to proceed would result in "another Cuba." Ambassador Bennett believed this and reported it on Wednesday, April 28, 1965, triggering massive American intervention. Five days later Ambassador Martin on a special mission for the president concluded that the revolution had indeed passed under Communist control. He told the president and said so publicly in Santo Domingo on Sunday May 2. President Johnson embraced this interpretation ambiguously on April 30, after several thousand paratroopers and marines had been landed, and openly on May 2 after Ambassador Martin's report. On the latter date, the president announced that in addition to saving American lives, the soldiers went into the Dominican Republic because "What began as a popular democratic revolution, committed to democracy and social justice, very shortly moved and was taken over and placed into the hands of a band of communist conspirators."

To repeat the point, gaps between belief and reality are important and can become exceedingly dangerous. If one believes he can fly, for example, and jumps from a high building the gap between belief and reality can even be deadly. Those who afterward come to study the shattered body on the pavement make a valid point by observing that there are no wings on the remains, but that method of reasoning will never bring them to understand why he had jumped. There is no reason to doubt that determination to stop a Communist takeover was a decisive factor in the American decision to intervene.

The third public objective of the American government was to protect the right of the Dominican people to self-determination or, as President Johnson declared on April 20: "Our goal in the Dominican Republic . . . is that the people of that country must be permitted to freely choose the path of political democracy, social justice, and economic progress." Here lies the core of American intervention, for saving lives and stopping a Communist takeover, imaginary or real, are negative accomplishments. The American government gave substance to the intervention when by their deeds they began to give substance to the words "freely choose the path of political democracy, social justice, and economic progress."

The United States chose to define Dominican self-determination through three successive missions, those of John B. Martin, McGeorge Bundy, and Ellsworth Bunker, the latter ostensibly an OAS mission. There is little public information about the missions of Martin and Bundy. After establishing a spotty cease-fire, Martin sought to form a coalition interim regime around Antonio Imbert. When this failed to attract the agreement of the loyalist revolutionaries under Colonel Francisco Caamano, a second mission arrived and took up the negotiations. Originally the mission was composed of the president's special assistant McGeorge Bundy, Deputy Secretary of Defense Cyrus Vance, Under Secretary of State Thomas Mann, and Assistant Secretary of State Jack Vaughn. The group soon allowed or accepted Bundy's enthusiasm for Juan Bosch's minister of agriculture, Antonio Guzman. According to Ambassador Martin, this attempt to build a loyalist-militarist coalition failed for three reasons. Imbert refused to cooperate because the attack he had been allowed to launch north of the American "international neutral zone of refuge" had succeeded, and apparently he thought he was strong enough to win alone. For their part, the loyalists refused to carry out the purge of "Communist influence" demanded by the United States. It may also have been impossible to choose chiefs of the armed forces and of the three branches of service acceptable to the loyalists, the military, and the United States.

After the Martin and Bundy missions came the OAS-Bunker mission, created on June 2 and composed of representatives of El Salvador, Brazil, and the United States. Because they were conducted ostensibly under the guidance of the OAS, Bunker's efforts to achieve United States objectives gained legitimacy. Actually, all military and political decisions, as well as dominant military power, remained in the hands of the United States Government.

The objectives and accomplishments of the OAS negotiating mission, dominated by Ellsworth Bunker, have been made public and conform to the general pattern of American intervention described earlier. On June 18, 1965, the OAS committee published its proposal for the solution of the Dominican crisis. This plan called for: 1) free elections "no earlier than six months but no later than nine months from the present date"; 2) OAS supervision of the electoral campaign and the voting; 3) full amnesty for all participants in the civil war, the military combatants to return to barracks and refrain from political activity, the civilian combatants to surrender their arms to the OAS; 4) the establishment of a provisional government to act as a "caretaker" and to hold elections and to be composed of "all sectors of the country"; 5) the OAS committee to advise for recognition and assistance to the provisional government; 6) the commitment of the newly elected Dominican government to hold a constitutional assembly. On August 31, an "Act of Dominican Reconciliation" was signed in Santo Domingo and, on September 3, a provisional government headed by Hector Garcia-Godoy was sworn. (See OAS Documents 280 and 281.)

Like the proposal of mid-June, the final agreement provided for a competent provisional government, free elections within nine months in which "all parties whose principles are compatible with representative democracy" might participate, general amnesty, and civilian disarmament. The act also arranged the dismantling of the loyalist zone in Santo Domingo and, in effect, left the withdrawal of the inter-American force in the hands of the provisional president, the United States, and the OAS. The day after Garcia-Godoy took office, the United States recognized his interim government and extended an immediate grant of $20 million. Elections were held on June 1, 1966, and Joaquin Balaguer, puppet vice president under Trujillo, won the presidency. The flow of American money continued, reaching some $228 million in the next five years. Balaguer won reelection to a second four-year term in 1970.

An Explanation of the Pattern of American Intervention

The discussion in the first section of this essay of the Mexican and Dominican interventions revealed that the United States sought not a counterrevolutionary but a reformist, democratic outcome. This response seems to antedate factors such as anti-communism and great power status.

The response may be explained in terms of the influence of a number of factors on the formation of policy. These factors are: 1) the attitudes and beliefs of American leaders; 2) the domestic political needs of the Wilson and Johnson administrations; 3) the comprehension of the local situation by policy makers; 4) the military capability possessed by the two governments at the time of intervention; and 5) the nature of the international situation.

The Attitudes and Beliefs of American Leaders. Attitudes and beliefs influence decision makers to see an obligation to intervene and a threat or benefit in the outcome of a revolution. Two beliefs deserve mention here. First, Presidents Wilson, Kennedy, and Johnson and their advisers believed the United States bears a special responsibility for the preservation and extension of democracy everywhere in the world. This belief alone fosters opposition to communism. Their belief in the unique responsibilities of the United States may be documented by reference to the writings and addresses of the presidents, notably the inaugurals of Kennedy and Johnson. Second, Wilson and every president since Truman believed that the success of radical revolutionary movements endangered the prosperity and security of the United States, particularly if the victorious revolutionaries were Communists. Gordon Levin has argued persuasively that Wilson used American power against imperialism and revolution in order to assure the prosperity and security of the United States. Referring to Vietnam on the eve of the Dominican intervention, President Johnson declared that defeat in South Vietnam would just encourage those trying to conquer every free nation within their reach. "Our own welfare and our own freedom would be in danger." In this way, Johnson and his predecessors linked Communist revolution, world war, and national security. The search for specific economic motives by which to explain American intervention may be a waste of time. The conceptions of Wilson, Kennedy, and Johnson were much broader than aiding American investment abroad. Rather, they envisioned the use of American power to create and preserve a safe and congenial world order composed of as many independent, democratic, capitalist nations as possible. In order to create a safe and congenial world order, the United States must assist in the transformation of revolutionary violence into democratic processes. The link between Soviet power and foreign Communist parties only served to heighten American determination to control revolution.

Domestic Political Needs. To attempt to discover the links between domestic political calculations and the conduct of foreign affairs is to enter a shadowy realm of implication and circumstantial evidence. What passes for an analysis of the linkage between domestic and foreign policy usually amounts to a recitation of newspaper editorials and speeches and resolutions in Congress and the inference from these an explanation of foreign policy conduct. To make things worse, what matters most is not the objective truth about the domestic political situation, but what the decision makers perceived it to be. When President Wilson asked Congress to approve the use of force against Mexico, the House agreed 337-37. What weight should that be given in Wilson's calculations? He acted without Senate approval. Would he have acted at all if he knew Congress would deny his request? What role should be given to the influence of John Kennedy's progressive supporters on the decision to make the Dominican Republic a showcase of the Alliance for Progress? To what extent did President Johnson's opposition to Communist revolutionaries stem from reaction to the conservative appeals of Senator Barry Goldwater during the presidential campaign? To what extent did Johnson act from a perceived need to preserve national unity in the aftermath of John Kennedy's assassination? To what extent did he use his anti-Communist foreign policy in order to gain leverage in persuading conservative congressmen to support sweeping social welfare legislation?

In a democracy, the government must win the enduring support for or toleration of intervention from the individuals, groups, and institutions that organize and express public opinion. The outcry after the seizure of Veracruz must have removed any lingering doubts of the president that there would be widespread popular support for war with Mexico. Before the spectacle of ceaseless slaughter in Europe, American opinion remained pacific; even when Villa crossed the border to murder American citizens in a desperate attempt to provoke American intervention.

In the 1960s the American people and Congress gave the president the money and moral support needed to create an unparalleled strategic and conventional force in the belief that such strength was needed to counter the open and real hostile intent of the Soviet Union. When the government began to use its new capabilities not against the Russians but against revolution in Santo Domingo and then against revolution in Vietnam, the support of the groups, individuals, and institutions that organize and express public opinion began to wane. The decline in support worked profound effects on American intervention over the span of seven or eight years. One president declined renomination and opened Vietnamese peace negotiations, the next president withdrew most of the American ground troops from Vietnam and shifted to a strategy of naval blockade and massive air assault. The Dominican Revolution of April 1965 benefited not at all from this general reduction in popular support for intervention. The country is too small, the intervention too early and too massive. Should a new outbreak of change occur in the Republic in the future, it will come at a time when a change in opinion and, possibly, presidents will have further reduced the likelihood of American intervention.

Comprehension of the Local Situation by Policy Makers. One can expect a wise response that is not accidental only to the extent that the intervening government possesses an adequate historical and political understanding on which to base policy. In simplest terms, to what extent does the intervening government understand which revolutionary faction is winning and why? President Wilson understood the reasons why revolution began in Mexico but, as Link observed, his understanding remained strictly political. He believed the Mexicans sought to destroy tyranny and create constitutional democracy. This explains both his puzzlement over the opposition of the Mexican revolutionaries to his proposals for a solution to the civil war, and his persistence in advancing those proposals after countless rebuffs. This also explains his failures to anticipate Mexican opposition to the landing at Veracruz and the Pershing expedition after Villa. Dead Americans and Mexicans sobered him. Wilson's understanding of the need for radical change in Mexico caused him to overthrow a military dictator but, after countless unsuccessful efforts at mediation, to avoid attacking the Mexican revolution.

One can speak less confidently about how well the Kennedy and Johnson administrations understood the local situation in the Dominican Republic. Ambassador Martin's book reveals the domination of Dominican society by the military and the oligarchy, and the weakness of communism in the Republic, a condition confirmed by Moreno, Rodman, and Wiarda. Even so, the ambassador and his staff worried more about communism than about rightists. The book is full of a sense of impending doom, of statements like: "This was the twilight of the old order. The Republic's political leaders did not seem to realize that this was their last chance at constitutional democracy. If they threw this one away, they were finished. The next revolution would be proletarian and Communist-led, and the present politicians would be among the first to go to the wall."

What followed was a military coup that destroyed the constitutional government of Juan Bosch and reinstated military-oligarchical control. That coup was followed by the revolution of April 1965. It is fruitless to speculate about what might have happened to the revolutionary movement had the United States abstained from intervention. There is no way to know. The effect on American policy of the actual situation in the Dominican Republic was superseded by the domestic American preoccupation with the twin desires to resist revolution and to spread democracy.

Capability. The size, mobility, training, and equipment of the armed forces of the intervening country exert great influence on the choice of means and objectives. The United States lacked the ability to intervene in Southeast Asia during the Laos crisis of 1961-1962 without calling general mobilization. In that case, President Kennedy settled for an international agreement guaranteeing Laotian neutrality. By 1965, pursuit of the strategy of "flexible response" had built a vast conventional force, as well as an extraordinary nuclear superiority over the Soviet Union. The Dominican Revolution occurred on the eve of massive American intervention in Vietnam. The military weakness of the United States in 1914 and 1916 restrained Wilson's interventions. Even the border with Mexico could not be defended without mobilizing the National Guard.

A Favorable International Situation. There are at least three factors here likely to have influenced the Mexican and Dominican interventions. The first is the absence of countervailing power. There is no nation able to oppose American power in the Caribbean outside of Cuba, and Soviet aid to Cuba has rather narrow limits. The result is to isolate the Central American and Caribbean republics in a most disadvantageous mismatch and to give greater weight to the influence of domestic opinion.

Second, the kind of situation most favorable to intervention would seem to be a division between one's chief opponents and a lack of involvement by the intervening government in other major conflicts. This situation existed at the time of Wilson's interventions in Mexico. The European nations were on the verge of world war, and the United States, although tangled in interventions in the Caribbean, stood outside any of the existing major conflicts. The deterioration of American-German relations and the approach of United States intervention on the side of Britain, France, and Japan restrained Wilson's inclination to interfere in the Mexican revolution.

In 1965, again, the United States was not involved in any major conflict. Granted, the "cold war" with the Soviet Union and the isolation of China continued, but by the middle of the decade the hostility between Russia and China was deep and serious. Within three years a Russo-Chinese war in Asia would seem likely. This division among its chief opponents and the extraordinary margin of American strategic superiority and conventional mobility gave the United States a freedom of action in 1965 that it had not possessed since World War II and might never possess again.

The final aspect of the international situation likely to have affected American intervention is the support or opposition of the nation's allies. Clearly British, French, German, or Japanese support is far less important to the United States government as it ponders an intervention than the reverse. The absence of allied support for the intervention in the Dominican Republic (or Cuba or Vietnam) makes little difference. There is, presumably, a point at which allied opposition, rather than tolerance or indifference, would begin to bear heavily on American policy. The allies are unlikely to express such opposition until American action begins to endanger their own security or domestic political fortunes.

An Assessment of the Mexican and Dominican Interventions

The thesis of this essay holds that the Wilson and Johnson administrations sought essentially the same objectives. President Wilson actively aided the overthrow of the military dictator, Huerta, while President Johnson blocked the reimposition of undiluted military rule. Both men sought to stop the revolutionary violence, establish an interim coalition government acceptable to all the major warring factions, hold free elections, and return the country to constitutional democratic rule.

Only President Johnson succeeded in these aims, because the Dominican Revolution was localized and narrowly based (the peasants outside Santo Domingo were hardly touched by the violence of April and May 1965), because the country is tiny, the traditional ruling groups retained some power and coherence (even if all was nearly lost for them by April 28), and he could apply overwhelming force instantly.

In regard to both the Mexican and Dominican cases, one may ask whether the American objectives were appropriate to the two revolutionary situations. One may answer unequivocally about Mexico. Wilson's objectives were so inappropriate as to be irrelevant to the struggle he sought to regulate and force into constitutional channels. The parties of Constitution and Convention were engaged in a fight to the death. The stakes were control of Mexico and the remaking of Mexican society along radical lines. Such a struggle for these goals is illsuited to adjudication by election. The parties themselves would have fought as desperately against American intervention as against each other.

The size and character of the Dominican Republic—a tiny country long broken and impoverished by a history of the bloodiest tyranny—obviously posed different problems for American leaders. A revolution potentially as profound as the Mexican broke out in Santo Domingo on April 24, 1965. At issue were power and the reconstruction of Dominican society along radical lines. The fissures and inequities in Dominican society that contributed to the outbreak were, just as in Mexico, unlikely to be ameliorated or adjusted by elections and constitutional government while traditional military and land-owning groups retained the power to block reform.

Abstention is no more preferable in principle to intervention, but only in relation to the accomplishment of foreign policy objectives. So long as those objectives are defined as Wilson, Kennedy, and Johnson defined them, there is probably no alternative to intervention. It is not the purpose of this essay to suggest an alternative set of objectives that might make abstention a feasible policy. Even so, one wonders whether the United States, protected by extraordinary nuclear and conventional power, might not choose, as did the British under Pitt, to remain indifferent to the nature of internal regimes in foreign countries. Grounds for intervention would then exist not in the chimera of constitutional democracy but in the accumulation by a powerful adversary of dangerous political, geographic, or economic advantage.

SUGGESTIONS FOR FURTHER RESEARCH

Research in intervention requires, first of all, adequate and accurate case studies and, second, some systematic methods for evaluating the information made available by the case studies. The development of further case studies on intervention, then, is an invaluable undertaking. Therefore, the systematic evaluation of the case studies can be greatly assisted by the contemporary analytic tools of decision-making and systems analysis. The most important area for further research perhaps lies in the area of the relationship between domestic politics and foreign policy. This area is to date little explored and therefore promises great reward for those who undertake studies of the relationship. Their studies, in turn, would be of utmost value to those who sought to understand and judge interventions. There is little I can suggest at this stage as to what might be the most fruitful approaches to the study of the relationship between domestic politics and foreign policy. Some tentative approaches have been scouted in the works of Singer, Rosenau, and others. The subject, nonetheless, remains essentially unformed and unexplored.

The chief problem for those who seek to establish the influence of domestic politics on foreign policy is, first, to define the two areas satisfactorily and, second, to discover the kinds of information that would substantiate influence in the normal operation of an administration. Solid evidence of links between domestic politics and foreign policy are information of such a sensitive character that they are kept secret with great care. It may be, therefore, that one must seek direct evidence of direct linkage through a systems approach or other analytical tools.

BIBLIOGRAPHIC NOTE

The explanation of foreign policy depends on two different kinds of intellectual effort: one must know what happened, and knowing this one may then attempt to say why, or at least how and for what purpose it all happened.

In regard to the first task, the collection of facts, scholars, political leaders, and journalists have contributed much information about both the Mexican and Dominican interventions. About Mexico, some of the more helpful works are Frank Brandenburg, *The Making of Modern Mexico* (Englewood Cliffs, N.J.: Prentice-Hall, 1964); Clarence Clendenen, *The United States and Pancho Villa: A Study in Unconventional Diplomacy* (Ithaca, N.Y.: Cornell University Press, 1961); Howard Cline, *The United States and Mexico,* rev. and enl. (Cambridge, Mass.: Harvard University Press, 1963); Charles Curtis Cumberland, *Mexican Revolution: Genesis under Madero* (Austin: University of Texas Press, 1952); K. J. Grier, *The United States and Huerta* (Lincoln: University of Nebraska Press, 1969); P. Edward Haley, *Revolution and Intervention: The Diplomacy of Taft and Wilson with Mexico, 1910-1917* (Cambridge, Mass.: MIT Press, 1970). Arthur S. Link's multivolume study of *Wilson* (Princeton, N.J.: Princeton University Press) is an invaluable aid. Robert E. Quirk has examined one of the numerous American interventions in Mexico in *An Affair of Honor: Woodrow Wilson and the Occupation of Veracruz* (Lexington: University of Kentucky Press, 1962), and John Womack's *Zapata and the Mexican Revolution* (New York: Knopf, 1968), is a biography of that colorful and influential figure.

On the Dominican Republic, Samuel Flagg Bemis's *Latin American Policy of the United States: An Historical Interpretation* (New York: Harcourt Brace, 1943) covers relations between the United States and the Dominican Republic to World War II. Sumner Welles, *Naboth's Vineyard: The Dominican Republic, 1844-1924*, 2 vols. (New York: P. O. Appel, 1966); Selden Rodman, *Quisqueya: A History of the Dominican Republic* (Seattle: University of Washington Press, 1964); G. P. Atkins and L. C. Wilson, *The United States and the Trujillo Regime* (New Brunswick, N.J.: Rutgers University Press, 1972), and Howard J. Wiarda, *The Aftermath of the Trujillo Dictatorship: The Emergence of a Pluralist Political System in the Dominican Republic* (Gainesville: University of Florida Press, 1965) cover the nation's tormented past and present.

Among the best books on the intervention of 1965 are Juan Bosch, *Trujillo: causas de una tirania sin ejemplo*, 2d ed. (Caracas, 1961) and *The Unfinished Experiment: Democracy in the Dominican Republic* (London: Pall Mall, 1966); Theodore Draper, *The Dominican Revolt: A Case Study in American Policy* (New York: Commentary, 1968); Abraham F. Lowenthal, *The Dominican Intervention* (Cambridge, Mass.: Harvard University Press, 1972); José Antonio Moreno, *Barrios in Arms: Revolution in Santo Domingo* (Pittsburgh, Pa.: University of Pittsburgh Press, 1966); Marcel Niedergang, *La révolution de Saint-Dominique* (Paris: Plon, 1966); Tad Szulc, *Dominican Diary* (New York: Delacorte Press, 1965); Jerome Slater, *Intervention and Negotiation: The United States and the Dominican Revolution* (New York: Harper and Row, 1970). John Bartlow Martin, the American Ambassador to the Dominican Republic during Juan Bosch's aborted tenure and a special adviser to President Lyndon Johnson during the intervention, has written *Overtaken by Events: The Dominican Crisis from the Fall of Trujillo to the Civil War* (New York: Doubleday, 1966), and Johnson's own *Vantage Point: Perspectives of the Presidency, 1963-1969* (New York: Holt, Rinehart, and Winston, 1971) gives the president's account of his reasons for ordering the intervention. The *Public Papers* of Presidents Kennedy and Johnson are a handy source of presidential speeches and other public pronouncements (Washington, D.C.: Government Printing Office, annual).

In the main text of the essay I avoided certain kinds of interpretive tasks: I have not, for example, questioned but have only recorded the moral justification given by the Wilson and Johnson administrations for the two interventions (self-determination, rightly understood); nor have I challenged the political basis for the dispatch of American troops to the Dominican Republic (an unwillingness to permit even the risk of Communist success, in the belief that such a success anywhere in the world endangered American security). This is not the result of moral obtuseness on my part or of political insensitivity. I am aware of the sometimes bitter debate about the bases of American foreign policy. If the rationale of American policy since 1945 was most cogently and eloquently explained and justified in Dean Acheson's *Present at the Creation: My Years in the State Department* (New York: Norton, 1969), it has been interestingly and thoroughly challenged, most effectively, perhaps, by William A. Williams's *Tragedy of American Diplomacy,* rev. and enl. (New York: Dell, 1962), Robert W. Tucker's *Nation or Empire? The Debate over American Foreign Policy* (Baltimore: Johns Hopkins Press, 1968), and Joyce and Gabriel Kolko's *Limits of Power: The World and United States Foreign Policy, 1945-1954* (New York: Harper and Row, 1972). The reader interested in basic moral and political questions as they apply to American foreign policy should study these works carefully. My comparison and the pattern of intervention I identified are meant not to replace or to divert but to inform the work of those interested in the study of foreign policy as well as of those interested in raising the fundamental questions.

Further Research

The limited relevance of American intervention to the Mexican and Dominican revolutions invites studies of the two kinds. First, new thought must be given to formulating goals of American foreign policy appropriate to the changed circumstances facing all nations in the last third of the twentieth century. In an interdependent world, increasingly beset by shortages of primary commodities, American leaders have already begun to find it unsuitable to continue indefinitely to respond to crisis in Robert E. Osgood's words "by the exercise and extension, rather than the abstention or retraction, of American power." (*Prob-*

lems of Modern Strategy, Part I, Adelphi Paper No. 54, reprinted as "The Reappraisal of Limited War," in Frank N. Trager and Philip S. Kronenberg, eds., *National Security and American Society: Theory, Process and Policy* [Lawrence: University Press of Kansas, 1973], p. 356.) The Nixon administration has attempted to give the United States new foreign goals and has described them at length in the annual "State of the World" messages. With one or two exceptions, particularly Stanley Hoffmann's "Weighing the Balance of Power," *Foreign Affairs* 50 (July 1972): 618-43, the new American goals have not been tested by intelligent national debate. Certainly the problem of finding new, workable policy goals has not elicited anything like the thought and panache applied to it by the Nixon administration's chief foreign actor, Secretary of State Henry Kissinger. Even the best of the revisionists have taken the old policy as a starting point, and this is plainly inadequate. The new goals must be something more than the negation of the old.

A second area of research invites attention, as well. It should be possible to shed more light than now exists on the sources of foreign policy. My findings suggest that domestic influences—particularly the need to be seen to be defending democratic self-determination—affect American intervention in important ways. The study of the influence of domestic factors on the formation of foreign policy has only begun. Not surprisingly, the best place to start is Henry Kissinger's "Domestic Structure and Foreign Policy," in James N. Rosenau, ed., *International Politics and Foreign Policy,* rev. ed. (New York: Free Press, 1969). The present accomplishments of political science in this area are well summarized by K. J. Holsti in Chapter 12, "Explanations of Foreign Policy Outputs," of his *International Politics: A Framework for Analysis,* 2d ed. (Englewood Cliffs, N.J.: Prentice-Hall, 1972). The chapter contains an excellent bibliography. As Holsti reveals this is an area of great importance to scholars and policymakers, and one that promises to reward effort with understanding that can bring greater knowledge and control of policy itself.

THE MANCHURIAN CRISIS, 1931 - 1932

Norman A. Graebner

FROM ITS INCEPTION the Manchurian crisis raised the issue of United States intervention in Asia as had no previous challenge to China's Open Door. Even as late as the months preceding the Mukden incident of September 18, 1931, United States officials adhered to the established notion that the Open Door principle defined no prevailing American interests in China and therefore need provoke no United States involvement in China's defense. When the news of the Mukden clash reached Washington, however, the Hoover administration revealed no inclination to escape responsibility for what occurred in Asia. This country not only was the world's most powerful but also, more than others, had identified its favored position in the Far East with the status quo in China. Because the United States had revealed greater concern for China's future than did the other powers, any successful Japanese assault on the East Asian settlement would pose a special challenge to American prestige and diplomacy.

Still the Japanese aggression of 1931, and the deep apprehension which it generated within the United States, questioned far more than this country's commitment to the Open Door and the state of its prestige. What the Japanese assault endangered was the credibility of the international treaty structure which supposedly had eliminated at last the employment of force in relations among nations. If the United States had rejected League of Nations membership, it had taken the lead in negotiating the Nine Power Pact of 1922 and the Kellogg-Briand Peace Pact of 1928. For Washington these two treaties comprised the world's greatest hope for global peace and stability. And Japan, in signing them, had agreed to share with other Pacific powers the responsibility for maintaining the treaty system in China. At stake in Manchuria, therefore, was less that region's future than the entire post-Versailles international order.

With good reason Chinese editors moved quickly to universalize the significance of events in Manchuria. Shanghai's *Shun Pao* warned its readers that a troubled China spelled trouble for the world. To Shanghai's *China Press* Japan threatened not only the safety of Manchuria but also the peace and security of all nations. "Unless immediate international pressure is exerted," ran its conclusion, "the Kellogg pact, the League of Nations Covenant, and other similar world declarations will be thrown into the dust-bin." Before long such themes filtered through the American press. Japan's war against China was serious enough, agreed the *Washington News,* but it was, in the words of that newspaper, "insignificant compared with the larger issue of rescuing the world's peace machinery." United States interests demanded no less than a serious attempt to sustain the post-Versailles peace structure. "If the United States Government cannot make these peace treaties operate—by diplomatic demands, or by economic boycott, if necessary," charged the *News,* "how does it expect the American people or the world to retain any faith in peace treaties and disarmament? We believe these treaties can be made to work. At least, the State Department can try."

United States officials readily defined the Japanese challenge in universal terms. Following the Mukden incident they still agreed that this country possessed no interests in China or Manchuria that justified war; United States and Chinese interests were scarcely congruent. But Washington assumed a worldwide community of interest in peace of sufficient strength to compel Japan's compliance with its international obligations. This assumption gave the United States both its guiding objectives and its anticipation of success in achieving them. Stanley K. Hornbeck, chief of the Division of Far Eastern Affairs, advised the administration to base any protests to Tokyo on the issue of international peace and not on the principle of the Open Door. United States Ambassador to China Nelson T. Johnson similarly admitted his indifference to Manchuria's future but not to the future of the Kellogg Pact and the League. As he warned the State Department late in November 1931, "The fate of Manchuria is of secondary importance compared to the fate of the League."

Secretary of State Henry L. Stimson, like Hornbeck and Johnson, was troubled less with Chinese integrity than with the structure of world peace. At a cabinet meeting on October 9, Stimson warned President Herbert Hoover against involving the United States in any humiliating position should Japan refuse to honor its signatures on the Nine Power and Kellogg pacts. But the secretary recorded in his diary the essential role of the Far Eastern treaty system in United States policy:

> The question of the "scraps of paper" is a pretty crucial one. We have nothing but "scraps of paper." This fight has come on in the worst part of the world for peace treaties. The peace treaties of modern Europe made out by the Western nations of the world no more fit the three great races of Russia, Japan, and China, who are meeting in Manchuria, than, as I put it to the Cabinet, a stovepipe hat would fit an African savage. Nevertheless they are parties to these treaties and the whole world looks on to see whether the treaties are good for anything or not, and if we lie down and treat them like scraps of paper nothing will happen, and in the future the peace movement will receive a blow that it will not recover from for a long time.

It was the presumed indivisibility of peace that rendered Japanese aggression a question of vital concern. An unopposed Japan, believed Stimson, would destroy the credibility of the whole system of collective security based essentially on the force of world opinion and operating through the world's peace system. For that reason he could offer Japan, as a signatory of the Nine Power and Kellogg pacts, no choice but to sacrifice its interests and ambitions to the higher goal of world peace, which, it so happened, underwrote the worldwide interests of the United States.

Even before the end of September Stimson had outlined a program to bring Japan to terms. Writing to Hugh Wilson, the American minister at Geneva, Switzerland, he made clear the United States preference for direct Sino-Japanese negotiations. If outside leadership were required, China and Japan should submit their dispute to the League. Or if such means failed, argued the secretary, the United States would consider some resort to sanctions. Early in October, when it became clear that China and Japan would not settle their differences peacefully, Stimson placed the available sanctions before the president: collective economic

sanctions against Japan; an exercise of diplomatic pressure, based on
the power of public opinion, to guarantee a fair settlement for China;
or a vigorous moral judgment against Japan to save as much respect as
possible for the peace treaties. Hoover rejected economic sanctions
outright, arguing in his *Memoirs:* "Ever since Versailles I had held that
'economic sanctions' meant war when applied to any large nation. . . .
no nation of spirit would submit to having her whole economy totally
demoralized and her people thrown out of employment and into
starvation. . . . Sanctions or the threat of them also meant rising emo-
tions, the development of incurable hatreds, and an insensated opposition to any remedial action."

Economic sanctions would produce war. But Hoover no more than
his predecessors in the White House dared contemplate the use of force
to protect American treaty rights in the Far East. The system of
unequal treaties in China, which the United States shared with the
other great powers, was the creation of British gunboats in the nineteenth century. The Open Door notes of 1899 and 1900 identified
United States purpose with the preservation of the established treaty
system, but before the Washington Treaties it was the Anglo-Japanese
Alliance of 1902 that maintained the status quo in China. By substitut-
ing the Four-Power Pact for the Anglo-Japanese Alliance, the Washington Conference freed Japan of the restraints of British policy and
released Britain from its traditional role as the guarantor of the treaty
system in China. Thereafter the United States confronted an increasingly expansive Japan alone. The Washington Treaties, moreover, restricted
the United States to its naval base in Hawaii. With the British fleet held
at Singapore, no Western naval power in the Pacific could contest
Japanese supremacy in the China seas. This trend against naval competition in the western Pacific received confirmation in the Pact of Paris
and the London Naval Treaty of 1930. American naval officers, convinced that the Philippines were indefensible and subject to conquest in
a war, had no desire either to hold the islands or to contest Japanese
ambitions in Manchuria. Thus Hoover commanded no force to carry
out a threat against Japan. And a war against Japan, his military
advisers assured him, would not bring victory in less than four years.

President Hoover defined the major ingredients of Washington policy
at a cabinet meeting in mid-October. Japan, he admitted, had behaved
outrageously toward the United States. "But the Nine-Power Treaty

and the Kellogg Pact," he added, "are solely moral instruments based upon the hope that peace in the world can be held by the rectitude of nations and enforced solely by the moral reprobation of the world. . . . We are not parties to the League of Nations, the covenant of which has also been violated." The United States would, therefore, confine its role in the Sino-Japanese conflict to friendly counsel, especially since it did not possess interests in China which would recommend a war over Manchuria. Still, Hoover charged, the United States had a "moral obligation to use every influence short of war to have the treaties upheld or limited by mutual agreement." The president discovered the means to uphold the Far Eastern status quo in two long-term sources of power, both of which would eliminate the necessity of military involvement. The first lay in world moral pressures, organized largely under the League. The second comprised China's "transcendant cultural resistance" which had demonstrated often its power to absorb or expel foreign intruders. Hoover's recorded statement defined the limits of United States intervention in Manchuria. Having rejected economic sanctions as merely a prelude to war, he placed his hopes for peace on the altar of moral sanctions alone. Still the reliance on moral suasion in no measure eliminated the prospects of success in stopping Japan. No nation, Hoover and Stimson agreed, could defy a united and outraged world opinion with any chance of success.

On October 8 news reached Washington that the Japanese were bombing Chinchow in southern Manchuria, distant from Mukden. "I am afraid," Stimson recorded in his diary, "we have got to take a firm ground and aggressive stand toward Japan." The administration responded with its initial move to confront Japan with countering pressure. Reluctant to act unilaterally, Stimson instructed the American consul in Geneva, Prentiss Gilbert, to sit with the League Council at its meeting on October 13. But Stimson limited Gilbert to possible League action under the Kellogg Pact. On October 17 the Council, in secret session, agreed to urge all signatories of the Kellogg-Briand Pact to remind China and Japan of their obligations to sustain the peace of the Far East. For Hoover and Stimson that was enough, for they would have the United States accept no responsibility for the Manchurian settlement. Indeed, on October 19 the secretary ordered Gilbert to avoid all League deliberations that involved the employment of League machinery rather than appeals under the Kellogg Pact. London and Paris argued that Gilbert's withdrawal from the Council would discredit the organization in a time of crisis and lend encouragement to Tokyo.

During subsequent days the boundaries of United States involvement in League action became clear. Stimson permitted Gilbert to "go on sitting at the damned table," as he complained in his diary. "He is, however," continued the secretary, "to keep his mouth shut and let it be shown in that way that he is nothing but an observer." Thereafter Washington followed the League at a distance. Stimson even held up his note to China and Japan under the Kellogg Pact for three days after Britain and France had sent theirs. On October 24 the League Council passed a resolution which called upon Japan to evacuate Chinese territory by November 16. This decision Stimson refused to endorse, for it might commit the United States to some future intervention with force. Hoover agreed. William Castle, under secretary of state, recorded in his diary on November 4 that the president had remarked at lunch that "he wants to get completely out of the League connection and thinks it might have been wise politically, to make Stimson keep out."

Actually much of the American press, taking seriously the universal implications of Japanese aggression, appeared far more venturesome than the administration. Indeed, some editors and writers lauded Stimson's limited cooperation with the League as a decisive and effective response to Japanese behavior. The *Brooklyn Eagle* termed it "the most important single development in American foreign policies since 1920." For unlike previous American deliberations with League officials on questions of opium production, disarmament, or trade, the United States now sought, through cooperation with the League, the prevention of a dangerous international dispute. The Great Depression, the *Saint Paul Dispatch* reminded its readers, had demonstrated that the United States was not isolated from the world economically; the Manchurian crisis proved that it could maintain its political isolation with no greater success. As a country deeply involved in the world community, the United States could well rely on the League and accept the responsibility which such reliance entailed. And it was far better that the United States acted with the League in Manchuria, argued the *New York Herald Tribune,* for any Japanese defiance of the League would flout, not the United States alone, but virtually the entire world. The broader the judgment against Japan, the greater the presumed restraint on Japanese behavior and the less the danger of military involvement.

Such newspapers demanded by late November that the Hoover administration, acting with the League, create the necessary deterrent against Japanese expansion. "If the Western world does not respond to the present call from the Far East," warned the *New York Journal of Commerce*, "it might as well cease to talk about plans for reducing outlays on armaments, based on formal renunciation of war as an instrument of policy." Similarly the *Norfolk Virginia-Pilot* admonished the Western governments: "The League of Nations and the signatories of the Kellogg and Nine-Power pacts must act with all the power at their command to prevent this high crime [of Japanese aggression] against the basic principles that form their common dedication." Japanese success in Manchuria, declared the *New York World Telegram*, would set off aggressions in Europe. "If Japan can break the treaties successfully today," ran its warning, "Germany and Italy and other nations will be encouraged to use force tomorrow." Some interventionist editors granted cautious approval to economic sanctions. For the *Detroit News* economic sanctions comprised "the one effective weapon." William Allen White's *Emporia Gazette* agreed that a boycott would bring Japan to terms inasmuch as its industrial life depended on international trade. With world peace at stake, argued the *Milwaukee Journal*, the president could scarcely hesitate to adopt an effective course of action. "He must know," declared the *Journal*, "that he would have the overwhelming approval of the American people."

Japan's open contempt for the November 16 deadline measured the League's ineffectiveness. Yet some editors viewed the League action of October as evidence that reason was indeed overcoming force in international affairs. The *Buffalo Courier-Express* termed the League's "interference" as a "notable victory for the organized opinion of the world against war as an instrument of national policy." The *Baltimore Sun* proclaimed with equal satisfaction, "The gain for peace is at once a vindication of the League and the Kellogg Pact. . . . The League has not, to be sure, imposed its demands on Japan in their entirety. But it has so mobilized the forces of world opinion and world diplomacy as to check Japan in her career of Manchurian aggression."

Recalcitrant isolationists were not convinced. They charged the administration with breaking faith with the American people who had made clear their rejection of the League in every election since Versailles. Stimson's instructions to Prentiss Gilbert, complained the *Louisville Courier-Journal*, suggested that the United States was about to enter the League through the front door. The Hearst press demanded that Hoover stop acting as if he were president of the world. Not all editors were convinced that sanctions—economic or moral—would achieve their objective of restoring the treaty structure in the Far East. For some the danger to world peace lay less in Japanese aggression than in the cleavage which sanctions would create between the Eastern and Western worlds. The *Philadelphia Record* termed a boycott both unwise and ineffective, leading not to the triumph but to the destruction of the League. The *New York Daily News* wondered why Washington was so insistent on preserving the status quo in Asia when this country protected no tangible interests in opposing Japan. "The answer as we see it," ran its judgment, "is that Japanese expansion is not going to stop. We believe that by sitting on the safety-valve, the United States is only piling up trouble for itself."

In endorsing no more than the Council's restatement of the Kellogg Pact, the Hoover administration, throughout November and December, attempted to maintain an official neutrality on the Manchurian question. Neither the president nor the secretary of state had any desire to antagonize Japan. When the League Council reconvened at Paris in mid-November, Hoover sent Ambassador Charles G. Dawes from London to represent the United States as observer and consultant. But Stimson informed Dawes that the United States would not join any League embargo against Japan although it would not interfere with such sanctions. Official Washington understood that Japanese militarists and nationalists had long awaited the opportunity to drive the moderates from power and commit their country to a program of austerity at home and expansion abroad. The worldwide depression which struck Japan in 1931, added to Chiang Kai-shek's reassertion of Chinese primacy in Manchuria, presented the militarists the occasion to attack. With good reason, therefore, Stimson feared that external pressure on Japan might strengthen the hand of the extremists in the Japanese government. His policy, he wrote, was "to let the Japanese know that we are watching them and at the same time to do it in a way that will help Shidehara [Japan's foreign minister] who is on the right side."

Having globalized American interests by binding them to the perpetuation of the treaty structure, Hoover and Stimson required some means to make that structure effective. No other course of action could close the gap between their desire to avoid trouble and their determination to stop Japan. Increasingly they contemplated some recourse to moral sanctions. During November Stimson concluded that it might be wise to "outlaw Japan and let her sizzle [under a Chinese boycott] and all the moral pressure of the world." Early in December Hoover offered for cabinet discussion a proposal that the League instruct its members not to recognize any changes in Manchuria which resulted from violations of the Kellogg Pact. If the United States could not prevent Japanese aggression, it could express its feelings of deep moral disapprobation toward events in Manchuria and thereby satisfy public demands that this country take its stand against Japan without involving itself in war. Columnist Walter Lippmann that month favored nonrecognition of treaties "negotiated at the point of a bayonet" as a promising vindication of the world's peace efforts. Through such nonrecognition, wrote Lippmann, the powers would compel the Japanese to contemplate the destruction of their legal position and with it the undermining of Japan's credit and prestige throughout the world. Japan's defeat in the face of legal sanctions would demonstrate that "the world's effort to establish law and order in international life had not been wholly vain."

Before the end of December the Hoover administration settled at last on the Wilsonian doctrine of nonrecognition as the means best designed to reenforce the treaty system. "We do not see how we can do anything more ourselves," Stimson informed Dawes, ". . . than to announce our disapproval and to announce that we will not recognize any treaties which may be forced by Japan under the pressure of military occupation." Stimson rationalized the administration's move toward nonrecognition in his memoirs. "If the fruits of aggression should be recognized," he wrote, "the whole theory of the Kellogg Pact would be repudiated, and the world would be at once returned to the point of recognizing war as a legitimate instrument of national policy. Nonrecognition might not prevent aggression, but recognition would give it outright approval."

On January 7, 1932, Stimson formally applied the American doctrine of nonrecognition to Manchuria by sending identical notes to Japan and China which declared that this nation could not "admit the legality of any situation *de facto* nor does it intend to recognize any treaty or agreement entered into between those Governments" which might impair either the treaty rights of the United States or the territorial and administrative integrity of the Republic of China. Three days earlier Hoover and Stimson had agreed that Britain and France should also publish statements of nonrecognition. Both European governments refused; they had no interests in Manchuria which would encourage even a legal sanction against Japan. Still the president believed that nonrecognition, backed by continued Chinese resistance, would frustrate Japanese designs. He argued that the Kellogg Pact was the great moral force against aggression and that the note of January 7 had effectively mobilized world opinion against Japanese behavior. Indeed, Hoover predicted that the note would stand as one of the country's great state papers.

With that judgment much of the American press agreed. The *Providence Journal* thought the note one of "clear and far-reaching importance in the history of twentieth-century diplomacy." The *Grand Rapids Press* regarded it "an act of far greater portent than the invoking of the League of Nations Covenant." Such major newspapers as the *Baltimore Sun* and the *Louisville Courier-Journal* joined the *Nation* in recommending that the United States back its doctrine of nonrecognition by withdrawing its diplomatic representation from Tokyo. In rationalizing his January note Stimson admitted that the United States had no quarrel with Japan's rights in Manchuria and no desire to influence the final Manchurian settlement provided that it did not violate the Kellogg Pact. Stimson was convinced, however, that if governments extended a similar warning of legal retribution to those who would break treaties anywhere it would place his note "on a more elevated and broader principle" and permit it to "appeal with greater force to a much larger number of nations in the world." Again Washington had declared that change to be legal also had to be peaceful. Unfortunately such doctrine, however laudable in the abstract, offered no hope of peace. For to satisfy Stimson's demands Tokyo would be compelled to give up its ambitions in Manchuria inasmuch as it could never improve the Japanese position in that region through peaceful means alone.

If Stimson's moral interventionism enjoyed wide approval in the American press, it did not impress some realists who wondered whether nonrecognition would serve the cause of peace at all. The *Chicago Daily*

News voiced the minority position with considerable clarity: "To remind Japan of its pledges or to reassert the open-door principle, seems harmless enough. But pin-prick notes irritate the sensitive and proud Japanese, and stiffen the attitude of the dominant military clique. China's ultimate interests may be served better by a policy of patience and discretion, by overlooking Japan's inconsistencies, and letting it restore order and security throughout Manchuria."

Such doubts were not limited to the press. In Tokyo United States Ambassador W. Cameron Forbes found Stimson's toughness a meaningless verbal exercise which would under no circumstance serve the interests of the United States. To Forbes the compelling rationales for American involvement in Manchuria—the Open Door as embodied in the Nine Power and the Kellogg pacts—had already lost their durability. Rhetorical recriminations based on such documents, argued Forbes, would merely aggravate tensions across the Pacific. Thus unilateral and multilateral denunciations of Japanese policy in Manchuria, which clearly no country intended to support with military sanctions, exceeded the bounds of common sense. The ambassador noted in his journal that "protests not backed up by the mailed fist only stir up ill-feeling without accomplishing anything." Mere threats would exacerbate the very danger of war that they were intended to eliminate. What controlled in Manchuria was Japanese power and interests, not Japanese legality. Far better, explained Forbes, to recognize the actual conditions which governed the Sino-Japanese relationship:

> I am more or less an "insurrecto" on the whole idea of trying to protect weak peoples against agression [sic]. If they are weak because they are small, that is one thing; if they are weak because they are rotten, that is another. It is a rule of Nature that rotten things shall fall and that live things should utilize the decayed substance of the other as fertilizer and material to further its own growth. I do not mean by this that I want to see Japan absorb China, but some change was necessary in the governmental structure of Manchuria, and Japan had the punch to provide it.

Stimson's protests, Forbes warned Hornbeck, would silence Japan's conservatives. Upon departing from Tokyo in March 1932, Forbes announced that his staff was unanimous in its opposition to the moral pressures emanating from Washington, convinced that they would ultimately lead the United States into war. Years later Forbes complained that it was the belligerent tone of official American rhetoric that permitted the Japanese extremists to paint the United States as Japan's primary antagonist and thereby prevent the moderates from making any energetic bid for power.

Forbes's immediate successors in Tokyo, Acting Ambassador E. L. Neville and Ambassador Joseph C. Grew, agreed that Japanese actions in Manchuria responded largely to economic and security interests. Grew warned Washington that force—perhaps a war—alone would stop Japan. "The Japanese government," he wrote in mid-1932, "intends to carry out its Manchurian program unless prevented by superior force. Furthermore, the elements now in control of the country believe that their cause is just and that this gives added strength to their determination. They regard America as their biggest stumbling block. They regard the Manchurian cause as one of superior and vital national interest, if not one of self-defense, and on that basis they are willing to fight if necessary." Inside the cabinet Patrick J. Hurley, secretary of war, took up the theme that force alone would save the treaty structure of Manchuria. Stimson responded simply that "the policy of imposing sanctions of force had been rejected when the United States made clear its refusal to support the League of Nations."

As some critics predicted, the verbal strictures against Japan had no apparent effect, for that country continued its assault along the Chinese mainland and finally, on January 28, attacked Shanghai, largely in retaliation against the Chinese boycott. Hoover ordered United States naval vessels to that city to protect American civilians. Stimson warned Tokyo that unless Japanese officers protected the International Settlement in Shanghai the result would be catastrophic. Many Americans shared Stimson's alarm but not his sense of outrage at the Japanese assault on Shanghai. More than events in Manchuria, those in Shanghai raised the specter of global war and dictated caution in like measure. Even as members of the press again condemned Japan for its brutality they demanded that the United States move with extreme delicacy. "The American people," declared the *Philadelphia Record*, "don't give a hoot in a rain barrel who controls North China." The *Ohio State Journal* added: "Until Japan deliberately and maliciously encroaches upon our rights, our place is at home." Stressing the need of caution the *Boston Herald* remarked characteristically, "To condemn Japan is perfectly justifiable. To carry that condemnation to the extent that it invites war is something to be avoided by all good citizens." But some believed, despite the renewal of Japanese aggression, that the continued outpouring of verbal recrimination would ultimately have the desired effect on Japan. The *Washington News* phrased the widespread American conviction that immorality in international affairs was self-defeating: "Japan has outlawed herself. That act carries its own retribution. No nation can live unto itself alone. Some day . . . Japan will come back and beg to be respected and trusted again. Then she will pay heavily for this madness."

Undaunted by Japanese bahavior and the doubts expressed by informed United States officials, Stimson determined to press forward in his moral and legal crusade against Japan. Hoover again argued against any verbal threat to use force, but Stimson, in partial disagreement, believed that "we had a right to rely upon the unconscious elements of our great size and military strength; that I knew Japan was afraid of that without telling her that we were not going to use it against her." For Stimson it seemed essential that the United States continue to give official recognition not only to the country's general pro-Chinese sympathy—made up of demanding economic sanctions—but also to its adherence to the principle of peaceful change. In addition, on February 16 the League Council supported the nonrecognition doctrine and called upon Japan to fulfill its obligations under the Nine Power Treaty. "As I reflected on it," Stimson recalled, "it seemed to me that in future years I should not like to face a verdict of history to the effect that a government to which I belonged had failed to express itself adequately upon such a situation." Indeed, Stimson hoped, as he confided to his diary, that Japan would not withdraw from Shanghai before the United States could pass moral judgment on the latest aggression.

To reaffirm the principles of the Open Door, Stimson drafted an open letter to Senator William E. Borah of Idaho, dated February 23, 1932. Basing his new appeal on the Nine Power Treaty rather than the Kellogg Pact, Stimson argued that nothing had occurred to challenge the validity of the treaty system. The two treaties, he wrote, "represent independent but harmonious steps taken for the purpose of aligning the conscience and public opinion of the world in favor of a system of orderly development by the law of nations." Stimson's letter included a warning to Japan that the American decision for nonrecognition, if taken by other governments of the world, "will effectively bar the legality hereafter of any title or right sought to be obtained by pressure or treaty violation, and which . . . will eventually lead to the restoration to China of rights and titles of which she may have been deprived." Never before had Stimson made such claims for the coercive power of nonrecognition. Addressing the American Conference on International Justice in Washington on May 4, during Stimson's absence, Acting Secretary William Castle carried even further the administration's faith in the burgeoning Hoover-Stimson doctrine. "The President," said Castle, ". . . realized that in the mechanism of international relations a stern deterrent of the use of force would be to make valueless the results of war. . . . I believe that this 'Hoover Doctrine,' accepted by most nations of the world, through the League vote, is welcomed because it accomplished as nearly as may humanly be possible the purpose of peaceful prevention of war."

Again nonrecognition enjoyed the public approval that Stimson had anticipated. For the *Christian Science Monitor* Stimson's letter ranked with the most important state papers in the country's history. The *Wall Street Journal* termed it "a lucid, forceful statement of the correct American attitude toward the dangerous outbreak of extreme nationalism in the Orient." The *Washington Post* heralded nonrecognition as "the most important contribution to the machinery of international justice since the Kellogg Pact was signed." Some were not convinced. Again a minority defined nonrecognition less an American response to Japanese aggression than a device to avoid the necessity of creating a response.

Neither Stimson's strong historical defense of the Nine Power Pact nor even his veiled threat of a naval race in the Pacific under the Washington treaties stopped Japan or brought any country to China's defense. During March 1932 the Japanese smuggled former Emperor of China Henry Pu Yi into Manchuria and installed him as head of the new puppet state of Manchukuo. On May 5, 1932, Japan and China signed a peace treaty. Before the end of that month Tokyo had withdrawn all Japanese troops from the Shanghai area. For the moment the stabilization of Manchukuo was challenge enough. Facing the continuing failure of nonrecognition as an effective sanction, Stimson knew scarcely where to turn. Clearly the president no less than the bulk of the

American press remained opposed to economic and military sanctions. What remained for Stimson, therefore, was another powerful assault on world opinion. The secretary arranged to make his statement before the Council of Foreign Relations in New York. There on August 8, 1932, he returned to the Kellogg Pact as the bulwark of peace. Declaring aggression illegal, he admonished the world to condemn Japan as a lawbreaker. This in itself would comprise an unassailable force for peace. "Moral disapproval," said Stimson, "when it becomes the disapproval of the whole world, takes on a significance hitherto unknown in international law. For never before has international opinion been so organized and mobilized."

Stimson received his customary adulation. The *New York World Telegram* now praised the Hoover-Stimson doctrine as "the most important international step taken by the United States since the World War." The Hoover administration had abandoned the American policy of splendid isolation. "It is little wonder," added the *Washington Post*, "that Japan is acutely concerned over the purport of the American exposition of the Kellogg pact and the consequences which are now sure to flow from a wilful rupture of the mutual pledge of all nations to remain at peace." The *Nation* agreed. "Public sanction on which rests the Kellogg Pact," ran its conclusion, "can be one of the most potent sanctions in the world." War had ceased to be a private matter; instead of nobody's business the Hoover administration had made it everybody's business. The pressure unleashed by a universal concern for peace would render war too unproductive and costly. With such rationalizations the nation escaped the Manchurian crisis without the necessity of either defining its interests in the Far East with some accuracy or subjecting the implications of moral sanctions to closer scrutiny.

What Manchuria made clear was that nonrecognition, like other broad generalizations, meant nothing or it meant war. Still much of the country's foreign affairs elite lauded the Hoover-Stimson response as commendable in principle and significant in achievement. Robert Shaw concluded in the November 1932 *Review of Reviews* that the doctrine of nonrecognition supplied teeth to the Kellogg Pact even while it permitted the world to avoid any commitment to the use of force. "Unlike the economic boycott," he wrote, "it does not hurt neutrals or lead to warfare. It annuls the fruits of victory in such a way that wars cannot pay in either prestige or easy economic exploitation." Pointing to the achievements of the four Hoover years in *Foreign Affairs* of April 1933, Stimson asserted that the administration had thrown its weight behind the Kellogg Pact to make it "a living force of law in the world." Later Stimson complained that the United States, in the face of a great moral crisis, walked by on the other side of the street.

That it had not done. The Hoover-Stimson decision to intervene morally did not commit the United States to action in the Manchurian crisis. Washington's physical abstention from the burgeoning tensions in the Far East illustrated simply that the Japanese challenge did not touch any immediate United States interests. But the Hoover administration, by promulgating the notion that peace was indivisible, had defined Japanese aggression as essentially a global threat which the United States could ignore only for the moment and which demanded that Japan, no less than the United States, ultimately accept the status quo in the Far East. Until Washington acknowledged openly that limited Japanese infringements on Chinese sovereignty endangered no fundamental United States economic and security interests, this country would continue to stand as a perennial barrier to Japanese ambition whether it chose to limit its interposition to moral pressures or not. As the special defender, not of its own interests, but of the treaty system in China, the United States would emerge as the enemy of Japan and the major source of that country's frustration. Thus the Hoover-Stimson commitment to the status quo, in defense of an indivisible peace, would as surely trap this nation in war as would the assault on any body of tangible and universally recognized American interests in the Far East.

SUGGESTIONS FOR FURTHER RESEARCH

Manchuria was scarcely a unique episode in United States history. Its challenge to the historian, therefore, does not lie in exposing in greater detail the attitudes and decisions that surrounded the crisis. The several studies of the Manchurian affair reveal in profusion the suppositions and purposes of national and world leaders and the limitations which the established institutions and modes of thought imposed. The problem of Manchuria, to be fully understood, must be placed in a broader context.

Japan's assault on Manchuria comprised the first major postwar challenge to the Versailles order and the treaties of the 1920s designed by the great democracies to institutionalize any changes in that order to the end that any recognized alteration in the treaty structure would be arrived at peacefully. In 1931 the Hoover administration could not, for two reasons, accept any Japanese-inspired change in the Versailles system. First, in a moral world no status quo (and thus moral) power could accept an immoral and illegal action without admitting that the world had failed in its great endeavor to reduce all international relations to peaceful procedures. Second, if one aggression succeeded where would the treaty system hold? Still despite the significance which Hoover and Stimson assigned to the treaty system they rejected the price of war in its defense simply because they recognized no threat to American interests in Japanese aggression. Their rationalizations for the Hoover-Stimson doctrine of nonrecognition reflected essentially their belief that Japanese behavior endangered world stability every-where. Yet they were willing to coexist with Japanese aggression against China presumably forever.

This inconsistency created a profound dichotomy between the ten-dency to denounce aggression as unacceptable because of its global ramifications and the refusal to act as if the nation's interests were threatened at all. It was this gap between purpose—to guarantee interna-tional conformity with treaty obligations—and physical abstention to avoid war that sustained the tension between the United States and Japan. If the United States rejected Japanese expansion as unacceptable it never confronted that country with understandable policies which reflected the national determination to uphold established treaties. It is this pattern of response to forceful change, whether the change is limited or not, which suggests the historic importance of the Man-churian crisis and the areas for further study. For that pattern of rejecting change while refusing to fight for the status quo established the character and limits of national behavior in a variety of interna-tional confrontations and interventions in the decades which followed. This suggests the need not only of understanding more precisely the intellectual framework in which leaders commit the country but also of knowing to what extent the State Department and White House accept or neglect the recommendations which emanate from the armed forces.

BIBLIOGRAPHIC NOTE

As an international crisis Manchuria embodied a clear challenge and a less-than-clear response both in the United States and in western Europe. The Japanese assault on the status quo of East Asia came first. Japan's motives and objectives were no mystery in 1931; subsequent writings merely added details. Even before the Washington Conference of 1921-1922 observers noted that Japan had not accepted the existing political and economic order in the Far East. They warned, moreover, that the only alternative to continued Western rejection of change was ultimate war. Two articles that stressed these themes were Arthur Bullard, "Expanding Japan," *Harper's Monthly Magazine* 139 (November 1919): 857-66; and K. K. Kawakami, "A Japanese Liberal's View," *Nation* 113 (November 9, 1921): 530-31. Japanese objectives at the time of the Manchurian crisis were clarified in Viscount Kikujiro Ishii, "The Permanent Bases of Japanese Foreign Policy," *Foreign Affairs* 11 (January 1933): 220-29; and George H. Blakeslee, "The Japanese Monroe Doctrine," *Foreign Affairs* 11 (July 1933): 671-78.

From the literature on Japanese foreign policy the following works are representative. On the beginning of the Manchurian crisis see Robert H. Ferrell, "The Mukden Incident: September 18-19, 1931," *Journal of Modern History* 27 (March 1955): 66-72. Several major studies of Japanese policy, which include the Manchurian episode, are Tatsuji Takeuchi, *War and Diplomacy in the Japanese Empire* (Garden City, N.Y., 1935); Arthur M. Young, *Imperial Japan: 1926-1938* (London, 1938); and Seiji Hishida, *Japan among the Great Powers* (New York, 1940).

President Hoover's reaction to the Manchurian crisis emerges clearly in his *Memoirs of Herbert Hoover: The Cabinet and Presidency, 1920-1933* (New York, 1952), vol. 2. Ray Lyman Wilbur and Arthur Mastick Hyde, eds., *The Hoover Policies* (New York, 1937), comprises a useful collection of basic documents. William Starr Myers has produced a laudatory study of Hoover in *The Foreign Policies of Herbert Hoover, 1929-1933* (New York, 1940). For Stimson's role in the Manchurian crisis the best starting point is Henry L. Stimson and McGeorge Bundy, *On Active Service in Peace and War* (New York, 1948). Also valuable is Stimson's *The Far Eastern Crisis* (New York, 1936). Stimson's retrospective judgment of the Hoover policies appeared in his article, "Bases of American Foreign Policy during the Past Four Years," *Foreign Affairs* 11 (April 1933): 383-96. Elting E. Morison has produced the standard biography of Stimson in his *Turmoil and Tradition: A Study of the Life and Times of Henry L. Stimson* (Boston, 1960).

Christopher Thorne's *The Limits of Foreign Policy: The West, the League and the Far Eastern Crisis of 1931-1933* (London, 1972) supersedes all previous studies of the Manchurian crisis in both scholarship and detail. But Sara R. Smith's older *Manchurian Crisis, 1931-1932* (New York, 1948) is still useful. Specifically on Stimson's role in the crisis is Armin H. Rappaport, *Henry L. Stimson and Japan, 1931-1933* (Chicago, 1963). Robert H. Ferrell's *American Diplomacy in the Great Depression* (New Haven, Conn., 1957) traces Stimson's reaction to Manchuria somewhat more briefly. For specific aspects of the Hoover-Stimson policy see Paul H. Clyde, "The Diplomacy of 'Playing No Favorites': Secretary Stimson and Manchuria, 1931," *Mississippi Valley Historical Review* 35 (September 1948): 187-202; and William R. Castle, Jr., "Recent American Policy in the Far East," *Annals of the American Academy* 168 (1933): 46-53.

For the United States the lasting contribution of the Manchurian crisis was the Stimson Doctrine of nonrecognition of change resulting from the use of force. Two highly laudatory evaluations are Quincy Wright, "The Stimson Note of January 7th, 1932," *American Journal of International Law* 26 (1932): 342-48; and Manley O. Hudson, *By Pacific Means: The Implementation of Article Two of the Pact of Paris* (New Haven, Conn., 1935). A more recent study is Robert Langer, *Seizure of Territory: The Stimson Doctrine and Related Principles in Legal Theory and Diplomatic Practice* (Princeton, N.J., 1947). Richard N. Current has distinguished between the two doctrines in his superb article "The Stimson Doctrine and the Hoover Doctrine," *American Historical Review* 59 (April 1954): 513-42. See also Current's *Secretary Stimson: A Study in Statecraft* (New Brunswick, N.J., 1954). On Roosevelt's adoption of the Stimson Doctrine see Bernard Sternsher, "The Stimson Doctrine: F.D.R. *versus* Moley and Tugwell," *Pacific Historical Review* 31 (August 1962): 281-89. Also important in the study of this transition from Hoover to Roosevelt are Joseph C. Grew's *Ten Years in Japan* (New York, 1944) and Grew's *Turbulent Era: A Diplomatic Record of Forty Years, 1904-1945,* ed. Walter Johnson, 2 vols. (Boston, 1952).

THE PALESTINE QUESTION: DOMESTIC PRESSURES ON THE PRESIDENT FOR INTERVENTION, 1944 - 1948

Dennis Deutsch

Introduction

Following the demise of the Ottoman Empire after World War I, the victors met to discuss the disposition of the conquered territories. Most of the land under consideration was divided by the British and the French and placed within their respective spheres of influence. Included in Great Britain's share was the region of the Middle East referred to as Palestine. In 1922, by the authority of the League of Nations, Palestine officially became a British mandated territory.

The British, however, were not the only ones interested in the fate of Palestine. By the end of World War I, world Jewry had developed nationalistic aspirations which it hoped would culminate in the establishment of a sovereign Jewish state in Palestine; the site of the biblical Jewish kingdom of Judea. In order to bring about their state, these Jews, known as Zionists, organized a worldwide political movement which had as its function the raising of funds and political support for their program. In 1917 the Zionists won their first concession from the British government with the issuance of the Balfour Declaration in which the British foreign secretary said: "His Majesty's Government view with favour the establishment in Palestine of a national home for the Jewish people, and will use their best endeavours to facilitate the achievement of this object." The intent of the declaration was never executed by the British, however, and subsequently during the years following the First World War the Zionists carried on a campaign to impel the British government to make good its promise.

In April of 1946 the president of the United States outlined the position of his administration on the question of a Jewish state in Palestine, a problem that was officially the concern of the government of Great Britain. Writing to Prime Minister Attlee President Truman explained, "the Jewish Agency proposed a solution to the Palestine problem by means of the creation of a viable Jewish State in control of its own immigration and economic policies in an adequate area of Palestine. . . . The proposal received widespread attention in the United States both in the press and in public form. From the discussion which has ensued it is my belief that a solution along these lines would command the support of public opinion in the United States. . . . To such a solution our government could give its support." Two years later, Truman again asserted his role as president and granted recognition to the fledgling state of Israel. What caused the president of the United States to intervene in the "foreign problem"? The answer lies in understanding the power and impact of public opinion and interest group politics in the United States.

United States Public Opinion and Pressure Group Politics

While the British Zionists were actively trying to influence their government, the Zionist Organization of America was using its resources to convince the United States government that it should intervene on behalf of the Zionists and proclaim its support for the establishment of a Jewish state in Palestine. As early as 1914, Justice Louis Brandeis, himself a Zionist, presented his political colleague and friend President Woodrow Wilson with an explanation and outline of Zionist goals and aspirations. The success of the Zionists, however, was minimal in the United States and no action was officially taken by the government on the proposal.

Some success was achieved during the inter-war years in convincing certain factions of the government that the Zionists should be given governmental support. By 1944 the political elite of the nation favored the notion of a Jewish Palestine. On June 27, 1944, the Republican National Convention adopted the following resolution supporting the Zionists:

> In order to give refuge to millions of distressed Jewish men, women and children driven from their homes by tyranny, *we*

call for the opening of Palestine to their *unrestricted immigration* and land ownership, so that in accordance with the full intent and purpose of the Balfour Declaration of 1917 and the resolution of a Republican Congress in 1922, *Palestine may be constituted as a free and democratic commonwealth.* We condemn the failure of the President to insist that the mandatory of Palestine carry out the provision of the Balfour Declaration and of the Mandate while he pretends to support them (italics mine).

The following month the Democrats followed suit at their convention: *"We favor the opening of Palestine to unrestricted Jewish immigration and colonization* and such a policy as to result in *the establishment there of a free and democratic Jewish commonwealth"* (italics mine).

Unfortunately for the Zionists, Congress was not actively involved in the foreign policy decision-making process. The problem as it was perceived by the Zionist leadership in the United States presumed a need for mass support in order to strengthen their position when confronting the president, since it would take the active support of the president for a Zionist success. They had good reason to hold this belief. As early as 1943 the American Zionist Emergency Council initiated lobbying efforts at local and federal levels and discovered, as the 1944 convention resolutions verified, that congressmen, senators, and grass-roots party officials were willing to support the Zionist idea. By the 1944 presidential election, support of politicized America for the Zionist program was clear. President Roosevelt, however, did not commit the nation to any action to implement this program or to intervene in what was, after all, a British affair. In spite of his unwillingness to act, Jewish support for Roosevelt in the November election was overwhelming. It appeared that the Jewish vote would continue to support the Democratic administration regardless of the president's position and his lack of action on the Palestine question. So the Jewish vote at that time could not be used as an effective ploy to persuade Roosevelt to act and declare American policy as officially favoring the establishment of a Jewish state in Palestine. A stronger, wider-based support for the Zionist program had to be secured in order to influence the president. The Zionists decided to conduct a massive effort to gain the support of the whole American people in order to use public opinion as a means of pressuring the president to act in their favor.

For this purpose the American Zionist Emergency Council began a national propaganda campaign. The Council launched it with a book, *America and Palestine,* which, it maintained, expressed "the attitude of official America and of the American people toward rebuilding Palestine as a free and democratic Jewish commonwealth." Of course, the conclusion reached in the work was that American support was already with the Zionists. The book was a fascinating example of expert manipulation of factual material to present a conclusion that deceptively appeared to be valid. The work traced the history of American attitudes toward the question of Jewish nationalism and Palestine. It noted the 1922 congressional resolution favoring the Zionist program and that "outstanding members of the United States Congress had previously manifested their warm interest in the movement for Jewish national restoration in Palestine. Governors, mayors, judges, and other federal, state, and municipal officials had clearly indicated their approval of the re-establishment of Palestine as a Jewish National Home." Then, in Chapter 8, the Council systematically listed those organizations, prominent individuals, and state governments, which by 1944 had declared themselves in favor of a Jewish Palestine. It refers to the American-Palestine Committee, formed in May 1932, which listed among its membership "thirty-six high-ranking government officials." When the Committee was reorganized in 1941, it boasted sixty-eight senators and over two hundred congressmen within its ranks. Statements from five presidents of the United States (Wilson, Harding, Coolidge, Hoover, and Roosevelt) were provided as evidence of a previous American commitment. It noted further that twenty state legislatures by 1944 had adopted resolutions favoring the establishment of a Jewish commonwealth in Palestine. Among other Zionist supporters listed in the book were such notables as Vice President Henry Wallace, Associate Justice of the Supreme Court Frank Murphy, and twenty-seven state governors. The book was a masterpiece of propaganda, for it presented its arguments well with substantial supportive evidence. Although it dealt adequately with the attitude of "official America," the book failed to present any evidence of support for the Zionist program from the mainstream of the American people. The reason is understandable. The intent of the book was to aid in creating a bandwagon effect in order to gain just that support.

What actually was the position of the American public at this time? Before being able to appreciate the meaning of American public opinion surveys (Cantril, Roper, Gallup, etc.) on the Palestine question, we must know precisely what issue the Zionists were emphasizing at the time the various public opinion surveys were taken. In order to accomplish this we can examine the directives sent from the national offices of Zionist organizations to their local chapter offices advising the locals which issues to concentrate on in their propaganda efforts. One such organization was the National Council of Jewish Women (NCJW). The Council is one of the more moderate Zionist affiliates which divides its programs between funding health and educational projects in Israel and serving as a domestic Jewish philanthropic group. The NCJW offers a fine illustration of Zionist activity in the United States. In February 1944 the Zionists were campaigning to achieve a reversal of the policies of the British White Paper of 1939 which had limited Jewish immigration to Palestine. Following the example set by the Zionist Organization of America the national offices of the NCJW issued a memorandum to regional and chapter presidents advising them to use the immigration issue in their campaigns within their communities. Mrs. Mildred Welt, national president of the NCJW wrote that all chapters were "to support all efforts toward the abrogation of the White Paper" and to limit their activities in their respective communities to this single issue. In December 1944 the National Opinion Research Center at the University of Denver conducted a survey which indicated that on the question of providing the Jews with a special chance to settle in Palestine after the war, 45 percent of the public favored giving the Jews such an opportunity.

> (December 1944) Do you think the Jews should be given a special chance to settle in Palestine after the war, or do you think all people should have the same chance to settle there?
>
> Jews 45%   All the people same 44%   Don't know 11%

In 1945 some five million Jews resided in the United States. This represented 3.7 percent of the total population. A response by 45 percent of the population in favor of giving the Jews a special chance to immigrate was indicative of a generally sympathetic viewpoint on this issue by the American public at the outset of the Zionist campaign. If the Zionists were to be successful in persuading Roosevelt to change his position and the position of the government, they would have to demonstrate an increase in that 45 percent.

The Zionists were active for the next three years in trying to increase their broad-based support. Local chapters were advised by their national offices to wire the president in order to speed action on the Zionist proposals. Each organization related in the telegram its size and strength. One telegram sent to President Truman by the American Jewish Conference in June of 1946, for example, begins: "On behalf of the American Jewish Conference, its 63 affiliated national organizations and the hundreds of communities represented in it." In order to further the bandwagon effect, local chapters were urged to issue to their community newspapers press releases written and distributed by national offices. If the impression of strength and unanimity could be made throughout the communities of the United States, the Zionists figured, then the popular support for their program would rapidly increase.

After one year of this kind of campaigning—press saturation and sending telegrams to the president—the Zionists had no success in changing the percentage of American support for their position. Whereas in December 1944, 45 percent of the population believed that the Jews should be granted a special chance to settle in Palestine after the war, in December 1945 a similar question elicited only a 44.5 percent favorable response. No significant change in support for the Zionists had taken place in a year's time.

An examination of further survey data indicates that support for the Zionist position continued to remain below the 50 percent level. In 1944 two issues were at hand: Jewish immigration to Palestine and the establishment of a Jewish state in Palestine. While 45 percent of the population favored giving the Jews a special opportunity to settle in Palestine after the war, only 36 percent of those surveyed believed that the British should set up a Jewish state in Palestine.

(December 1944) There are over a million Arabs and over half a million Jews in Palestine. Do you think the British, who control Palestine, should do what some Jews ask and set up a Jewish state there, or should they do what some Arabs ask and not set up a Jewish state?

The British should set up a Jewish state	36%
Did not know	32%
The British should follow neither Arab nor Jewish wishes	10%
The British should not set up a Jewish state in Palestine	22%

Substantial support for the Jewish state already existed. When the question came closer to home, however, requiring the government to commit itself to intervene on behalf of the Zionists, support diminished considerably with only 20 percent of the population believing that the United States should officially establish a policy calling for a Jewish state in Palestine.

(December 1944) Do you think the United States government should officially demand that Palestine be made into a Jewish state, or don't you think so?

United States should officially demand that Palestine be made into a Jewish state	20%
United States should not demand a Jewish state	30%
Don't know whether or not the United States should demand a Jewish state	18%
British should not set up a state or don't know	32%

If the Zionists were to prove successful in changing Roosevelt's position, they would have to show that a shift in American public opinion was taking place. At this point it was not.

Another six months of campaigning elapsed and the Zionists achieved no further success. In fact, support for their program decreased about 5 percent.

(May 1946) Do you think this [allowing 100,000 Jews to settle in Palestine] is a good idea or a poor one?

Good	40% (of the total population)
Poor	7%
No Opinion	4%

(The remaining 49 percent had no idea what the issue was about.)

After two and one-half years the Zionists still had not gained the mass public support which they needed in order to impress FDR. But at the same time a quirk of history which was to prove a great advantage to the Zionists took place. In April 1945, with the sudden death of President Roosevelt, Harry S. Truman assumed the office of the president of the United States. There were numerous differences in the personalities and backgrounds of the two presidents and the Zionists would make every effort to capitalize upon these differences. For one thing, Truman was already somewhat favorable to the Zionist program. As a United States senator Truman delivered a speech on the floor of the Senate in which, when confronted with a resolution calling for the Senate to declare itself favorable to a Jewish Palestine, he had declared, "My sympathy is, of course, with the Jewish people." Furthermore, good friends of the new president had close association with the Zionist movement. One such friend was Eddie Jacobson. Prior to his entrance into politics Truman had shared the proprietorship of a men's haberdashery with Jacobson. When Truman assumed the presidency the Zionists were quick to remind Jacobson of his Jewish affiliation and used him as an instrument to influence the president. It is interesting to note that Margaret Truman, in her extensive study on her father, discounted Jacobson's influence on the president. She claimed that any belief that Jacobson actively discussed any political issues with Truman is unfounded. Very recently, however, the diary of Eddie Jacobson was uncovered in a Kansas City attic. Through his diary, Jacobson proves conclusively that, in reference to the Palestine issue specifically, he often made contact with the White House between November 1947 and May 1948.

The value of these contacts is reflected in the remarks of retired State Department Assistant Director of the Office of Near East and North African Affairs Edwin Wright. Referring to a period in 1948 when Truman refused to see anyone on the Palestine question, Wright explains the president's sudden reversal, and his agreeing to see Chaim Weizmann of the World Zionist Organization, as the direct result of the friendship between Truman and Jacobson. Wright claims that the president saw Weizmann "because of the intervention of Eddie Jacobson. [Jacobson's entry for March 13, 1948: 'Arranged meeting with Pres. and Dr. W.[eizmann] Pres. very bitter—had to use argument about his idol Andrew Jackson.'] But he never saw the State Department (officials). . . . When the pressures are put on, the White House would repudiate the State Department and would go along with the Zionist pressures."

The successes that the Zionists began to have with Truman were reflected in the aforementioned letter from Truman to Prime Minister Attlee in which Truman based his position on favoring the issuance of

100,000 visas for immigration to Palestine on the support of American public opinion.

By 1946 it was clear to the Zionists that, although they had failed to create the support they wanted from the American public, they had created an effective myth of support which had prompted Truman to act on their behalf. The increase in public support was not evident, but the Zionists had successfully influenced the president to take a positive position on the Palestine question. If they wished the president to take further action and make a greater commitment, the Zionists would have to employ new tactics.

Their opportunity for new tactics developed early in 1947 when anticipation of the 1948 presidential election created political stirrings throughout the United States. The Zionists saw a new means of influencing the president; they would try to capitalize upon the power of the Jewish vote. While this factor had failed to be of much relevance in the previous election, the Zionists hoped that the political climate was favorable for the Jewish vote to be a factor with which the Democrats would have to reckon. Zionist leader Abba Silver recalls in his *Vision and Victory*, "The approaching November elections offered a favorable opportunity. It is at such times that government in a democracy is more sensitive to the expressions and sentiments of its citizens. A Political Action Committee was organized to demand, in the name of American principles and American commitments, action from our government. In connection with Palestine, the pressure of aroused and indignant public opinion was great." The Zionists used the election effectively. They applied pressure on the president from all areas. In March 1948 the Democratic party publicity director, Jack Redding, wrote to the president: "We have the Zionist Jews in the office everyday and the pressure is building up a terrific head of steam." Another tactic used by the Zionists is illustrated by the advice offered the president by Robert Hannigan, chairman of the National Democratic party, when he reminded Truman that many who had contributed to the Democratic campaign of 1944 were pushing for administration support of the Jewish position on Palestine.

Even the president's personal staff was not left unaffected by the Zionists' tactical infiltration. In a memorandum of November 1947, presidential aide Clark Clifford indicated to Truman just how crucial the Jewish vote could be in carrying New York in the election. Since the Jewish population there was roughly 18 percent of the total, it was necessary, indeed, that Truman have respect for this large block of votes.

The Zionists also made effective use of congressmen to pressure the president. One story told by Edwin Wright, who at the time was serving as a United Nations specialist in the State Department, illustrates how effective an assertive congressman can be.

> Emanuel Celler came in with a group of Zionists [to Truman's office] and told Truman that Dewey was coming out with a speech in which he was going to favor 100,000 Jews being sent to Palestine. And Celler said to him, "Now, Harry, you've got to beat Dewey to it or he's going to get the Jewish support and the Jewish vote and if you don't come out for a Jewish state (and the story was that Emanuel Celler pounded on the desk) we're going to vote you out of office and we'll run you out of the city." That's the threat. And I think it's true as far as I can tell because Emanuel Celler was one of the most avid of the Zionists in Congress.

Exposed to all these pressures from his party, from his political advisers, and from Congress, it appeared as though Truman could not escape the Palestine question.

Then, shortly after the incident with Celler, the president decided to remove himself from the Palestine problem entirely, informing his secretaries that he would not speak with anyone on the issue. For the Zionists, however, this was not the end of the question. They had received word from their sources that the Jewish Agency in Palestine was preparing to declare the establishment of the Jewish state regardless of the decision reached in the United Nations which was in the midst of debating the issue. If the new state was to survive, it would need prompt recognition by various world governments. The American Zionists had to convince Truman that he would have to take a leading role and respond to the Israeli declaration. The president, however, was resolved not to meet with anyone concerning the issue; least of all more Zionists. The obstacle was overcome by the intervention of the president's friend Eddie Jacobson, who, on behalf of the Zionists convinced Truman that he should meet with Chaim Weizmann. Weizmann was flown from London to the White House for the historic meeting which was crucial for the future of the Zionist movement. Although not all the specifics of that meeting have ever been fully revealed, undoubtedly it was Weizmann's eloquence and forensic abilities which were instrumental in persuading Truman to assert his authority as the chief executive. The "State of Israel Proclamation of Independence" was issued in Tel Aviv on 14 May 1948. On May 15 the president extended United States recognition to the provisional government of Israel. The Zionists finally had succeeded through the use of public opinion and pressure politics in influencing the president to intervene in a problem which was not germane to American affairs.

Comment

The research conducted during the last decade by Lee Benson, Lester Milbrath, V. O. Key, Howard Childs, and other public opinion and interest group theorists has effected a reversal from earlier points of view on the relative influence of interest group politics and public opinion on the foreign policy decision-making process. In his 1967 article "Interest Groups and Foreign Policy," Milbrath concluded that "interest group influence on foreign policy is slight." Similarly in 1969 Lee Benson, in "An Approach to the Scientific Study of Past Public Opinion," wrote "that public opinion significantly influences policy has long been assumed. How much hard evidence exists to support it, however? Rather little." Scholars from earlier decades, however, have maintained that United States foreign policy historically has in fact been a reflection of the whims and wishes of the public. A classic study from this earlier period is Thomas A. Bailey's *The Man in the Street: The Impact of American Public Opinion on Foreign Policy,* written in 1948. Bailey maintained that "what the government in Washington does or fails to do in the field of foreign affairs will depend largely on the wishes of our citizens, and what our citizens demand or fail to demand will affect mightily the destiny of this planet."

Perhaps the total reversal of opinion which took place in the 1960s went a bit too far. As the case just presented illustrates, it was entirely the politics of the American Zionists as a pressure group which impelled the president to intervene in the fate of Palestine. If there had not been a significant Zionist group in America, United States interest in the Zionist cause would have been negligible. Public opinion and interest group pressures are still of significant importance in the American political process. Potentially each administration is vulnerable to the pressure of certain interest groups in America.

The American Jewish community is a group that historically has had greater success in influencing the Democrats than the Republicans. In the 1944 presidential election the Democrats were confident of full electoral support from the American Jewish community. Their confidence was well founded, since Jewish support for Roosevelt was overwhelming. In the 1948 election, the Zionists were successful in forcing the Democratic leaders to doubt the continuance of that support unless they affirmed the Zionist program. The Republicans on the other hand have not had to rely on the Jewish vote. Their support has traditionally come from other sectors of society. The absence of this dependence is reflected today in President Nixon's policy toward Israel. He has not been liable to the manipulation of the American Zionists. The delivery of arms to Israel has been cautiously administered by the president, much to the chagrin of the Zionist community and the Israelis. It was only after the failure of the president in many months of diplomacy in which Nixon tried to force the Middle East belligerents to negotiate a settlement that he reaffirmed the friendship of the United States with Israel. In January of 1970 the president made a policy statement in which he declared his intention to maintain a balance of power in the Middle East. This position, coupled with continual Soviet military support to Egypt, eventually led to the delivery of additional Phantom jets to Israel. Those who had demanded through the long months of diplomatic action that the president deliver jets were primarily the Zionists, certain black groups, and the AFL-CIO—groups that had backed the Democrats in 1968 and were not in a position to exert any real pressure on Nixon. The additional jets were provided not in response to domestic pressures, in this case, but were delivered due to Nixon's personal perception of Israel as an important anti-Communist ally in the Mediterranean world.

Although in a democratic society it is conceptually ideal to have a government which is responsive to its constituency, great care must be taken when a response involves international politics. If any special interest group is capable of influencing policy to the degree that the Zionists were able to do so during the late 1940s, we risk the real possibility of losing whatever democratic value is left in our political system. The president of the United States should not be liable to political pressures from interest groups to the degree that Truman was during his tenure of office. To intervene in foreign affairs on behalf of a minority of Americans is to jeopardize the rights of all the American people as well as the rights of the people of the nation in which we are interfering. Whether it be corporate, religious, or private interests, we must take care to limit the power of both the president and lobbies in America so that the interests of all the American people and the sovereignty of all the peoples of the world is not impaired.

Epilogue

There develops from this particular case two serious questions relevant to most foreign policy and domestic issues: what role should interest groups play in the decision-making process, and, once this role is defined, how can the activities of such organizations be limited to that role? I have illustrated the way in which interest group pressures are powerful enough to direct American foreign policy. Other recent events in American history serve to illustrate further the immense strength of pressure groups. From the International Telephone and Telegraph (IT&T) exposé of 1972 we saw that interest groups in corporate form are capable of circumventing justice and tainting our judicial branch of government. The legislative branch, too, has not been beyond the reach of interest group politics and its negative aspects. Government contracts and corporate legislation have often been all too favorable to private interests at the expense of the general public. Some congressmen have actually overstepped the bounds of the law while responding to such pressure. One case often cited when referring to the problem of political ethics is the example of Senator Thomas Dodd in the early 1960s in which the pressure to which he succumbed came in the form of campaign and other contributions in return for contracts and favorable legislation.

   Certainly the voices of the American people must be heard. In many cases the only way information and opinions from the public can become an effective force is through a cooperative effort. We should encourage such activity. However, we must also develop the means for controlling this input so that it remains an input of opinion and an illustration of electoral support or disapproval, and not simply a matter of which group has the largest treasury.

Some rudimentary steps have been taken in this direction by the passage of laws requiring that political parties and candidates reveal their income sources. A much more difficult and complex problem remains for further analysis and action: the development of a system in which information flows freely into the government without the consequence of political patronage and dominating pressure groups.

SUGGESTIONS FOR FURTHER RESEARCH

Events are moving quickly in the Middle East: so quickly that questions which were raised only a few months ago are now moot and seemingly unimportant with respect to new queries and theories that are now prevalent. This paper was a consideration of a democratic presidency during a period when the American Jewish community had to make its presence felt in the White House via an intermediary, an apolitical personal friend of the president. Today we have a Republican administration (traditionally more responsive to large corporate concerns than Zionist interests) and a Jewish secretary of state. How are the Zionists responding to this precedent in American history? Are the oil lobbies drastically changing their strategy and tactics or do they feel that the same reasoning and approach that they used on John Foster Dulles will be equally successful with Henry Kissinger? These are the kinds of questions that presently deserve consideration.

During the Yom Kippur War Nixon was quick to resupply Israel with the arms she needed to counter Russia's airlift to the Arab states. Why? My own thinking is that the Soviet airlift was a tactical blunder from the political point of view. The Republicans, and Nixon in particular, have historically been slow to respond to Jewish-Zionist demands here in the United States. My own speculation is that Nixon's resupplying of the Israeli's was due totally to his lingering Cold War perspective and that if Russia had remained passive during this last round of the Arab-Israeli War, there could have been no domestic pressure large enough to move Nixon toward resupplying Israel, sans Arab occupation of Tel Aviv. We will look forward to some later studies examining the interplay between the president and the Zionists which took place during these early October days which led to Nixon's actions making him a Zionist hero.

With the exception of John Kennedy's short tenure in office, the past four administrations (two of which were Republican and two

Democratic) have had to contend with an Arab-Israeli War. Using our policy toward Israel under each of these administrations, with a full comparative study of the foreign policy decision-making process in each would be an excellent way of examining the basic questions which this paper raised: do public opinion and interest group politics play a role in the structure of governmental process, and to what extent should they?

In order to get a more complete picture of the domestic pressures on a president which attempt to influence his foreign policies, studies, of course, should not be limited to the Middle East or, for that matter, Vietnam. To varying degrees, for every area to which our foreign policy is directed, we have both corporate interests and public interests concerned with the decisions the president will make. In some cases these interests are identical. In most instances the two interests conflict. Where each conflict arises, there is a basis for a case study of the presidency and its accompanying domestic pressure which should be explored.

BIBLIOGRAPHIC NOTE

In order to appreciate fully the complexity of the foreign policy decision-making process with respect to Israel, it is essential that one first have a basic knowledge of the history of modern Zionism and the Jewish state movement. Although there are innumerable volumes on virtually every aspect of Zionism and Israeli history, a good beginning is in the reading of Walter Laqueur's *A History of Zionism* (New York, 1972), which develops the rise of modern Zionist thought and its political maturation in the nineteenth and early twentieth centuries. See also Israel Cohen, *A Short History of Zionism* (London, 1951), and Rufus Learsi, *Fulfillment: The Epic Story of Zionism* (Cleveland, 1951). Progressing chronologically to the period between the World Wars, one should read Christopher Sykes, *Crossroads to Israel* (London, 1965; Bloomington, Ind., 1973). Sykes's coverage of the troublesome "Mandate Years" is superb and provides the reader with one of the most objective accounts written on the period. For those interested in pursuing the history of Israel after the creation of the state, I suggest Nadav Safran's *From War to War* (New York, 1969). While doing any reading on the history of Israel and the Arab-Israeli wars, it is essential that *The Israel-Arab Reader* (New York, 1969) be kept as a "vade mecum." Laqueur has accumulated in this short volume all the pertinent agreements, declarations, and policy statements made from the Bilu

Manifesto of 1882 through the Six Day War. Every history of Israel will make reference to these vital documents and it is extremely helpful to have the texts available while reading.

There too are some important studies dealing specifically with United States foreign policy and Israel. For a survey of early United States involvement in the Middle East see James A. Field, Jr., *America and the Mediterranean World, 1770-1882* (Princeton, N.J., 1969). See also Joseph L. Gabriel, *Protestant Diplomacy in the Near and Middle East: Missionary Influences on American Policy, 1810-1927* (Minneapolis, Minn., 1971). The role which oil interests have historically played in shaping our policies is explored in George Lenczowski, *Oil and State in the Middle East* (Ithaca, N.Y., 1966).

Of course there are always personal accounts that emerge from any period in history which add to our perspective. In this respect we have, inter alia, *The Autobiography of Sol Bloom* (New York, 1948) which reflects the thoughts of this Zionist protagonist of the Roosevelt and Truman eras. See also Cordell Hull, *Memoirs,* 2 vols. (New York, 1948), Walter Millis, ed., *The Forrestal Diaries* (New York, 1951), and the two volumes of Truman's *Memoirs* (New York, 1955).

Turning to the analytical studies of the presidency, foreign policy, and public opinion, we find an abundance of materials. Perhaps the best-known study of the role of public opinion in the United States and the theories behind it, is V. O. Key, *Public Opinion and American Democracy* (New York, 1961). For a more historical perspective of the role of public opinion in shaping our foreign policy, there are two works of interest by Ernest May: *American Imperialism: A Speculative Essay* (New York, 1968) and "An American Tradition in Foreign Policy: The Role of Public Opinion" in *Theory and Practice in American Politics,* ed. William Nelson (Chicago, 1964).

Although the foregoing suggestions are certainly a selected bibliography, they should provide the reader with a fairly thorough introduction to the history of the period as well as an appreciation for the theoretical aspects of the factors involved in the making of foreign policy.

U.S. INTERVENTION & ABSTENTION
IN GREECE, 1944 - 1970

Theodore A. Couloumbis & M'Kean M. Tredway

THE FORMAL VISIT of Secretary of State William Rogers to Athens on 4 July 1972 gave rise to the following interesting and somewhat paradoxical set of reactions: Parliamentarians such as Panayotis Kanellopoulos and George Mavros, the leading spokesmen of the unified political opposition in Greece, boycotted the Fourth of July celebrations at the United States Embassy in Athens and denounced Rogers's visit as signifying blunt acceptance and condonement of a dictatorial regime that has systematically violated the ideals of the North Atlantic Treaty Organization (NATO) and the Western World. This visit in their view was a clear "interference in Greece's internal affairs."

On the other side, reacting to insistent press reports to the effect that Secretary Rogers, while in Athens, had pressed for elections to democratize Greece, First Deputy Premier Stylianos Pattakos angrily denounced these reports as unfounded rumors, adding that it would be "naive" to believe that Rogers had come to Athens "to order us to declare elections." Byron Stamatopoulos, the Greek government's official spokesman, reacting to similar rumors retorted, "We do not interfere, but neither do we tolerate interferences."

So we find ourselves in the perplexing situation where a single event, the Rogers visit, has given rise to complaints against "interference" by members both of the opposition movement and of the military government.

But let us go further and give some more examples of governmental and nongovernmental activities in the United States which have both direct and indirect (albeit hard to measure exactly) effects on the internal political situation of Greece: The platform of the Democratic party (approved by the 1972 convention in Miami) contains a plank: "Cease American support for the repressive Greek military government." To the average Greek, involved in politics, this means that a George McGovern victory in the November 1972 elections would cause a decisive shift of existing United States policies and even, possibly, result in the toppling of the regime by the Greeks themselves.

On the other side, there has been a continuous string of high-level diplomatic and military visits to Greece, including such top echelon administration dignitaries as Secretaries Maurice Stans, Melvin Laird, Rogers, and, not the least, Vice President Spiro Agnew. These visits have been clearly interpreted as symbolic of the Nixon administration's substantive support for the Greek colonels.

A group of students and professors pickets a Greek Embassy function in Washington, D.C., because it is being attended by high-level U.S. officials. On the other side, a consortium of New York banks authorizes a multimillion dollar, short-term, loan to the Greek government, at a time when balance-of-payments pressures on the Greek economy seem to be on the rise.

Committees of concerned Greeks and Americans are lobbying through Congress and the media are arguing for or against the military government, depending on their roots and orientations.

Congressional hearings both in the Senate and the House reveal serious bipartisan opposition to the administration's "business as usual" handling of Greco-American relations. Simultaneously, U.S. media afford a full opportunity to the Greek regime's exiled critics to tell their side of the story, expose oppression and torture, and plead for the return of democracy to their homeland.

On the other side, at a solemn ceremony in Norfolk, Virginia, Greece's ambassador to the U.S., Vassilios Vitsaxis, cheerfully proclaims the continued solidarity of the Greco-American alliance, as he accepts a converted U.S. destroyer for the Greek fleet.

A teach-in is held at the Massachusetts Institute of Technology protesting U.S. support for the "fascist militarists" in Greece, while on the other side one witnesses mushrooming combinations of Greco-American priests and businessmen presiding over the bustling traffic of Greek-Americans who yearly flock to the homeland cities, islands, and countryside in search of rest and old roots.

From all these examples one can easily be led to the conclusion that there exists considerable U.S. influence in Greece.[1] But this influence, it is obvious, is not monolithic and unidirectional but diverse, fragmented, and mutually nonreinforcing. On one side, most of the Johnson and Nixon administrations' activities seem to favor the perpetuation of the post-1967 political status quo. On the other side, serious congressional opposition, pressure groups, and the media are strongly behind the causes of the democratic opposition forces in Greece. All this is, at best, a function of an open, pluralist, and fragmented democracy such as the United States. Governmental influence in the United States cannot be easily orchestrated through private and independent institutions, as would be the case in well-controlled totalitarian and authoritarian regimes.

Background to Influence

Decisive foreign influence in the domestic and external affairs of Greece is not a contemporary phenomenon; it can be traced back to Greece's birth as a modern nation. Great-power influence, in its various forms, has been a way of life for this small, strategically located nation since 1821. The post-World War II period has been no exception to this rule. The chief difference, now, lies in the fact that the main source of influence has shifted from Britain to the United States, while the principal challenger still remains Russia.

Shortly after World War I there was a massive infusion of close to

[1] The terms influence, intervention, interference, and penetration will appear repeatedly in this chapter. As these writers define them, *intervention* is reserved for large-scale military and economic presence of one nation within the borders of another, which is designed to preserve or change the structure of political authority in the target nation (e.g., British intervention in Greece 1944-1946 or Soviet intervention in Hungary and Czechoslovakia 1956 and 1968, respectively). *Interference* is used to connote a single act designed to affect the target nation's political process (e.g., a United States ambassador's public or private endorsement of a given politician, political party, specific policy, or aspects of the political system and process). *Penetration* stands for a long-range, aggregate condition which permits the representatives of one nation to participate authoritatively in the political process of the other nation (e.g., members of advisory military and economic missions of donor nations serving in close, day-to-day cooperation with the relevant bureaucratic divisions of the recipient nations). *Influence* is used generically and impressionistically so as to provide a catchall, umbrella term for the other three defined above, and it contains elements of not only intergovernmental influence but also people-to-people influences including dependencies in the economic, social, and cultural fields.

1.5 million refugees from Asia Minor into a country of only 5 million. The effects of this event have not been clearly gauged to this day. Whether the migrations caused the frequent political upheavals reflected in the unbridled rivalry between republican and royalist elements or whether they merely aggravated an inherently unstable situation remains an open question. Military factionalism and frequent coups for power were the rule rather than the exception. But in 1936, in line with authoritarian and fascist trends throughout Western Europe, General John Metaxas established a dictatorship in Greece. The dissolution of political parties and the disorganization of related pressure and protest groups, which followed Metaxas's takeover, may have created the political vacuum which, in part, accounted for the bitter postwar struggle for political power in Greece.

A Decade of Tragedy

In 1940 Greece was attacked by Italy and in 1941 overrun and occupied by Germany and her Balkan Axis allies. During the 1941-1944 occupation a strong resistance movement developed. The largest and most effective organization was the National Liberation Front (EAM), which was controlled at the top by the clandestine remnants of the Greek Communist party. By the time the Germans evacuated in October 1944 and the British, together with the Greek government in exile, had reentered Athens, the Communist-controlled guerrilla forces were in firm charge of large portions of the country.

Bad politics on all sides and a series of miscalculations precipitated the December 1944 battle of Athens. The British—with total Soviet acquiescence—proceeded to crush the EAM bid for a greater share of power in the Greek government. Greece, by the "percentages agreement" made in Moscow between Stalin and Churchill on October 9, 1944, had been placed in the British sphere of influence. Both Greece and Turkey were considered two strategic links for the British lifeline to India and the Far East. The Russians, in return for a free hand in Eastern Europe, did not interfere while their Greek comrades were being crushed in Athens.

The initial Communist defeat was followed by an uneasy truce between the warring factions. Postwar Greece adopted the constitutional process by holding internationally observed elections on March

31, 1946. The question of the monarchy was also settled by plebiscite on September 1, 1946. Sixty-eight percent of those voting opted for the return of King George II and for constitutional monarchy. An unfortunate, perhaps tragic, decision was made by the Communists and some of the Center-Left politicians to abstain from the March 1946 elections. Perhaps, had they participated, they might have integrated themselves into the "system" and, possibly, the bloody civil war which ensued might have been averted.

The year 1947 was a terrible one in Greece. Communist guerrilla hostilities were rising rapidly at a time when the British had given notice of their inability or unwillingness to continue aiding the Greek and Turkish central governments. Most of rural Greece was in Communist hands and the situation was rapidly deteriorating further. Simultaneously Greece's Communist neighbors were vilifying mercilessly the allegedly fascist and authoritarian Greek government. The economy was in a state of near paralysis, beset by rapid inflationary spirals. The non-Communist politicians were bickering and refusing to coordinate their activities, still nursing prewar grudges. At this second, and even more critical, bend of Greece's postwar tragedy the British deus ex machina gave way to an American one. The succession act was named the "Truman Doctrine" and it appeared to signal a revolutionary departure from traditionally isolationist and noninterventionist United States policies in peacetime Europe. The intricacies of how the Truman administration pushed the multimillion dollar bill to aid Greece and Turkey through a skeptical and sedentary Congress are masterfully detailed in Joseph Jones, *The Fifteen Weeks.*

It is important, given this chapter's thesis, to illustrate the near total dependency of the Greek nationalist government on external British and later American support. The late 1940s was not a time for Greek politicians to worry about the niceties and outward appearances of autonomy. It was a time when political survival was at stake. They would not bite the hand that fed them. No one perhaps has better captured this dependency than Dean Acheson, probably the real father of the Truman Doctrine: "All this time," he said, "Greece was in the position of a semiconscious patient on the critical list whose relatives and physicians had been discussing whether his life could be saved. The hour had come for the patient to be heard from. On March 3 [1947] with the support of kind friends and their guidance of a feeble hand, the Greek government wrote asking for help—financial, economic, military and administrative."[2] Apparently the diplomatic hand of Greece was so "feeble" at the time that even the request for American help had to be drafted in the United States by American officials.[3]

The Greek government realized very well that United States assistance would entail some limitation of its sovereignty. The Minister Councilor of the Greek Embassy in Washington, for instance, reported to his home office that "the United States Plan would be accomplished by a limitation in some measure of the sovereign rights of Greece."[4]

While Greece's nationalists were clinging desperately to Washington's support for survival, its Communists were looking for Moscow's support in their obstinate bid for power. But although guidelines, slogans, and aphorisms from the Soviet Union abounded, substantive material aid was not forthcoming. It is now generally conceded by most analysts that Stalin and the USSR were opposed to the Greek Communist bid for power, which, in their view, had no chance for success but which threatened the stable and settled balance of power in the Balkans.

Stalin's clearest expression of his attitude toward the Greek Communist guerrillas emerged in a conversational exchange with Yugoslavia's Milovan Djilas. Stalin said: "No, they have no prospect of success at all. What do you think, that Great Britain and the United States—the United States, the most powerful state in the world—will permit you to break their line of communication in the Mediterranean Sea? Nonsense, and we have no navy. The uprising in Greece must be stopped and as quickly as possible."[5]

The Greek guerrillas received considerable aid, however, from their Communist neighbors, especially Yugoslavia. The latter undoubtedly offered assistance in the hope that a Communist regime in Greece (which would be dependent on Yugoslavia) might be pressed to make territorial concessions in Macedonia. After the Soviet-Yugoslav split in 1948, however, the Greek Communist leadership opted for a pro-Soviet

[2] Dean Acheson, *Present at the Creation* (New York: W. W. Norton Co., 1969), p. 221.

[3] Joseph Jones, *The Fifteen Weeks* (New York: Harcourt, Brace and World, 1964), pp. 77, 146.

[4] Stephen G. Xydis, *Greece and the Great Powers: 1944-47* (Thessaloniki: Institute of Balkan Studies, 1963), p. 480.

[5] Milovan Djilas, *Conversations with Stalin* (New York: Harcourt, Brace and World, 1962), pp. 181-82.

orientation and purged its Titoist elements. The Yugoslavs in retaliation sealed their border with Greece, and Yugoslavia served no more as a privileged sanctuary for the Greek guerrillas. The closing of the Yugoslav border, the revitalized Greek armed establishment (heavily aided by the United States), and the disastrous battlefield tactics of the Nikos Zachariades-led guerrillas tipped the scale in favor of the Central government and by early 1949 the Communists fled the country mostly to sanctuaries in Albania and Bulgaria.

Scholarly debate continues today as to whether without British and later American interventions postwar Greece would have been taken over by the Communists and turned into a "People's Democracy." Revisionist scholars seriously question whether the Churchill-Acheson cold-war concept of postwar Greece is accurate. It portrays Greece as a country saved from the clutches of the Moscovian world Communist movement thanks to the massive and timely support provided by the British (1944-1946) and the Americans (1946-1949). The revisionist scholars argue, on the other hand, that the West tragically misjudged matters, by equating the liberal-democratic forces in Greece with Communism thus eventually rendering this miscalculated guess into a self-fulfilling prophecy. Also, by backing conservative, royalist, and even some Nazi-collaborationist elements in the Greek political arena—elements that were expected to serve best the short-term military interests of the Western leaders—the Anglo-Americans were contributing to the long-range polarization of forces within the Greek political system.

Regardless of the merits and demerits of this debate, the fact remains that Greece's fate was settled by direct agreement between the British and the Soviets, with the tacit approval of the United States, on October 9, 1944. Once this fact is well understood, and the determination of both great powers to live up to this agreement is well established, then the whole fratricidal upheaval in Greece between 1944 and 1949 is reduced to a bloody exercise in tragic determinism.

Greece, throughout the civil-war period, can be best characterized as a multipenetrated polity. The two sides—in their fratricidal conflict—sought and accepted foreign aid and influence in order to prevail against their domestic antagonists. Once the Communists were defeated, and the Northern Balkan tap was shut off, the sources of influence and penetration moved primarily into the United States.

The 1950s: Reconstruction and Development

The legal framework for the longer-range United States presence in Greece was provided by the latter's entry into NATO early in 1952 and by a "bilateral facilities agreement" signed on 4 February 1953. This arrangement made available to the United States a naval communications station north of Athens, installations and port sites in Crete, Military Airlift Command facilities at the Athens Airport, and fuel and storage facilities in Piraeus, the port of Athens. There are some additional, but unlisted, facilities which have been made available by special agreements.

The presence and influence of the United States in the post-World War II years has been so apparent that the Greek political culture has come to assume that "nothing of significance ever happens in Greece unless the United States wants it." This, of course, takes on special significance when examining the political crises of the 1960s, the subsequent coups d'etat, and post-1967 Greek-American and Greek-NATO relations.

Throughout the 1950s the United States diplomatic representatives interfered quite overtly in Greek political affairs in order to maintain a pro-Western stability. Despite strong public reactions by press and politicians, the United States managed to have its way in Greek affairs, namely, to discourage the governmental instability which results from a multiparty system (a Greek tradition); to keep the Greek Armed Forces in a state of modernized readiness; and to insure that the Greek Communist party would never be given an opportunity to seize power.

In a recent revisionist account, Constantine Tsoucalas, a Greek sociologist in Paris, described the method and style of American influence as follows:

> Through bargaining over the amount and use of the money given, the USA had a stronger hold over Greek governments than Britain had ever managed to get. An implied threat to stop, reduce or even postpone the aid was enough to make Greek ministers fall flat on their faces. This goes far to explain the ease with which the USA could impose governments, policies and personalities even after the civil war was over. This was a change from the past. British influence had been based on an elaborate and carefully developed system of "agents"—who possessed or acquired key positions in the decision-making process in Greece. Under normal

circumstances, British intervention was never blatant or explicit, since it was channeled through diplomatic and "covered" activities. American influence, on the contrary, soon became a recognized institution.[6]

Jean Meynaud, one of the most prolific writers on Greek politics, offers perhaps the fullest, if somewhat exaggerated, descriptions of the style and manner of American influence over Greek affairs.[7] Americans, according to his account, were generally more casual in style than their stiff and formal British predecessors. United States ambassadors such as John E. Peurifoy were often given to public pronouncements on Greek domestic affairs as compared to the subtle and discreet "behind-the-scenes" British approach. United States presence and support in Greece was multifunctional, often resulting in direct and parallel relationships between the military functionaries and bureaucrats of both nationalities. Thus, the United States had a heavy input on decisions dealing with the Greek economy, the armed forces, and the police apparatus.

Further, the United States interfered directly in the political process and clearly tilted the balance in favor of men such as Alexander Papagos (premier 1952-1955) and later Constantinos Karamanlis (premier 1955-1963). According to Meynaud, the main instrument for this influence has been the direct link between Greek and United States security/intelligence agencies with and without the knowledge of the Greek government. Other methods of exerting influence would include a long list, among which were threats to terminate or reduce American aid, showing of the United States flag by frequent naval visits in Greek ports (though the NATO agreements allowed this), contacts of Greek military officers serving in NATO facilities with their American counterparts, American movies which accounted for nearly 50 percent of the shows projected before Greek audiences, cultural exchanges and visits of influential functionaries or parliamentarians, Greek exchange students studying in the United States, heavy U.S. private investments (close to 50 percent of all foreign investments in the years 1953-1970), the all-important effect—primarily through immigrant remittances—of

[6] Constantine Tsoucalas, *The Greek Tragedy* (Harmondsworth, Mddx.: Penguin Books, 1969), p. 106.
[7] Jean Meynaud et al., *The Political Forces in Greece* (Athens, 1966), pp. 408ff.

nearly 2 million Greek-Americans, and, finally, the gradual development in Greece of a binational subculture which has been dependent
on, and hopeful for, a heavy and continuing U.S. presence in the
country. The most famous people in this category include Aristotle and
Jackie Onassis, and Tom Pappas, the well-known Greek-American in-
dustrialist and Republican financier.

During the 1950s the foundations were laid and the firstfruits were
reaped of what has come to be known as "the Greek economic
miracle." Generally, the 1950s could be characterized as a period of
rapid economic development as well as political stabilization. Yearly
GNP growth rates ranged from 6 to 8 percent until this trend was
briefly interrupted in the year following the 1967 coup. The multiparty
system of the 1946 and 1950 elections—in the latter of which forty-
four parties competed—gave way to fewer and fewer parties, reaching
the "healthy phenomenon" of essentially only three major parties
competing in the 1964 elections.

The 1950s also contained one important structural source which
rendered the coups of the 1960s more probable. The Greek military
enjoyed disproportionate time, attention, aid, training, and the U.S.
dollar, compared to other political and social structures such as political
parties, the bureaucracy, trade unions and other pressure groups, and
institutions of higher learning. According to official U.S. statistics, the
total number of Greeks (mostly officers) trained in the U.S. under the
Military Assistance Program (MAP) between 1950 and 1969 amounted
to 11,229. To this number one should add 1,965 students trained under
the MAP at overseas installations. Considering the total number of the
Greek officer corps, approximately 11,000, and despite retirements and
other turnovers, these training figures assume a staggering significance
in terms of influence. The assumption, here, is that U.S. trained officers
are likely to develop ties, both ideological and professional, that will
render them friendly to the United States.

Gradually there developed in Greece a hypertrophic military establishment, enjoying virtual independence from civilian control, dominated primarily by officers of conservative orientation, and consistently corroded by secret military organizations, which, in turn, were
treated with considerable laxity and circumspection by the civilian
authorities.

In the foreign policy area, NATO's solidarity was severely tested as a result of the Cyprus crisis, which heated up around 1955 as a result of conflicting interests of the British, Greeks, and Turks. The positions of the three allies were diametrically opposed. The British wished to continue their colonial sovereignty over the island. The Greeks desired self-determination which was likely to lead to Enosis (or union with Greece) in view of the 80 percent majority of the Greek Cypriots on the island. The Turks wanted either perpetuation of British governance or Taksim (partition of Cyprus between Greece and Turkey), but in no way would they tolerate union with Greece. Despite frequent outbursts straining relations to the point of rupture, and continuous Greek-Cypriot guerrilla activities from 1955 to 1959, the first phase of the Cyprus issue was settled in 1959 by the NATO-inspired Zurich and London treaties, hammered out away from the glaring lights of United Nations public diplomacy.

The events of the Cyprus crisis in the 1950s provide a fascinating opportunity for research in the styles of NATO and U.S. influence in the relations between Greece and Turkey. It would not be unreasonable to speculate that without mutual dependency on the U.S., Greece and Turkey might have found themselves embroiled in a catastrophic war over Cyprus any time from 1955 on. So here was a situation where great power interference (and penetration in general), in the interest of maintaining NATO solidarity, reduced for both Greece and Turkey the likelihood of war over an extremely emotional and explosive issue. A fascinating study could be made comparing the analogous effect of Soviet penetration in Eastern European countries, for instance, the degree to which USSR penetration in Bulgaria, Romania, and Hungary has defused their traditional nationalist/irredentist quarrels.

The 1960s: Crisis and Military Intervention

The 1960s will remain an intriguing subject for historians of the future. At present, interpretation of these events must be based upon incomplete and impressionistic data. It appears that the so-called crisis years, which began with the disputed elections of October 1961, represent the growing pains of a rapidly modernizing country.

With continued rapid economic development (the Gross Domestic Product growth rates in the 1960s averaged yearly close to 8 percent), rapid urbanization, increased participation in the educational process, and the cold war detente atmosphere of the early 1960s, the Greek people began pressing hard on their relatively inadequate institutions—especially the political parties and the monarchy—articulating demands vigorously and expecting more authentic participation in the governance of the country. The political parties had been ineffectively organized and they suffered from polyarchic and centrifugal tendencies. Both constitutional monarchs, King Paul and later King Constantine, were prone to intervene in the political system. These incursions undoubtedly strained the spirit if not the letter of the Constitution.

In 1963, after two years of continuous pounding by the Center coalition forces—led by the veteran Greek politician George Papandreou—and as a result of some royal maneuvering by King Paul, Constantine Karamanlis and his ruling party (National Radical Union [ERE] gave way after eight years of rule to a Center parties' coalition government, which assumed power, after the February 1964 elections, with an unprecedented 53 percent popular mandate. However, relations between Papandreou and King Constantine (who succeeded King Paul after the latter's death early in 1964) quickly deteriorated especially over the issue of control over the armed forces. In July of 1965 the old politician and the twenty-five-year-old king reached a total impasse.

Papandreou was forced to resign on 15 July 1965, and an abnormal political situation developed in Greece. His Center Union party split into majority and minority factions. King Constantine delayed the electoral process and maneuvered the minority faction under Stephanos Stephanopoulos into power, while the Greek people broke out into frequent and vocal, but not violent—by United States standards—demonstrations, demanding elections and a new parliament.

The 1965-1967 crisis period is extremely instructive. The two large, non-Communist parties, for the first time, paid attention to grass-roots organization and sought to modernize their bureaucratic structures. For instance, both the National Radical Union and the Center Union set up youth groups to attempt to reach a segment of the population previously courted exclusively by the Leftist—Unified Democratic Left (EDA)—party.

The political crisis was reflected primarily in the military establishment, with charges and countercharges between ERE and the Center Union that each was trying to pack, politicize, and control the armed forces. The mirror-image "Pericles" and "Aspida" affairs are instructive to this effect. "Pericles" involved an alleged military plan to pressure Greek voters in favor of ERE in the 1961 elections. "Aspida" was an organization of officers uncovered early in 1965, which was allegedly Leftist and "Nasserite" in orientation. Dramatic trials on both affairs were held in 1966.

The crisis was further exacerbated by the foreign-policy climate. Beginning with December of 1963, the Cyprus question erupted again and brought Greece and Turkey once more to the brink of conflict. The United States pressed, pleaded with, and cajoled both allies to refrain from force and settle peacefully. This, naturally, brought about the enmity and the chagrin of both, each feeling that the United States was siding more with its opponent.

Andreas Papandreou (an important member of his father's cabinet), for instance, made an election issue of American interference in Greece's domestic affairs. He argued for more independence and equality in their mutual relations. His rhetoric, of course, was not at all palatable to American representatives who had not been accustomed to hearing such slogans from non-Communist politicians.

Despite the excitement, confusion, and occasional jitters cultivated by an overanimated press, the Greeks appeared to have been marching out of the crisis on the eve of the 1967 military coup d'etat. Following an agreement between George Papandreou and Panayotis Kanellopoulos (who had replaced Constantine Karamanlis as leader of ERE following the latter's departure from Greek politics in December 1963), Parliament was dissolved, and Kanellopoulos headed a government that was scheduled to conduct elections on 28 May 1967.

The colonels' coup of 21 April 1967, however, denied the Greek people the opportunity to settle the great issues. Charging political corruption, chaos, and imminent Communist danger, the colonels suspended the parliamentary process and promised to reshape a healthy democracy sometime in the future. King Constantine led an unsuccessful countercoup against the colonels on 13 December 1967. When it failed, he moved to Rome in a semiofficial status while his duties were carried out by General George Zoitakis, the regent. In 1972, Zoitakis was succeeded by George Papadopoulos who was both the leader of the 1967 putsch and currently premier.

The Papadopoulos government drafted and partially applied a new constitution, lifted censorship—which was replaced by a Draconian press law—and released most of its political prisoners. On the other hand, it continued to consolidate its control over all the political and social institutions of Greece. Martial law remained in effect in the major urban centers.

United States policy vis-à-vis the colonels' regime has been one of dilemma. The deputy assistant secretary for Near Eastern and South Asian Affairs, Rodger Davies, told the U.S. Senate in early June 1970: "We disagree with the political system which prevails in Greece and consider a return to parliamentary rule essential to the long-term stability and prosperity of Greece. At the same time, we must preserve our important strategic interests in Greece as a valuable geographic area in the critical Eastern Mediterranean region. Balancing these often conflicting interests has been the major concern of U.S. policy toward Greece since the coup."

Greek View of United States Policy

The preponderance of the Greek politicians, whether left, center, or conservative, find themselves in strong opposition to the military regime. There is a consensus among them that the United States, at worst, connived and, at best, knew of the coup, but failed to warn them. Further, they feel that, despite modest rhetoric to the contrary, the United States is supporting the colonels, responding to their bluff that they might look to the Soviets or the French for an alternative patron or reduce U.S. access to Greek territory and facilities.

Most Greek politicians feel that, if the United States makes it clear and unequivocal that it wishes the genuine restoration of democracy in Greece, the U.S.-oriented Greek military will force the ruling junta to comply. Of course, there are many variations to this theme. Some politicians, for instance, merely wish to see the United States stop aiding the colonels and leave the "solution" to the Greek people.

Paradoxically, the military government in Greece is also complaining about U.S. interference. Arguing that the two countries have mutual strategic interests, the colonels insist that the United States has no business intervening in Greek domestic affairs, pressing for democracy, and generally dictating from without.

United States policies have been equivocal and vacillating—the dilemma again—thus managing to antagonize both sides in the Greek drama.

Immediately after the coup of April 1967, the United States suspended delivery of heavy arms shipments to Greece. This embargo was secretly violated, however, by the Johnson administration, and, since September 1970, the Nixon administration has lifted it altogether.[8]

Following the departure of Ambassador Philips Talbot from Greece in January 1968, the selection of the new ambassador, Henry Tasca, appeared to have been delayed a few months, so that in fact he did not arrive in Athens until January 1970. This apparent delay was, however, canceled out by frequent, high-level U.S. military and diplomatic visits, which were prominently publicized by the controlled Greek press.

Over five years have passed since the April 1967 coup. The United States must review its Greek policy and its strategy in the Mediterranean. Resolving this "dilemma" could become a traumatic experience for American decision-makers.

United States Interest in Greece

The issues are many, and at best they can be raised in terms of questions.

1. What specifically are the national interests of the United States in Greece—bases, access to Greek territory, denial of Greek territory to the Russians? Are U.S. interests to be defined in terms of purely military criteria or more inclusive political and economic ones? If so, are U.S. interests threatened by a return to parliamentary rule? Are they threatened by a perpetuation of the present regime?

2. What is the attitude of the Greek population toward the colonels' regime? Assuming the hostility of the Greek people (otherwise why the perpetuation of martial law?), how useful will U.S. military bases be if they are surrounded by a hostile population? How long before active resistance might place the United States in a dilemma of "pulling out" or fighting against yet another popular insurgency?

3. What about the issue of NATO supporting a dictatorship for narrowly defined military reasons? The preamble of the NATO charter and article 2 provide for an association of free and democratic nations. What are the duties, if any, of NATO vis-à-vis Greece? Should the U.S.

[8] See "Greece, Spain, and the Southern NATO Strategy" (U.S. Cong., House, Hearings before the Subcommittee on Europe of the Committee on Foreign Affairs, Washington, D.C.: Government Printing Office, 1971), p. 55.

be concerned about the coloration, quality, popularity, and effectiveness of the occasional Greek regime, or merely worry about the regime's "friendliness" and compatibility with U.S. "interests"?

4. In the last analysis, one must ask: What leverage does the United States have in Greece, how can this leverage be best applied if at all, and to what end?

A superpower such as the United States is locked into an interventionary position with all its allies. Inequality plus contact spell intervention in any relationship. No matter what the United States does in the future with respect to Greece, it will be considered either a form of passive acceptance of the status quo or support for the revisionists, depending on who has the upper hand.

So the question remains: How can the United States best "intervene" prudently and in its own best, enlightened interests, if indeed it should at all?

SUGGESTIONS FOR FURTHER RESEARCH

The bibliography suggests many angles which remain to be explored. From the standpoint of American diplomacy, relations with Greece in various eras could stand further exploration, especially where the role of Congress is concerned.

The question of the establishment of bases overseas in general and in Greece in particular deserves more study as does the whole history of the Sixth Fleet in the Mediterranean.

BIBLIOGRAPHIC NOTE

For useful literature in political science devoted to the theoretical study of concepts such as "intervention" and "civil conflict," see the following: T. R. Gurr, "A Casual Model of Civil Strife: A Comparative Analysis Using New Indices," *American Political Science Review* (December 1968); *Journal of International Affairs* 22, no. 2 (1968) (the entire issue is devoted to the study of intervention); C. R. Mitchell, "Civil Strife and the Involvement of External Parties," *International Studies Quarterly* (June 1970); J. N. Rosenau, ed., *International Aspects of Civil Strife* (Princeton, N.J.: Princeton University Press, 1964);

also by Rosenau, ed., *Linkage Politics* (New York: Free Press, 1969); and R. J. Rummel, "Dimensions of Conflict within and between Nations," *General Systems Yearbook, 1963,* 8: 1-50.

For Greece's modern history and culture, the following English-language readings are recommended: E. S. Forster, *A Short History of Modern Greece, 1821-1956* (London: Methuen, 1958); W. A. Heurtley, *A Short History of Greece* (Cambridge, Eng.; Cambridge University Press, 1965); N. Kaltchas, *Introduction to the Constitutional History of Modern Greece* (New York: Columbia University Press, 1940); L. S. Stavrianos, *The Balkans since 1453* (New York: Rinehart, 1959); and I. T. Sanders, *Rainbow in the Rock* (Cambridge, Mass.: Harvard University Press, 1962).

Moving to the post-World War II period, we should turn to J. M. Jones, *The Fifteen Weeks* (New York: Harcourt, Brace and World, 1960), as the book which provides a carefully documented blow-by-blow description of how the "Truman Doctrine" was sold to the U. S. Congress and the American people. J. O. Iatrides, *Revolt in Athens* (Princeton, N.J.: Princeton University Press, 1972), is a careful and detached study of the prelude to the Greek civil war and some of the British miscalculations which helped bring this war about. Also by Iatrides is the *Balkan Triangle* (Hague: Mouton, 1968) which is quite helpful because it focuses on postwar Greek relations with Balkan neighbors. A. Kedros, *La Resistance Grecque: 1940-44* (Paris: Laffont, 1967), is a book sympathetic to the left-dominated resistance movement in German-occupied Greece. On the other side, the book by D. G. Kousoulas, *Revolution and Defeat* (London: Oxford University Press, 1965) is a standard cold-war interpretation of history pinning the blame for Greece's strategy primarily on conspiratorial Greek Communists. More than balancing the Kousoulas treatment is L. S. Stavrianos, *Greece: American Dilemma and Opportunity* (Chicago: Henry Regnery, 1952), who views the left as angels and the right as devils. S. G. Xydis, *Greece and the Great Powers, 1944-47,* is a meticulously documented traditionalist study of the transition from British to United States influence in Greece immediately after World War II. T. A. Couloumbis, *Greek Political Reaction to American and NATO Influences* (New Haven, Conn.: Yale University Press, 1966), is an account that reflects on attitudes of Greek political parties (from left to right) on postwar American presence in Greece. Perhaps the most insightful and useful account of the postwar Greek political system (the authors admit clearly to a socialist orientation) is by J. Meynaud et al., *Les Forces Politiques en Grece* (Paris, 1965).

The final category of books to be discussed in this annotated bibliography includes books that have appeared since the military coup of April 21, 1967. Here one can readily identify the following subcategories: books descriptive of the coup from a journalistic viewpoint; books opposing the colonels' regime; books supporting the colonels' regime; and finally, a small category of works attempting to be "objective and scientific."

In the journalistic category entries would include books such as J. F. Chauvel, *La Grece à l'Ombre des epées* (Paris: Laffont, 1968); and M. Marceau, *La Grece des Colonels* (Paris: Laffont, 1967).

In the category opposing the colonels there is a long list. (It should be added that many of the authors in this category, as well as the category to follow, claim to arrive at their judgments [and sometimes they do so] objectively): Anonymous, *Inside the Colonels' Greece* (New York: Norton, 1972); James Becket, *Barbarism in Greece* (New York: Walker & Co., 1970); R. Clogg and G. Yannopoulos, eds., *Greece under Military Rule* (New York: Basic Books, 1972). It should be said here that the Clogg and Yannopoulos book is a very well-documented and executed anthology of writings with emphasis on the analytical rather than purely descriptive orientation to the subject matter; M. Genevoix, *La Grece de Caramanlis* (Paris: Plon, 1972); John Katris, *Eyewitness in Greece* (New York: Dutton, 1971); M. Mercouri, *I Was Born Greek* (London: Hodder and Stoughton, 1971); A. Papandreou, *Democracy at Gunpoint: The Greek Front* (New York: Doubleday, 1971); M. Papandreou, *Nightmare in Athens* (Englewood Cliffs, N.J.: Prentice-Hall, 1970); A. Rousseas, *The Death of a Democracy* (New York: Grove Press, 1968); M. Theodorakis, *Journal of Resistance* (New York: Coward, McCann and Geoghegan, 1973); C. Tsoucalas, *The Greek Tragedy* (London: Penguin, 1969); Helen Vlachos, *House Arrest* (London: Andre Deutsch, 1970); also Vlachos, ed., *Free Greek Voices* (London: Doric Publications, 1971); and C. M. Woodhouse, *The Story of Modern Greece* (London: Faber & Faber, 1968).

For works rationalizing, supporting, and/or praising the military regime(s) see the following: D. Holden, *Greece without Columns* (New York: Lippincott, 1972); George Papadopoulos, *To Pistevo Mas (Our Creed)* (Athens, 1968), seven vols. (continuing); B. Stockton, *Phoenix with a Bayonet* (Ann Arbor, Mich.: Georgetown Pubs., 1971); and K. Young, *The Greek Passion* (London: Dent, 1969).

With some hesitation (we still have reservations as to the possibility of arriving at "value free" literature in the social sciences) we would list in the category of "objective" studies the following: K. R. Legg, *Politics in Modern Greece* (Stanford, Calif.: Stanford University Press, 1969); and J. Campbell and P. Sherrard, *Modern Greece* (London:

Ernest Benn, 1968). It is interesting that one goes to non-Greeks to find so-called objective studies.

Finally, our readers should be referred to Senate and House hearings and debates in order to arrive at United States policy "debate points." Of special value are the following: U.S., Cong., House, "Greece, Spain, and the Southern NATO Strategy," Hearings before the Sub-Committee on Europe of the Committee on Foreign Affairs, 92nd Cong., 1st sess., 1971. Also by the same subcommittee as above, see hearings entitled, "Political and Strategic Implications of Homeporting in Greece," April 1972; and "Implementation of Homeporting in Greece," July 1973.

UNFINISHED BUSINESS – INTERVENTION UNDER THE U.N. UMBRELLA: AMERICA'S PARTICIPATION IN THE KOREAN WAR, 1950 - 1953[1]

P. Wesley Kriebel

TWENTY-TWO YEARS after the beginning of the Korean War, a military armistice is still in effect in the divided peninsula. Armies still face each other across the Demilitarized Zone, which separates the Republic of Korea (ROK) from the North. The United Nations is still faced each year with the Korean Problem. The United States continues to maintain powerful land and air forces in the Republic of Korea and supports the ROK government with significant amounts of military and economic assistance. The Korean War is not a closed chapter of history. It is still very much unfinished business which affects relations between the two parts of Korea; relations among Korea's neighbors, Japan, the People's Republic of China, and the Soviet Union; and the relations of all these countries with the United States. A review of the Korean War is not simply an examination of the exercise of power by the United States in a specific situation in the past: it is preliminary to understanding America's continued involvement in Asia, and particularly the dramatic change that began in the summer of 1971, in America's relationship with the People's Republic of China.

Korea was hardly more than a place name to Americans before the Second World War, although the relationship was older and more complex than most Americans realized. In the generation before 1910, when Korea was annexed by the Empire of Japan, Koreans struggling to modernize their long isolated nation turned, in many instances, to American ideas and models. American missionaries, educators, and businessmen played influential roles. The mission movement, in partic-ular, became inextricably caught up in the Korean independence movement under Japanese rule. Korean leaders lived and were educated in the United States. But this association was largely unknown to the American soldiers who went ashore in September 1945.

At the end of World War II, the United States accepted the surrender of Japanese forces in Korea south of the Thirty-eighth Parallel, and the Soviet Union accepted the surrender of those Japanese forces north of the Parallel. The line of division had been intended only to facilitate Japan's surrender, for both the United States and the Soviet Union were pledged to a free and independent Korea; the United States by the Cairo Declaration of 1943 and the Potsdam Declaration of 1945; the Soviet Union by its explicit acceptance of the Potsdam Declaration in its Declaration of War against Japan in August 1945. Even before it became clear that the two could not agree on the terms for a unified Korea, friction between them hardened the Thirty-eighth Parallel into a political boundary. South of the Parallel, the United States found itself unexpectedly responsible for a people whose last independent government, forty years earlier, had been a weak, antiquated, absolute monarchy. The Koreans wanted their independence immediately and they wanted a united country. The Americans were unconvinced of the Koreans' readiness for self-government and still believed some agreement with the Soviet Union on a unified and independent nation would be possible.

In September 1947 the United States, convinced at last that no such agreement could be negotiated, took the question of Korean nationhood and unity to the United Nations. A commission was created by the UN General Assembly to oversee elections for a national government for all of Korea, but it was not permitted to function in the Soviet-controlled area north of the Thirty-eighth Parallel. In August 1948, following UN supervised elections, the Republic of Korea government was formally inaugurated. This government was subsequently certified by the UN General Assembly as a lawful government and, in the words of the resolution, "the only such government in Korea." In September 1948 the Soviet Union created the Democratic People's Republic of Korea in the North. The political division of Korea had been formalized.

In general, the United States did not consider the Korean peninsula

---

[1] This article for publication represents the views of the author and does not necessarily reflect the official opinion of the Department of State.

important to its national security. This view was widely known, even prior to Secretary of State Dean Acheson's now famous speech of January 1950 when he explicitly declared Korea to be outside the United States defense perimeter, which, he said, ran from the Aleutian Islands through Japan and Okinawa to the Philippines. The United States, in fact, wished to disengage its troops from Korea. By 1949 the last units had departed, leaving a young and lightly equipped Korean constabulary (which was supported by a United States military advisory group), a fragile, largely agrarian economy, and a fractious political scene. In the North, the Soviet Union created a well-equipped army, a tightly disciplined government, and the rudiments of an industrial economy based largely on earlier Japanese development. On June 25, 1950, North Korea's army smashed across the Thirty-eighth Parallel, sweeping aside all resistance.

The principal events of the Korean War are well known: the retreat to the Pusan Perimeter, the counterthrust of the Inchon landings and Chinese intervention in 1950; stalemate and armistice from 1951 to 1953; and the abortive political conference in Geneva in 1954. The critical decisions were the American commitment of ground forces and Chinese communist intervention. Both decisions dramatically changed the nature of the conflict. Neither could have been forecast in advance with certainty, although in both instances the possibilities were known. In both, the opponents concluded that the other side would not act or could not act in a manner which would materially affect the outcome of the conflict.

The United States Commitment

The Korean peninsula, by explicit, official statement, lay outside the security perimeters of the United States. Yet America was to incur 142,000 casualties in defense of Korea and commit an enormous treasure to the war. After three years the United States was willing to settle for a stalemate which seemed to do little more than return the situation to its position before the attack in 1950, but at much higher levels of tension and armament on the parts of both Korean protagonists. The first decision seemed to contradict the security analysis and the second appeared to disregard the enormous American, Korean, and allied loss of life. In both situations, the determining factor was the perception of the world by American leaders in the early 1950s.

The victory over Nazi Germany and Imperial Japan in the Second World War had turned to ashes in the mouths of America's people and leaders by 1950. The promise of a prosperous and stable world order under the guidance of the wartime allies working through the United Nations had not materialized. In American eyes, the reason lay in the unwillingness of the Soviet Union to forgo either the imperial ambitions of its Czarist predecessors or the ideological world revolution of its Communist rulers. There was ample evidence for this view in Soviet pressure against Iran, support for Communist guerrillas in the Greek civil war, and the harsh incorporation of the East European states into the Soviet system. Above all, there had been the Berlin blockade of 1948 when the Soviet Union appeared willing to risk armed conflict with the West, and the collapse of the Chinese Nationalist Government on the mainland of China in 1949. The subsequent development of the Moscow-Peking alliance raised the specter of half the world organized against the United States.

At the same time, it had become clear that Western Europe could not recover from the ravages of war without massive assistance over a long period of time from the United States. The colonial empires of Europe which had kept the peace in Africa and Asia were crumbling with consequences no one could foresee. The American armed forces, particularly the army, had been allowed to run down, and the United States had only begun to revive its wartime political alliances. The danger of a third World War seemed very real.

In considering the troubles facing the nation, American leaders accepted as an article of faith the premise that the primary cause of the Second World War had been the failure of nerve of the Western democracies in the face of nascent aggressions of Germany and Japan in the 1930s. When North Korea launched its attack in June 1950, it seemed that an organized and militant communism had thrown down the battle gage. To take it up was to risk danger, but there was also the possibility that the adversary would be checked. Failure to respond could only lead down the path of appeasement and, ultimately, to the world conflict the United States sought to avoid. President Truman says in his memoirs that on flying from Missouri to Washington on the Sunday of the North Korean attack, he thought of how the failure of the democracies to act in the 1930s had encouraged aggression in Manchuria, Ethiopia, and Austria. "If South Korea were allowed to fall," he concluded, "Communist leaders would be emboldened to override nations closer to our own shores. If the Communists were permitted to force their way into the Republic of Korea without opposition from the free world, no small nation would have the courage to resist threats and aggression by stronger Communist neighbors. If this was allowed to go unchallenged, it would mean a third World War, just as similar incidents had brought on the Second World War." No doubt he also recalled how the apparent impotence of the League of Nations in 1931 had led to Japanese expansion.

In deciding to go into Korea, the United States chose to do so under the still new but already tarnished emblem of the United Nations. Conceived in war and based on the assumption that the wartime alliance could be maintained in peace, the United Nations was viewed by the United States as a substitute for the disastrous political and military confrontations of the first half of the century and a partial substitute for armed strength itself in the sense that the collective weight of the international community could be brought to bear on those who would break the peace. At first, this hope seemed reasonable, even without the cooperation of the Soviet Union, because the membership of the United Nations in those years was mainly of states like-minded with the United States. This community of interest seemed only to confirm that it was Soviet intransigence alone which prevented the attainment of the United Nations Charter goals. To the United States, the concept of collective action under the Charter was no less at stake than was the nerve of the leaders of the non-Communist world.

The Korean question had been before the United Nations for nearly three years before the North Korean attack. A UN commission was in Korea at the time of the attack. There was, therefore, the logic of favorable past experience and practice to support the United States decision to seek UN endorsement for the commitment of American forces to Korea.

The American response to the North Korean attack was cautious in terms of its own commitment and in its invocation of UN support. The first move was a resolution in the UN Security Council (the Soviet Union was boycotting the Security Council and was not present to veto this and other resolutions) on June 25 calling for a cessation of hostilities and a withdrawal of North Korean forces to the Thirty-eighth Parallel, and calling on all UN members to render assistance to the organization in the execution of the resolution. On the same day President Truman authorized the use of air and naval forces to safeguard the evacuation of American nationals from Korea. Early on June 27 the United States announced that, pursuant to the June 25 resolution, it had authorized air and sea support of ROK forces, sent the Seventh Fleet to interdict the Straits of Formosa, intended to strengthen American forces in the Philippines, and accelerated military assistance to that government and to French forces in Indochina. A second Security Council resolution on June 27 recommended that all UN members furnish assistance to the Republic of Korea to repel armed attack and to restore peace and security. On June 30 the United States committed ground forces to the battle. On July 7 the Security Council established a unified command and asked the United States to designate the commander. General Douglas MacArthur was named commander-in-chief of the UN forces. Fifteen nations besides the United States eventually provided forces to the unified command, and five others furnished medical units. At this point, the commitment of the United States and of the United Nations was to end aggression, to restore the territorial integrity of the Republic of Korea, and to establish peace and security in the area. The possible interpretation of the UN resolutions was not an issue. The UN forces were fighting for their lives in the Pusan Perimeter.

When General MacArthur landed his forces at Inchon in September 1950 and broke the back of the North Korean army, a wholly new situation emerged. The effort to end the aggression became entangled with the dormant United Nations plans for a unified Korea, with the wishes of Republic of Korea President Syngman Rhee to unify the nation by force, and with MacArthur's belief that Korea was the battlefield on which to defeat world communism. There was now—in the words of Secretary of State Dean Acheson—no military power to frustrate UN and ROK goals. By this time the Soviet Union had resumed its seat in the Security Council and the locus of UN action had shifted to the General Assembly where there was no great-power veto. On October 7 the General Assembly passed a resolution establishing a commission for the unification and rehabilitation of Korea (UNCURK) and recommending that steps be taken to ensure conditions of stability throughout Korea. General MacArthur, citing this resolution, declared on October 9 he would take such military action as was required to enforce the decisions of the United Nations. To the growing unease of his own and allied governments, he sent his Eighth Army and ROK forces northward, ignoring or giving his own interpretation to the restraints his government attempted to impose on him. For a time it appeared that he would be successful in occupying all Korea.

The Intervention of Chinese Forces

As early as October 26 it had become apparent that Chinese forces were operating in Korea. There was uncertainty and confusion in Washington and in MacArthur's own headquarters in Japan as to their numbers, location, and intention. The blow fell on November 27, 1950, when Chinese armies under the thin cover of "People's Volunteers" attacked the extended and exposed UN forces, forcing a withdrawal that was not to end until February 1951, well south of Seoul. The Chinese intervention shattered for good the prospect of a militarily united Korea under UN auspices and created a new problem of immense dimensions for the United States and the United Nations. The United States was forced to reassess its war aims. Government leaders were convinced that the Soviet Union desired to entrap it into a prolonged war with Communist China on the mainland of Asia in order to drain resources and attention away from Europe. America's allies, particularly the United Kingdom, shared this view but they were also afraid the American response to Chinese intervention might include use of nuclear weapons and the triggering of an uncontrollable series of events ending in general war. Subsequent decisions made clear the United States would limit the war to the Korean peninsula and that it was not prepared to engage its full strength against the Chinese Communists. General MacArthur bitterly opposed these decisions as ham-stringing him as a military commander and as failing to recognize the global significance of the Korean battlefield in the fight against communism. Syngman Rhee, believing that military conquest of the peninsula was no longer possible and seeing his dream of a united Korea indefinitely delayed, became an increasingly recalcitrant ally. At home a disillusioned populace, believing that a just settlement and deserved victory had been snatched away by the Chinese, wavered between frustration over the decisions which would deny the possibility of the military victory over the Chinese and a fear of widening the war and increasing American casualties. The UN forces gradually reestablished their military line north of Seoul, but the balance of forces committed to Korea by the two sides permitted neither one the opportunity for a military decision. The United States turned to the possibility of a cease-fire.

Efforts to promote a cease-fire had gone forward in several channels for a period of months. In March 1951 the United States Government was preparing to put forward a proposal aimed at exploring the possibilities for cease-fire negotiations when General MacArthur preempted this with his own March 24 proposal to meet with the enemy commander and a warning in belligerent terms that the war might be widened if the fighting continued. Time has dimmed the furor caused by this action, but it resulted in General MacArthur's dismissal by President Truman, an inflamed public debate in the United States over the president's decision and over the conduct of the war, an exhaustive congressional inquiry into United States policy in Asia, and a four-month delay in the beginning of cease-fire talks. Preliminary discussions between the two sides about a cease-fire finally began on July 7. The negotiations themselves were to continue for a little more than two years with the principal issue becoming the forcible repatriation of prisoners of war. President Eisenhower took office in January 1953 after a campaign in which a major pledge was to end the fighting. On July 23, an armistice agreement was signed by the commander-in-chief United Nations Command, the supreme commander of the Korean People's Army (North Korea), and the commander of the Chinese People's Volunteers. No representative of the Republic of Korea signed the armistice, but President Syngman Rhee on August 7 in a joint statement with United States Assistant Secretary of State Walter Robertson pledged to honor the armistice.

The Armistice Agreement recommended that a political conference be held within three months. In fact, it was not convened until April 1954 when discussions on peace in Indochina and Korea were held in separate sessions in Geneva. The Korean Conference was unable to come to agreement. The points insisted upon by the United States and fifteen allied delegations and rejected by the Communist side were: 1) the United Nations should have a role in a Korean settlement, 2) elections must be free and with proportionate representation in both

North and South Korea, and 3) UN forces should be retained in Korea until a unified, independent, and democratic government had been created. There the matter rested. There has never been a political settlement.

The Geneva Conference left the armies in place. Although there had been no agreement on a political settlement, the United States could claim that two of its aims embodied in UN resolutions had been achieved: the aggression had been stopped and the territorial integrity of the Republic of Korea had been preserved. A third aim, the restoration of peace and security, had been only partially achieved. Of the other issues, the right of collective action by the international community had been sustained. Korea was not unified and that issue was more deeply entangled in great-power politics than ever. The significance of the Korean War on the global competition between the United States and the Soviet Union was, at that point, hard to determine. It could be argued that Communist probes to determine whether aggression could be successfully used against the non-Communist world had been blunted. At the same time, the reluctance of the United States to try to force a military decision against the Chinese could be cited as evidence of weakness that increased the prospects for general war, rather than diminished them.

But the legacy of Korea was more extensive and enduring than the immediate consequences. Not only was the aggression stopped, the war did not resume. Despite periods of tension and of harassment from the North, the peace in Northeast Asia has been kept. An uneasy and unspoken consensus developed among the great powers that Korean unification would not be sought by force. Behind this fragile armistice, Japan, stimulated by United States expenditures for the Korean War, and protected by strong American conventional and nuclear forces, began the economic transformation which in another decade would raise it to great-power status and eliminate once and for all the fear of Communist exploitation and takeover. The bitter hostility generated by the Korean War between the United States and Communist China froze for a generation the possibility of a modus vivendi which had seemed to be developing slowly in the wake of the collapse of the Nationalist Government.

The Republic of Korea was restored in territory but the enormous destruction and continued military confrontation across the Demilitarized Zone completely changed the prewar relationship between the Republic and the United States and in time transformed Korea itself. Korea's military forces were rebuilt. A mutual security treaty was concluded between the United States and the Republic of Korea at the time of the armistice as assurance of support if there were another attack from the North. American divisions manned the most likely corridors of attack until mid-1971, when these portions of the Demilitarized Zone were turned over to ROK forces. This close involvement with Korea required the maintenance of military bases in Okinawa and in Japan. These in turn gave America a capability for military intervention anywhere in East Asia, a capability that helped determine its actions in Vietnam. The Republic of Korea itself has grown from its weakness into a sturdy and respected middle power with a voice of its own in international affairs. The Korean War reenforced America's commitment to the Nationalist Chinese Government on Taiwan and stimulated an ever deeper involvement in Indochina. Korea and Indochina were regarded as the two arms of Communist probing in Asia. Truce in Korea concentrated attention on Indochina.

The right of the United Nations to undertake a collective military action became less significant as the limitations on the capacity of the organization to take such action were recognized. The circumstances that caused the Soviet Union to be absent from the Security Council early in the Korean War were unlikely to be repeated. If the Security Council were paralyzed by the veto, the General Assembly had only limited capacity to act as a substitute. Although fifteen other nations had joined with the United States in providing ground forces to assist the Republic of Korea, most of these were little more than tokens. Events demonstrated that all the participants were more concerned with their individual interests than they were with an abstract concept such as collective security. The United Nations was to experiment later with approaches to the problem of collective action, but the lesson the United States drew from its Korean experience was that collective security must be based on close community of interest if it were to be effective. The United States vastly expanded its system of mutual security pacts, and before the 1950s were over, America had security arrangements with forty-two separate countries. The unsatisfactory operation of the UN collective security concept helped reverse Amer-

124 P. Wesley Kriebel

ica's attitude toward rearmament. The momentum begun in the Korean War has carried forward ever since, and the nation has created stronger conventional and nuclear armaments than it had ever had in peacetime. The draft became a major element in peacetime security for the first time in American history. The president was given emergency powers during the Korean War, which remain unrevoked.

Conclusions

In reflecting on the Korean intervention and its near and long-term consequences, the importance of clarifying and reviewing national goals is very apparent. The conclusion that Korea was not inside America's security perimeter was not so much wrong as it was incomplete. The assessment failed to give proper weight to the political implications of the loss of a nation which had been created and sustained under American tutelage, and which lay within the range of American military power. The intentions of the United States in the month between the destruction of the North Korean Army and the intervention of the Chinese were not clear, in spite of all that has been written about that period by the principals. It seems that the United States was unprepared to deal with this unexpected political and military vacuum and so let matters drift. Later decisions to limit goals and the expenditures of forces may in part have been forced on the United States, but they were also the product of conscious decision: Full-scale war with China was to be avoided; concentration was to be in Europe. The United States did not exploit the full military potential of the forces it did employ in Korea, because the goals that had been set by that time made such exploitation meaningless.

As with the importance of goals, reflection shows some of the limitations on lessons of the past. The appeasement of the 1930s weighed heavily on America's leaders. The lesson of that experience was that aggression had to be met with force at the outset. The lesson was one of hindsight and offered little guidance as to the consequences of actually meeting aggression with counterforce. It was expected that only limited American military effort would be required to defeat the North Korean aggression. This analysis proved correct, but the conflict did not end. The Chinese intervention faced Americans with a problem new to their experience. If they employed sufficient force to bring a military decision, they faced the possibility of the very holocaust the Korean War was fought to prevent. To carry on in a limited fashion, not bringing to bear the full weight of existing and potential American power, meant forfeiting a clear-cut and satisfactory ending to the conflict. American frustration was great. The argument that large-scale conflict could be thwarted by immediate and forceful resistance failed to recognize the difficulty and hazards in attempting to control events through the rational and limited use of force.

No review of the Korean War from the American side can escape the conviction that the strong personalities of President Truman and General MacArthur greatly influenced events. Probably the critical moment in the war was during that first week in June when MacArthur recommended and Truman approved the commitment of United States ground troops. The two men seemed to have had the same perceptions of the cause and origins of the conflict, but they came to differ completely on the response, and on the analysis of the consequences of a limited war. Truman's view of the authority of the president and of the Communist aim to weaken America preconditioned him to strong, forceful action. MacArthur's confidence in his own abilities, his twenty years service in the Pacific, and his view of the singular importance of the Korean conflict made it impossible for him to accept a limited response to the aggression in Korea. It is futile to ask if America would have gone to war in Korea without Truman, or whether the Eighth Army would have collided with Chinese forces under the disadvantageous circumstances of November 1950 without MacArthur. However, there was nothing inevitable about either event.

Americans generally do not regard the Korean War as a satisfactory chapter in their history. The inconclusiveness of the outcome and the limited engagement of American power are out of character with American preferences for clear decisions and finished business. Yet one must hazard an attempt at deciding whether the intervention was worthwhile or whether there must be an embarrassed and bitter silence in the presence of 33,000 American dead. The passage of years since 1953 has shown that Korea was something of a watershed experience. Events in Korea are important because the interests of three great powers converge there. Events in Korea have an influence on the relations among the great powers which extends beyond the Korean peninsula. The decisions to resist aggression in Korea and then deliberately to limit that resistance were essentially sound, just because of their impact outside Korea. America was aroused and its allies were strengthened. The time of military vulnerability had passed. There is unfinished business in Korea. The problems there can be resolved only as the United States, the Soviet Union, and People's Republic of China complete the process of accommodating their differences.

SUGGESTIONS FOR FURTHER RESEARCH

Little is available in English on the attitudes and perceptions of the Communist states participating in the Korean War or on the influence which that conflict had on relations between the Soviet Union and the People's Republic of China. Similarly, the Republic of Korea's experience during the war has received only cursory attention in English and that primarily in terms of its effect on United States actions. Admiral Charles Turner Joy has written on the negotiations at Panmunjom which led to the Armistice Agreement of 1953 *(How Communists Negotiate* [New York, 1955]). Since that time there have been a number of professional and popular periodical articles on the Military Armistice Commission established to supervise the agreement, but there has been no systematic study of the commission's operation over the nearly twenty years since the fighting stopped. Americans tend to dismiss the commission if they think of it at all, but it is a functioning reminder of the American intervention in Korea and still influences American policy toward the Korean peninsula.

BIBLIOGRAPHIC NOTE

The basic documents on the Korean War can be found in three Department of State publications: *American Foreign Policy, 1950-1955,* Department of State Publication 6446 (1957); *The Record on Korean Unification, 1943-1960,* Department of State Publication 7084 (1960); and *The Korean Problem at the Geneva Conference,* Department of State Publication 5609 (October 1954). The presentation is intended to support the United States Government's position, but it makes easily accessible the relevant texts. The Department of State has in preparation volumes in its *Foreign Relations* series covering the beginning of the Korean conflict, which will make available a great deal of previously classified material. The congressional hearings following MacArthur's dismissal provide statements by many of those involved in decisions relating to Korea and convey something of the national feeling of frustration at the time, as well as the division in the country over the president's dismissal of his commander in the Far East: "Military Situation in the Far East," Hearings before the Committee on Armed Services and the Committee on Foreign Relations, United States Senate, 82d Cong., 1st sess., 1951.

Standard, readable accounts of the Korean War include David Rees, *Korea, the Limited War* (New York: St. Martins, 1964), and T. Fehrenbach, *This Kind of War* (New York: Macmillan, 1963).

Most of the principal figures have written on the Korean experience. These accounts are highly personalized and represent the considered views their authors wished to stand on the public record. They are in that sense of limited value but remain, nonetheless, important statements on the conflict. President Harry S. Truman's *Memoirs* (Garden City, N.Y.: Doubleday, 1955) reflects the haunting memory of the appeasement of the 1930s which was a significant conditioning factor in post World War II thinking in the United States. Secretary of State Dean Acheson *(Present at the Creation* [New York: Norton, 1969]) describes the frustrations of dealing with MacArthur and the gaps in United States knowledge and planning during the critical period between the Inchon landings and the full-scale intervention of the Chinese. General MacArthur's view of the necessity for a military confrontation in Asia with an aggressive monolithic communism is recounted in his *Reminiscences* (New York: McGraw Hill, 1964). General Matthew Ridgeway *(Korean War* [Garden City, N.Y.: Doubleday, 1967]) and General Mark Clark *(From the Danube to the Yalu* [New York: Harper, 1954]) give essentially soldiers' accounts. They reflect the tensions over the restraints placed on the use of military power in a limited war and the anxieties of military planners over military overcommitment in Korea and the possibility of weakness in Europe. Other accounts are given by Secretary of State John Foster Dulles, *War or Peace*, rev. ed. (New York: Macmillan, 1957), and Dwight D. Eisenhower, *White House Years* (Garden City, N.Y.: Doubleday, 1963).

America's pursuit of its Korean objectives in the United Nations is examined by Leland M. Goodrich in *Korea: A Study of United States Policy in the United Nations* (New York: Council on Foreign Relations, 1956). His account highlights the preponderant influence of the United States in the United Nations and the consequences this had for American views on collective security action by the international organization. The crucial first week of the war is examined by Glenn D. Paige (*The Korean Decision: June 24-30, 1950* [New York: Free Press, 1968]) in a case study on decision-making in a severely constricted time frame.

THE CONSEQUENCES OF ECONOMIC
ABSTENTION: THE ASWAN DAM

Janice J. Terry

THE ASWAN OR HIGH DAM project was described by Egyptian President Gamal Abdal Nasser as "more magnificent and seventeen times greater than the Pyramids." As the cornerstone of Nasser's program for Egyptian economic development, the Aswan Dam was intended to improve the living standard for all Egyptians by increasing agricultural output and providing low-cost electrical power for industrialization. Upon its completion the dam increased reclaimed agricultural land by one-third and provided 10,000 million kilowatt hours of electricity. Nasser Lake, the world's largest artificial lake, 500 kilometers (approximately 300 miles) long, was formed as a result of the dam. Originally 120 feet high, and recently enlarged to 122 feet, and a mile wide, the dam was to be the most extensive project of its type in the world.

Critics have noted the failure of the improvements provided by the dam to keep pace with Egypt's fast growing population; they have also questioned the expenditure of vast sums of money which might have been more efficiently used on a series of smaller irrigation projects along the Nile. Ecologically the dam has also had far-reaching effects, many of which were not widely anticipated when the project was formulated. Because it is no longer flushed by annual flood waters Egyptian soil has increased in salinity. The volume of the Nile flood waters, with its accumulated silt which previously flowed into the Mediterranean, has diminished. The result has been a marked decrease of plankton, organic carbons, sardines, and crustaceans in the Eastern Mediterranean. Although the planned fishing industry in Nasser Lake may mitigate some of this loss, the dam will have dramatic ecological consequences. While much of this criticism, particularly the ecological considerations, has validity, it fails to take into account the importance of Aswan as a symbol for the new Egyptian. The Aswan Dam gave Egyptians a sense of pride and, importantly from Nasser's viewpoint, something around which Egyptians could be rallied for other political, social, and economic programs.

As leader of the 1952 Egyptian revolution Nasser had three main goals: first, the eradication of the corrupt monarchy of King Farouk; second, the removal of all vestiges of imperialism; and, finally, economic and social development. Through Egypt's economic transformation Nasser sought to fashion a new Egyptian. For Nasser the new Egyptian was an individual who was proud to be an Egyptian and who was treated as an equal in the international community, particularly in the West. Once in power, Nasser attempted to create those circumstances which he deemed necessary to fulfill his goals. In his political activity Nasser was less motivated by ideologies than by pragmatic considerations of what seemed advantageous for Egypt. A charismatic leader, Nasser became the political model not only for Egyptians but for Arabs in general. Both the Egyptians and the Arabs were striving to rid themselves of the inferiority feelings induced by colonial domination and economic weakness. Thus Nasser realized that for Egyptians the psychological benefits to be gained by building the Aswan Dam were at least as significant as its economic potentialities. However, United States officials tended to emphasize the latter. With his keen insight into Egyptian public opinion, Nasser recognized that the Aswan project represented Egypt's newly won control over its own future and tremendously strengthened public support for himself and the Revolutionary Council.

Obtaining Financial Aid

Once Egyptian leaders had decided to build the dam the problem was to secure financial aid for it. Great Britain, the United States, and the World Bank were cautiously favorable. As early as 1953 the World Bank began feasibility studies on the project. The costs were variously estimated at $516 million by the Egyptian government to $1.5 billion by the World Bank.

For United States policy-makers, financing the Dam offered an opportunity to improve over an extended period U.S. relations with

Egypt, and with the Arab world in general. From 1953 to 1955 most State Department and Pentagon officials operated on the assumption that they could work with Nasser to the mutual benefit of both. United States relations with Nasser were, however, strained by the Baghdad Pact, which was a western attempt to form a NATO-type defensive alliance in the Middle East, and by the Arab-Israeli conflict. While anxious to increase the amount of foreign aid Egypt received, Nasser clearly would maintain cordial relations with the U.S. only insofar as these did not impinge on his determination to free Egypt from all imperial controls. Secretary of State John Foster Dulles was disturbed by Nasser's growing tendency toward neutralism and by his steadfast refusal to see the Soviet Union as the major threat in the Middle East.

As a cold war politician, Dulles viewed any refusal to be firmly aligned with the West as a pro-Soviet statement. He was opposed to neutralism, believing it to be Communism in disguise. A Republican, from an aristocratic background, Dulles had been reared in a strict, moralistic Calvinism; these factors had played influential roles in forming his political outlook. A rather aloof personality of noted intelligence and commitment to Christianity and the western system, Dulles was a direct contrast to Nasser. Dulles neither understood nor condoned Nasser's political neutrality in the Cold War. But he concluded after his 1953 visit to the Middle East, and on the recommendations of his advisers, that Nasser offered the best chance for stable leadership in the Middle East at that time.

Acting from these diverse and perhaps mutually exclusive motivations, United States, western, and Egyptian officials began serious negotiations over financing the Aswan Dam in 1955. Since the financing was a long-term project, both the World Bank and the U.S. demanded assurances from Egyptian leaders that they would operate under stringent economic prescripts to discourage inflation, curb outside spending, and channel their major efforts toward building and financing the dam. They also asked for a firm agreement between Egypt and the Sudan over use of the Nile waters. Eugene Black, President of the World Bank, conducted a long, complicated series of negotiations over these various stumbling blocks, but remained convinced the project was one which the West ought to support.

While these discussions were in process, Nasser continued to move toward open neutrality, consistently refusing to be tied down by long-term assurances to the U.S. concerning Egypt's economic or political future. In 1955 the Lavon affair, in which several Israeli agents were found to be planning to bomb U.S. buildings in Egypt in an apparent attempt to discredit Egypt in the United States, became known. This caused widespread reverberations in Israel and the Arab world; it resulted in David Ben Gurion's return to power as Israeli defense minister which, in turn, eventually led to the Israeli raid on Gaza in February 1955. This raid indicated to Nasser the relative weakness of the Egyptian army. With this in mind he began to look for additional armaments. When repeated requests for arms from the U.S. were refused or delayed, Nasser looked elsewhere. In April he attended the famous Bandung Afro-Asian Conference where he was cordially treated as an equal among Nehru, Tito, and Chou En-Lai. After Bandung his position in the third world improved considerably while his neutrality became more marked. Simultaneously, Egypt—ironically, acting upon a suggestion by Chou En-Lai—began discussions for armaments with the Soviet bloc. After the British disclosed the deal, Nasser was forced to reveal in September that Egypt would be getting arms from Czechoslovakia. Intelligence sources in the U.S. knew of this, but probably not the full extent of it, several months prior to the public announcement.

In spite of Egyptian moves toward more friendly and closer relations with the Soviet bloc, negotiations with the West for Aswan Dam financing continued. These were further complicated by conflicting reports that the Soviet Union had also offered to help finance the project. Finally in December 1955 it was announced that the U.S. was willing to provide $56 million and that Great Britain agreed to provide for the purchase of British goods $14 million in blocked sterling funds which were owed Egypt for services in World War II. The announcement also noted that the U.S. and Britain were ready to "consider sympathetically in the light of then existing circumstances further support toward financing the later stages" of the dam's construction. As, however, hostile activities along Arab-Israeli borders had increased, the Eisenhower administration initiated a series of plans and diplomatic approaches designed to implement a final settlement based on treaty agreements over boundaries, increased foreign aid for economic development, and water irrigation schemes with compensation and resettlement of the refugees. Nasser refused to consider tying any economic aid for Aswan to the much larger and infinitely more complex issue of the Arab-Israeli conflict.

Discussion over World Bank loans continued in Cairo between Egyptian leaders and Eugene Black. Having previously described Aswan as "an inspiring project," Black in February 1956 concluded an agreement whereby the World Bank would loan Egypt $200 million. This offer was accepted "in principle" by Egypt, but the details and actual acceptance were not finalized. Both the U.S. and World Bank offers were given on the assumption that further Soviet incursions into Egypt's financial and political spheres would cease. Black publicly underscored Nasser's pro-western sympathies in an attempt to diminish criticism over Nasser's growing contacts with the Soviet bloc. Although some officials later tried to link the eventual U.S. refusal of aid for Aswan to the Egyptian-Czech arms deal, U.S. and World Bank offers of aid were given several months after the deal had been announced and, indeed, after shipment of the armaments was well under way.

After negotiating the World Bank agreement in February 1956, Nasser wrote to the U.S. and Great Britain saying that he did not agree with all the conditions placed on the grants and asked that they be altered. In the meantime Dulles began to reconsider the original offer. Several factors caused the secretary of state and officials in Washington, as opposed to those in the field who continued to advocate U.S. aid, to conclude that support for Nasser's regime would not be beneficial to U.S. interests. Nasser's continued cordial relations with the Soviet bloc, which had initially hastened the Aswan Dam offer, after some months caused increased hostility among those officials and congressmen who opposed proffering U.S. aid to neutral third world nations. The Egyptian recognition of the People's Republic of China in May exacerbated that irritation. In a news conference Dulles remarked that "it was an action that we regret." He also made it quite clear that the U.S. would not cooperate on the Aswan project with the Soviet Union. In Washington it appeared increasingly as if Nasser were merely delaying a decision on the U.S. offer in order to wrest more favorable terms by bargaining between the U.S. and the Soviet Union. This apparent "playing one side against the other" was highly objectionable to most officials. Indeed, many were willing to call Nasser's bluff and let the Soviet Union try to finance the project, something that most officials felt would be exceedingly difficult for the Russians to do.

Then, too, there was some Congressional criticism from Southern senators who feared Egyptian competition in the cotton market; some Zionist opposition to the project was also exerted. These factors were not major considerations in the decision to withdraw the offer. Far more important in this respect was the growing disenchantment with Nasser's leadership as it related to U.S. interests in the Middle East. The question centered on whether or not the U.S. could continue to work beneficially with Nasser over the ten to fifteen years that the Aswan Dam would be under construction. The issue of whether Egypt, in light of its extensive financial commitments to the Soviet bloc, would be able to sustain the economic demands of the project was also raised.

In addition, both France and Great Britain, the closest allies of the U.S., were disturbed with Nasser. The French were angry over Nasser's support and aid for the Algerians in the Algerian Revolution which had begun in 1954. The British blamed Nasser for the dismissal in February 1956 of Glubb Pasha as commander of the Arab Legion in Jordan. Although he was not directly responsible for either of these, Nasser was blamed for these reversals of western dominance in the Arab world.

Finally, there was the perennial problem of the Arab-Israeli conflict which the U.S. had hoped Nasser would help to settle. After the U.S. diplomatic gestures toward settlement floundered, it was clear that the dispute could not be resolved without Nasser's leadership. Nasser refused to participate in direct negotiations with Israel and used Jordanian King Abdullah's assassination as an excuse. Abdullah was assassinated by a Palestinian in 1951 when it became public knowledge that he had participated in direct negotiations with the Israelis. David Ben Gurion rejected indirect discussions, whereupon the attempts to secure a settlement reached an impasse which was only broken following the fourth Arab-Israeli War in 1973.

In light of these considerations, the U.S. dragged its feet on responding to Nasser's requests to alter the terms of the offer. In June 1956, Black again visited Cairo and urged Nasser to accept. Actually, Nasser was quite anxious for the U.S. to aid the project, but wished to secure the best possible terms. Accustomed to protracted bargaining Nasser was genuinely puzzled by the failure of the U.S. to answer his proposals on alterations of the terms.

United States Withdraws Its Offer

After talking in Rome with Henry Byroade, U.S. ambassador to Egypt, who was returning from Washington, Black hurried back to persuade officials to affirm the U.S. offer. Time was an important factor because the fiscal year ended June 30; with growing congressional and bureaucratic opposition to aid for Egypt it would have been difficult, although not impossible, to obtain the appropriations for the next fiscal year. In spite of Black's arguments for aid, Dulles and his advisers decided on the basis of the aforementioned factors—congressional opposition, financial considerations, growing Egyptian neutrality and commitment to the Soviet bloc, Zionist lobbying, and general dissatisfaction with Nasser—to withdraw the offer. Because it was public knowledge that Egyptian ambassador Ahmed Hussein planned to accept the offer, the decision to withdraw it was made conclusive several days before Dulles's scheduled meeting with Hussein on 19 July.

Ambassador Hussein returned from Cairo with what he thought was the happy news that Nasser had decided to accept the U.S. offer. His somewhat early arrival caused Dulles and others to conclude that the U.S. had to withdraw the offer promptly, or be faced with the Egyptian acceptance of an offer which was no longer part of U.S. foreign policy. At the time, Nasser along with Nehru was visiting Tito in Yugoslavia. Nasser fully expected that a firm agreement for U.S. aid would be concluded between Egyptian and U.S. officials in Washington. In a reversal of policy, and to the surprise of Egyptian leadership, when Dulles met with Hussein in the presence of several other U.S. officials, he withdrew the offer. The withdrawal was based on the grounds that it was "not feasible in present circumstances to participate in the project." Dulles remarked both to Hussein and in his published statement concerning the reversal of policy that he was uncertain of "the ability of Egypt to devote adequate resources to assure the project's success." This was a direct and public criticism of Egyptian economic stability which was offensive to Nasser. The U.S. withdrawal also caused the World Bank and Great Britain to refuse aid for the Aswan project.

Contrary to some analyses, Dulles did not withdraw the offer in a "fit of pique," but only after rather careful scrutiny and with the support of a number of State Department and other government officials. It was the manner in which the offer was withdrawn more than the decision to abstain from economic involvement which caused the repercussions which had such disastrous results for the West. With the benefit of hindsight, both Egyptian and U.S. leaders have noted that it was this which caused the reactions in Egypt.

Before deciding to abstain from involvement, U.S. policy-makers had carefully analyzed the possible ramifications of the withdrawal. Most believed that Nasser would be angry and that United States-Egyptian relations would suffer temporarily. The possibility that Nasser might nationalize the Suez Canal was discussed, but was dismissed as improbable because the Canal was to revert to Egyptian control in a few years. Officials also discounted Egyptian ability to run it. Some officials who were aware of the importance of Aswan in Nasser's political scheme hoped that he would be overthrown when he failed to implement the plan. The possibility of Nasser's downfall was pleasing to many advisers. They felt he had outlived his usefulness and, in fact, was a threat in the area to U.S. interests—the free flow of oil to western allies, the maintenance of open communication lines and defense bases, the existence of Israel, political stability, and resistance to Soviet penetration in the Middle East. Events that followed proved all these assumptions fallacious. The repercussions of the policy reversal, some of which are still being felt, might have been avoided had Dulles withdrawn the offer in a less open manner, or had he continued to delay concluding the agreement. Nasser was informed of the withdrawal as he was returning with Nehru to Cairo; by the time he heard the news it was practically public knowledge. This prevented the Egyptians from formulating a face-saving diplomatic response to the economic and political setback.

In Cairo the refusal to grant aid was interpreted as an insult to Egypt and as a direct slap in the face to Nasser. He was particularly incensed by the inference impugning the soundness of the Egyptian economy. Nasser might have understood quiet diplomatic reasoning from Dulles— that owing to U.S. domestic pressures the grant could not be assured. However, he did not understand either the abrupt manner in which the offer had been withdrawn or the immediate public announcement of the decision. The withdrawal was greeted with praise in western capitals and with jeers and open hostility in Cairo and in the third world generally. However, the Russians did not immediately step in with offers to replace western aid.

Speaking publicly, Nasser attacked the British and the U.S. on 24 July. The speech was critical of U.S. allusions that the Egyptian economy was unsound and reaffirmed Egypt's determination to build the Aswan Dam. On 26 July, the anniversary of the 1952 revolution, Nasser publicly nationalized the Suez Canal, to the astonishment of most western officials. It was his biggest political coup, made possible by the United States' refusal to finance the Aswan Dam. It is probable that the canal would have been nationalized at some later date. Certainly the efficient takeover of the canal implied that plans had been made considerably in advance of the action of 26 July. The U.S. disengagement offered the perfect opportunity to nationalize the canal without reprobation from the third world community and to considerable political advantage to Nasser.

Furious, the British and French were determined not only to take back control of the canal, but to topple Nasser as well. Anthony Eden, British prime minister viewed Nasser as another Hitler who planned to dominate the entire Middle East. Influenced by World War II, Eden rejected any form of appeasement which he was certain would only encourage Nasser's dictatorial ambitions. Some members of Eden's cabinet refuted the parallels between Hitler and Nasser, but Eden overruled their objections. The French government was also anxious to overthrow Nasser in order to halt his support for the Algerians. For political and military reasons, the Israelis were also willing to discuss joint actions with the French and the British. As fedayeen activities along Israeli borders intensified and Nasser more loudly proclaimed Arab opposition to Israel, the Israeli government began to consider methods to break the Arab-Israeli stalemate and perhaps to force a settlement. With this in mind Israeli officials engaged in discussion with the French and, ultimately, with the British for a military action against Egypt. An agreement was eventually reached whereby Israel would launch an attack against Sinai, but would stop short of the canal. The British and French were then to intervene between the Israeli and Egyptian forces and occupy the canal. The scenario also anticipated the immediate downfall of Nasser and the establishment of a more malleable Egyptian administration.

United States Reactions

Throughout the intensive and often arduous diplomatic maneuvering which followed nationalization, the U.S. worked to secure a diplomatic settlement which would avoid armed intervention. As an international lawyer, Dulles felt that Nasser had acted within legal bounds. In fact, Nasser had been particularly careful to accede to the legal prescripts governing nationalization. Since no legal contraventions had occurred, the Eisenhower administration was reluctant to support a military solution which would have contradicted U.S. policies for peaceful solutions to international conflicts and for the application of international justice. Dulles as a lawyer decided to adopt what he considered to be a principled and correct stand on the matter of the canal's nationalization. Not surprisingly, the British and French were dismayed by U.S. hesitation to force an immediate settlement. The oil that was shipped through the Suez Canal was vital for the continuation of British and French industrial complexes—to say nothing of domestic use. When it became apparent that the U.S. did not intend to supplement the oil losses, the British and French determined that they would have to force their own settlement.

Negotiations dragged on throughout the summer months, complicated from the U.S. point of view by the approaching presidential election. After it became evident that a negotiated settlement would not achieve their desired ends, the British, French, and Israelis launched their military attack against Egypt. This resulted in British and French occupation of the Suez Canal and in the Israeli invasion of the Sinai Peninsula. Subsequently, the U.S. was in the awkward position of having to oppose its closest allies, Britain and France, in the public forum of the United Nations. This divergence contributed to strained relationships with Britain and the other NATO allies which lasted for some time. Eventually, the British, French, and Israeli forces withdrew from Egyptian territory, although Israel secured free access through the Straits of Tiran to Eilat. This acquisition was to be the *causus belli* for the 1967 Arab-Israeli war which has had such imponderable consequences, and which again led to armed conflict in October 1973.

The Suez nationalization and the war, which Egypt lost militarily but won politically, created limitless political support for Nasser in Egypt and throughout the Arab world. Through the nationalization of the canal and the western occupation of Egyptian territory, Nasser came to epitomize the third world leader who stood up to the superpowers and who refused to be dominated by them. The western military action against Egypt only reinforced the belief in the third world that the West was still engaging in neocolonialist endeavors. Rather than Nasser's precipitous downfall, which the West had anticipated, the year 1956 marked the zenith of his popularity. As a result the Middle East was swept with a series of pro-Nasser military coups, many of which were not directed by him, but which were certainly inspired by his actions over Aswan and Suez. These culminated in 1958 when Syria formed a union with Egypt, the pro-western King Faysal/ Nuri Said regime in Iraq was overthrown, and when both the Jordanian and Lebanese governments had to ask for and receive British and U.S. military assistance to prop up their governments against forces sympathetic to Nasser.

In fact, the December 1958 Soviet-Egyptian agreement to build the Aswan Dam almost escaped notice amid this effusion of political and military activity. Construction on the dam began in 1960; the basic structure was completed in 1969. The secondary projects were finished in 1971, thereby implementing a plan that had been proposed almost twenty years earlier.

Conclusions

In helping to finance the Aswan Dam, the Soviet Union achieved influence over Egyptian development and gained inestimable goodwill from the people. By abstaining from economic involvement the U.S. opened the door for Soviet presence in the Middle East, the event it had sought to avoid. Since many U.S. officials viewed postcolonial nationalist leaders as potential threats to western hegemony in the Middle East, they were divided as to what policies to adopt either in support of or opposition to such leaders. While the U.S. sought to assure itself of their loyalty, or at least adherence to the West, it also desired that they adopt overtly anti-Soviet policies. Most of the Arab leadership, of which Nasser was an outstanding example, perceived neutrality as the best means to maximize foreign aid and at the same time demonstrate their independence.

While U.S. officials living in the Middle East generally understood and coped with Nasser's neutrality, policy-makers in Washington tended to view his neutrality as thinly disguised pro-Soviet sentiment. For this reason, U.S. sympathy for Nasser declined in almost direct proportion to his neutral dealings with the great powers. Negative opinions of

Nasser were reinforced by domestic economic pressures and the Zionist lobby. The U.S. had only considered aiding the Aswan project as a means of assuring Nasser's continued pro-western stand. Once this assurance was not forthcoming, the reasons for aid ceased to exist. Some U.S. officials prophesied that U.S. involvement with the Aswan project would only increase sources of potential friction. But they had not foreseen that the abrupt manner in which the offer was withdrawn would have such widespread reverberations. Even with the benefit of foresight most would have decided not to provide aid, although the withdrawal undoubtedly would have been effectuated in a different fashion.

Following Nasser's nationalization of the Suez Canal, the U.S. resisted attempts to force a settlement by military means, thereby alienating its closest allies who perceived their vital interests were at stake. The U.S. then found itself in a position where its influence with Britain and France practically disappeared, and in which there was a corresponding failure to secure an increase of goodwill in Egypt and the Arab world. Such an open rupture among the great western powers over a crucial issue was almost unthinkable in light of cold war politics. The division was heightened by the reluctant appearance of the Soviet Union and the United States on the same side of the issue. This circumstance was particularly embarrassing in light of the Hungarian revolution and the Soviet military action against it. The split among the western powers caused recriminations on political levels; it also marked the end of an era in which the U.S. was the determining force in European international affairs.

In the Middle East the consequences were perhaps even more profound. The Soviet presence in Egypt set the stage for a decade of Soviet-United States rivalry in the area. After 1956, the superpowers continued to strengthen their alliances with Middle Eastern nations. Soviet policies in the Middle East also were based on furthering its self-interests; the recent ousting of Soviet technicians and military advisers from Egypt indicates that third world nations like Egypt consider attempts to dominate or control them as unacceptable. It was also an unsuccessful attempt by Anwar Sadat, Nasser's successor, to encourage the U.S. to use its influence with Israel and the Soviet Union to remove the stalemate of "no war, no peace" which had been the result of the 1967 Arab-Israeli war. The failure of this maneuver to incite any U.S. diplomatic initiatives was the backdrop for the 1973 war. In the long run, both economic and military intervention, whether from the western or Soviet blocs, which is interpreted as neocolonialist will eventually be rejected by the third world. It is likely that official doubt concerning the efficacy of U.S. aid for Aswan was correct. Abstaining from involvement in the Aswan Dam project probably did not harm U.S. interests in the Middle East over the long run. In the short term the manner in which the offer of aid was withdrawn definitely had negative effects which could have been avoided. The method of implementing the policy reversal was the catalyst in a series of events which resulted in the nationalization of the Suez Canal, the 1956 Suez War, and the decline of U.S. and western influence throughout the Middle East.

SUGGESTIONS FOR FURTHER RESEARCH

Studies investigating the economic and political impacts of the completed Aswan Dam project are now in order. In light of 1973 events, namely the fourth Arab-Israeli war and growing paramountcy of the U.S. in the Middle East, Soviet gains secured from the financing of the dam need to be reevaluated. Soviet influence appears to have been far more ephemeral than originally estimated in the post-Suez war period. Indeed, foreign policy-makers seeking long-range ascendancy in the Middle East would be well advised to review the efficacy of economic intervention as a means of securing permanent client-patron relationships. Recent events underline Egyptian determination to demark a more neutral stance and to refuse being cast in the client role for any superpower.

The importance of the Nasser era and his leadership in Egypt and the Arab world merit knowledgeable analysis. Many of Nasser's decisions have been discredited by Anwar el Sadat's less flamboyant but perhaps more effective political maneuverings.

Finally, research contrasting the Manichean world view of Dulles in his conduct of U.S. foreign policy with the consummate "art of the possible" diplomacy of Kissinger would provide provocative material for observers of international relationships. As the Aswan case study indicates, the purely mechanical methods of implementing the policies of abstention or intervention can sometimes be as crucial as the decisions themselves. In such cases the personalities of the key leaders, their abilities to present policies in the most favorable light, and their capacities to work easily with their colleagues—domestic and international—are of paramount importance.

BIBLIOGRAPHIC NOTE

The best primary source material on the Aswan Dam and U.S. involvement in the project are the Dulles Papers at Princeton University Library. These papers contain extensive material regarding U.S. policy in Egypt during the Eisenhower administration; the papers include an oral history project of interviews with most of the key foreign policy decision makers in both the U.S. and European governments during the Suez crisis. The Egyptian government has also published, in English, a number of official descriptions of Aswan including Gamal Abdal Nasser, President of the U.A.R., "Address on the Occasion of the High Dam Celebration," January 9, 1963, Cairo Information Department, 1963. The U.A.R. *The High Dam, Miracle of the XXth Century,* Cairo Information Department, 1964, contains the Egyptian government's description of the project. For Nasser's personal analysis of his goals see Gamal Abdal Nasser, *The Philosophy of the Revolution* (Buffalo, N.Y., 1959). The U.S. Senate Investigations on Aswan are published in U.S., Cong., Senate Committee on Appropriations, 84th Cong., 2d sess., January 26, 1956, Washington, D.C., 1956.

A good study of the Aswan Dam project from a historical perspective is Tom Little's *High Dam at Aswan: The Subjugation of the Nile* (New York, 1956). Another summary of the project is in J. E. Dougherty, "The Aswan Decision in Perspective," *Political Science Quarterly* (March 1959).

A fairly complete study on Aswan and Suez is Herman Finer's *Dulles over Suez* (Chicago, 1964), which is based on interviews and primary material. A new revised look at Dulles, in a more favorable light, is found in Michael A. Guhin, *John Foster Dulles: A Statesman and His Times* (New York, 1972). Peter Calvocoressi in *Suez: Ten Years After,* ed. Anthony Moncrieff (New York, 1966), presents a series of interviews with the leaders involved in the 1956 Suez crisis.

Kenneth Love in *Suez: The Twice Fought War* (New York, 1969), provides a complete historical analysis of the crisis, while Terence Robertson in *Crisis: The Inside Story of the Suez Conspiracy* (New York, 1965), focuses upon great power politics.

For the story of British involvement see Anthony Eden, *The Suez Crisis of 1956* (Boston, 1968), reprinted from his memoirs, *Full Circle*. Anthony Nutting in his *No End of a Lesson* (London, 1967) provides an opposing British point of view: Nutting, minister of state, resigned over British involvement in the Suez war. His biography entitled *Nasser* (New York, 1972) also presents a lengthy description of Nasser's regime.

Jacques Berque's *Egypt: Imperialism and Revolution* (London, 1972) is a masterful portrayal of the social situation which led up to the 1952 Revolution in Egypt and Nasser's regime. Mohamed Heikal in *Nasser: The Cairo Documents* (New York, 1972) gives an interesting, albeit biased, firsthand account of Nasser. A more objective account of Egyptian politics and Nasser may be found in Peter Mansfield, *Nasser's Egypt* (London, 1965).

For descriptions of the military aspects of the Suez War see A. J. Barker, *Suez: The Seven Day War* (London, 1964); Edgar O'Ballance, *The Sinai Campaign 1956* (London, 1959); Moshe Dayan, *The Diary of the Sinai Campaign* (New York, 1967), for a personal account of the war from the Israeli viewpoint.

P. J. Vatikiotis in *The Egyptian Army in Politics* (Bloomington, Ind., 1961) analyzes the role of the army in Egypt; Patrick O'Brien in *The Revolution in Egypt's Economic System: From Private Enterprise to Socialism, 1952-1965* (London, 1966) focuses on Egyptian economic development.

For information on Aswan and the Suez War as related to the international political sphere see Malcolm Kerr, *The Arab Cold War,* 3d ed. (London, 1971); Walter Z. Laqueur, *The Soviet Union and the Middle East* (New York, 1959); George Lenczowski, *The Middle East in World Affairs,* 3d ed. (Ithaca, N.Y., 1962); and Guy Wint and Peter Calvocoressi, *Middle East Crisis* (London, 1957).

Miles Copeland's *The Game of Nations* (London, 1969) is an ex-CIA agent's "inside" story of U.S. involvement in the Middle East. Finally, Robert Murphy in *Diplomats among Warriors* (New York, 1965) discusses "behind the scenes" political activities and negotiations of U.S. diplomats. Based on factual material and personalities, Edward Shechan's *Kingdom of Illusion* (New York, 1967) is a fictional treatment of negotiations between important western diplomats and an imaginary third world government, which is Egypt thinly disguised.

THE CONSEQUENCES OF ECONOMIC
INTERVENTION: PERU & CHILE

James C. Carey

Background

United States intervention in Latin America is an old story, but economic intervention was not widespread until the twentieth century, and dollar investment in Chile and Peru was not significant until after World War I. The background for such economic expansion came with Theodore Roosevelt's Corollary, the construction of the Panama Canal, and Taft's assurance that the flag followed the dollar. There is much in common in the history of U.S. economic penetration in Chile with that in Peru. England had moved in first and Germany and Italy followed, while all three kept their investments fairly widely distributed in agriculture, industry, finance, and shipping. When the Yankee dollar came along, it first went mainly into the extractive industries, especially minerals. Later, private loans to governments helped to provide a wedge for gaining concessions. Percentage figures on imports into the two countries, not high compared to Mexico and Central America, show the impact of World War I, when the increase between 1913 and 1926 was from 16.7 percent to 32.6 percent in Chile and from 28.8 percent to 46.2 in Peru. The years 1930 to 1960 with World War II showed the continued growth of U.S. influence over the foreign markets of Chile and Peru.

The need for outside capital and technology rendered Peru and Chile ripe fields for large Yankee mining and petroleum concerns. The *Commerce Reports* show that the U.S. Department of Commerce encouraged large-scale, rather than small-scale, investments. The Peruvian field was made even more attractive when with the backing of the U.S. government Augusto B. Leguía fortified his position in an eleven-year dictatorship (1919-1930) and in turn opened wide the door for private U.S. loan sharks and investors in the mines and oil fields. The record of private loans to Peru in the 1920s was indeed a seamy one. It was capped with a $416,000 bribe to President Leguía's son, Juan, from J. & W. Seligman and the National City Company of New York; this inducement was designed to encourage the Peruvian Government to request a loan. The ultimate purchasers, U.S. bond-buying citizens, were the real losers who had given $567,000 in loans. The 1929 crash on Wall Street meant that the stream of capital from North America, channeled through New York, was cut off abruptly. As soon as President Leguía was ousted by a coup, Peru defaulted on most of the bonds and the search for a negotiated settlement dragged on for many years. The U.S. benefactors proved to be those grafters and somewhat reliable but careless financiers who collected initial commissions on the loans as well as the U.S. business concerns which gained either new concessions or broader latitude for existing concessions in Peru.

Along the way, official Washington had cautiously encouraged the lending program to Chile, Peru, and other Latin American nations while rationalizing that U.S. private loans would lead to U.S. business opportunities. Also it was believed that U.S. money, rather than European, might be a factor in lessening the chances of violations of the Monroe Doctrine, for there was the possibility that an outside nation would use force to try to collect unpaid debts as in the Venezuelan incident of 1895.

Following the loan agreements, U.S. private investments entered into new avenues of commerce and industry, but the giants in Peru continued to be Cerro de Pasco Corporation (mining), W. R. Grace and Company (sugar, textiles, import-export, and the passenger as well as freight shipping enterprises), and International Petroleum Company (IPC) which was a subsidiary of Standard Oil of New Jersey that had tapped the rich, readily available, northern coastal oil fields. It was estimated that IPC exported about 90 percent of Peru's outgoing petroleum by the mid-1920s. Other important U.S. businesses which developed were All-America Cables, Pan American-Grace Airways, Frederick Snare Corporation, the Vanadium Corporation, National City Bank of New York, the trading firm of Wessel Duval Company, and other smelting and manufacturing, banking, and trading concerns.

Major U.S. investments in Chile were instituted a bit later than were the Peruvian ones where W. R. Grace had started a small operation in 1850 and Cerro de Pasco had opened activity in 1901 in Peru. But in Chile as in Peru the emphasis was on the extractive industries where U.S. firms were to become dominant in nitrate and copper production which led the way to a thirty-five fold increase in U.S. investments in Chile for the years 1914 to 1928. In 1913 Bethlehem Steel Corporation obtained the important iron mines in Coquimbo, and soon the Braden Copper Mines Company (later associated with Kennecott) began to develop the Rancagua mines. Associated with William Braden, New York, were the Guggenheim interests which started operation in Northern Chile at Chuquicamata, at that time the largest known copper deposit in the world. Anaconda was soon also in business there. By 1928 private United States investments in Chile were estimated as a minimum at $618,285,300, distributed as follows: government securities, $216,785,300; mining industries, $385,125,000; manufacturing, $11,285,000; merchandising, $22,500,000; public utilities, $6,500,000; banking, $600,000; miscellaneous, $2,500,000. By 1928 these investments were rapidly overtaking British capital which had held the upper hand. Loans to the Chilean government increased in toto from $100,000,000 in 1925 to $216,785,300 in 1928 and, as in Peru, there would be some negotiation difficulties over default. In addition W. R. Grace and Company, American Smelting and Refining Corporation, All-America Cables, International Telephone and Telegraph Corporation, National City Bank, and a smattering of trading and manufacturing enterprises were also involved. The Guggenheim interests purchased nitrate lands in 1924 and soon expanded their operations in this traditionally British field, as on a smaller scale did W. R. Grace and Du Pont.

Intervention

Under the broad, ephemeral canopy of laissez-faire, American businessmen operating in the two countries secured solicitous treatment from the United States diplomatic and consular offices. Both before and, for a time, after the First World War the U.S. government promised protection for property as well as lives of its citizens South of the Border. In Chile and Peru, as in most nations in that area of the world, American embassy representatives called for visits of U.S. armed vessels as an indication that Uncle Sam "might spank" those who threatened U.S. lives and property. In some cases the ambassadors suggested that the ships merely drop anchor off the coast and not approach the ports directly.

The *Papers Relating to the Foreign Relations of the United States* for both Chile and Peru show that to a significant extent the views of businessmen were important in determining the U.S. policy for those countries. An example of this in Lima was when the chargé d'affaires took the manager of Cerro de Pasco Corporation with him on his first visit to the newly installed chief executive of Peru, Luis M. Sánchez Cerro, who had recently unseated Leguía. Harold Kingsmill, the Cerro manager, had suggested the advisability of having "war vessels" brought to Peru. At this point, even before U.S. recognition of the new government, the Cerro manager wanted to discuss his company's affairs with the new chief of state. This was not the first time, nor the last, that business interests would be deeply involved in determining whether or not full diplomatic recognition should be accorded a new government in Peru and elsewhere. That U.S. firms did not remain aloof from Chilean domestic politics either is shown by these two examples. In 1925 Alfred Houston, attorney for the Braden Copper Company, asked the U.S. ambassador in Santiago to intercede with junta officers (who had just ousted another military junta) so as to protect from violence three Chileans of the first junta. In January 1928 Secretary of State Frank B. Kellogg concerned himself on behalf of W. R. Grace and Company with customs rebates which the Chilean government was considering granting domestic shipping on two classes of articles. Ambassador William M. Collier reported promptly to Washington that "I have finally after repeated representations secured the withdrawal of the objectional provision from the tariff bill and the bill thus corrected has passed both Houses of Congress." Max Winkler found that by 1928 extractive industries accounted for the major portion of Chile's export trade as copper and nitrates with by-products comprised over 80 percent of the total exports. U.S. dominance of Peru's exports presented a somewhat similar picture, although a more diversified one.

During World War II, U.S. investments continued to grow and to receive protection from the departments of State and Commerce. The Good Neighbor Policy had widened the official approach from Washington and brought cultural exchange offices into Lima and Santiago. In addition, a hemispheric defense emphasis after the outbreak of war in Europe soon led to a bolstering of personnel in the various military attaché offices and new or expanded development of military missions in Santiago and Lima. Peru, which back in 1920 had been the first in the world to receive a formal Naval Mission under the act of that year, found itself encouraged to accept extensive military development programs and equipment. Only Brazil, of all Latin America, obtained more U.S. military assistance money from July 1945 to June 1960 than Peru with its more than $94 million if loans are included. Military hardware was marketed in this as well as other parts of Latin America while official Washington whispered, "If we don't sell this, some other nation (possibly an unfriendly one) will do so." In this mood, an Export-Import Bank loan was used to finance submarine purchases for Peru. As that country cooperated more readily with Washington during World War II than did Chile, it came in for a larger share, but both nations received sizable inputs of Yankee capital through Lend-Lease agreements and loans from the Export-Import Bank. Both nations put the money to work (some for procurement of U.S. goods or services) only to find that most or all of it was to be eaten up by inflation and earthquakes. The former was especially disastrous in Chile from 1940 to 1955 where the cost of living index rose from a 1940 base figure of 100.0 to 2,887.1 in 1955.

The mighty dollar rendered its power obvious in all the main avenues of the Chilean and Peruvian economies during the 1950s. The book (one can only guess at the real) value of American private investments in Peru rose from $82 million in 1940 to $354 million in 1956, and in Chile from $414 million to $677 million over the same span. By the late 1960s the three large U.S. firms estimated their Chilean copper holdings to be worth $744 million. When added to this are the expanding U.S. government investments and the economic import of financial and technical assistance programs, there developed apprehension among the nationalistic-minded citizens who began to fear for the economic independence of their nations. Even assistance programs including AID projects, many of which had been designed to avoid charges of interference, caused some nationals to view them as invidious forms of "Yankee intervention." Wherever American technicians or techniques were employed there was indeed such a risk because monies from grants and loans were usually tied to procurement of goods and services from

North of the Border. With more and more public money from the United States following private money southward, the complex relationship between United States government interests and those of private citizens became all the more enigmatic. It became increasingly difficult for *Anglos* as well as *Latinos* to distinguish between U.S. public and private enterprise.

These countries depended primarily upon minerals (including petroleum in the case of Peru) for their foreign exchange. Since the mineral industries were primarily in the hands of U.S. concerns, it was natural that suspicion and distrust would grow at the same time that nationalism developed. By 1960 approximately 96 percent of direct foreign investment in Peruvian mining came from the U.S. and an even greater percentage of petroleum production was controlled by Standard Oil's subsidiary, IPC, following the 1957 absorption of the British Lobitos interests. Two-thirds of the direct foreign interests in Peruvian manufacturing were owned by U.S. firms. Chile's "subservience" to Yankee dollars was even more apparent, for copper had long been the main base for export income, providing upwards of 60 percent of the nation's sales in the world market. Almost all the copper industry belonged to the three giant U.S. concerns, Anaconda, Kennecott with the Braden subsidiary, and the Cerro Corporation. Of course there were limited short-range domestic economic benefits, but in the main the net income from such enterprise did not remain and accumulate in these two nations—because what did not leak out was usually used to pay for imported U.S. products of the immediate consumption type. Wartime trade patterns, in the two major world conflicts, had made Chile and Peru even more dependent upon one or two foreign-owned industries.

After the *Latinos* had cooperated with Washington in the Second World War, and the Northern Giant failed to provide a Marshall Plan for South of the Border, resentment built up as the rising tide of expectations soured in the reality that misery and poverty were constants. The rough reception—stones and spittal—for Vice President Richard Nixon in Lima, 1958, provided a window through which official Washington could see the surface of Chilean and Peruvian complaints against economic imperialism. The frustrated masses, in their feeling of inferiority, hurled charges against the powerful and wealthy U.S. and its outright or concealed intervention which had brought domination over the key industries in their world trade. Products pulled from the bowels of the earth, as copper or petroleum, seem to spur more direct antagonism than do many other development products. Possibly the contrast between a highly and a slightly industrialized nation is spotlighted against plenty and poverty. It was apparent to many nationals in Chile and Peru that the most easily exploited minerals were being siphoned off and that future production might be much more costly and difficult.

The idea grew that U.S. companies used Chile and Peru as pawns while those countries were gradually losing their birthrights to some of the richest mineral deposits of the world. Critics of U.S. import quotas and tariff provisions along with the general domination of markets pointed out how little the *Latino* miner or oil worker received in comparison to the selling price of the product in world markets. Charges were levied in the congressional halls of Santiago and Lima that Yankee firms did not pay their share of national taxes. Chilean and Peruvian tax assessment and related collection problems, always complex and not without considerable manipulation for or by the influential, leave a picture so confusing that it is very difficult to determine in any realistic manner what might have been fair taxes for foreign firms. Also it would be difficult to prove that U.S. businesses were not good employers, at least as judged by local standards; still resentment rose higher against what appeared to be and what was said to be "economic aggression." It seemed as if more enlightened policies were expected from outside capitalists than were required from the domestic ones. One thing was certain, the main foreign businesses were giants and thus, as anywhere, open to attack. Some nationalists argued that since money, one way or another, had such great influence then the northern interests should accept leadership responsibility commensurate with that great strength—and if they did not do that then their properties should be nationalized.

Ordinary citizens in Chile and Peru joined the young nationalistic economists in challenging outside capital and its imported technology. Protestors insisted that the *Latinos* received too low a price for their raw materials and manual labor while in turn they paid too much for the imported capital and technological skills. Peruvian Aprista intellectual Luis Alberto Sánchez stated the problem in even larger terms: "Many American politicians and financiers consider Latin America only a source of raw materials, purchased, of course, at a very low price. That means that we have been reduced to a very low standard of living and cannot, as a result, be consumers. In consequence, the powerful industries of the U.S. have lost many millions of buyers in Latin America. This is a contributory factor in the social failures and unemployment among certain workers in your country." Peruvians lamented that with all the oil produced in their land, there was not a single plant which produced high-test gasoline; thus a premium price had to be paid to import it for cars and airplanes. Some Chileans and Peruvians expressed unhappiness due to their belief that gold was being hidden in copper ingots or ore when it was shipped to the U.S. or elsewhere for refinement. Daily laborers and supervisory employees were aware of rankling inequalities, for U.S. citizen employees in Chile and Peru received higher (often far higher) pay for the same training, experience, and ability. (This has presented a problem, and it should be noted that American employees brought in from the U.S. are almost always accustomed to a higher standard of living than are nationals.) But, also, the highest salaried and most responsible positions were seldom, if ever, opened to the Chileans and Peruvians—and especially not until recent years. Ever galling was the fact that in the early 1960s no place in the world (not even Africa) produced copper as cheaply as did the key operations in Chile and Peru—and all this while the companies had been netting a handsome profit over a span of many years.

Through the 1950s the discontent rising against foreign economic power was mainly a middle-class grass-roots movement, for the governments of Chile and Peru were seeking a route between the leftist protestors and the rightist domestic and foreign entrepreneurs. Nationalists, in general terms, continued to charge U.S. investors with alliances with domestic monopolies, thus further stifling the growth of a more progressive economic atmosphere. Evidence of discontent with these conditions showed itself in the form of wider protests and strikes. By the 1960s some of the higher clerics and important military figures (traditionally more inclined to be proponents of the status quo) began to criticize or condemn capitalism for its failure to alleviate the misery of the masses. The Chauffeurs' Federation of Peru, protesting IPC's monopoly of petroleum production and an increase in gasoline prices (not exorbitant by world prices), went on strike in 1958. Even W. R. Grace (usually closely identified with national welfare and in recent years careful not to be offensive by dabbling in local politics) found 2,000 workers on strike at its Paramonga sugar estate in Northern Peru.

There police and workers fought a pitched battle resulting in three deaths and sixteen injuries. On several occasions, the National City Bank headquarters in both Chile and Peru came under attack by strikers. Clashes in the mining areas increased in the 1950s and 1960s. Police shot eight demonstrators, killing two, at the Peruvian port of Ilo where work for the Utah Pacific Company was halted (1957). The year 1960 saw various battles in the Peruvian highlands. When Indians, led by the mayor of Cerro de Pasco City, moved onto one of the Cerro company farms the ensuing conflict left three Andino Indians dead and twenty-five policemen injured. This encounter was not only an outburst against foreign mine ownership but also part of the larger movement seeking broad agrarian reform. Yet the opposition to outsiders there in the Cerro mining region was deep-seated, for as early as 1930 two U.S. citizens lost their lives in the anti-foreign outburst at the time that President Leguía was ousted. When in 1942 I visited the Cerro de Pasco residential area near Oroya, foreigners were then under "protection" of an armed Peruvian soldier who stood guard at the entrance to the living quarters. Presumably the guard was there to give assurance to the residents, mainly U.S. citizens and some Canadians, and to check on the nonresidents who wished to visit. Difficulties spread in both Chile and Peru during the 1960s. Early in 1966, some 10,000 workers at the Braden Copper Company's *El Teniente* mine struck. Other Chilean copper miners joined in spite of the government's orders to return to work. Before it was over, eight miners were killed and thirty-five wounded as a thousand miners battled a hundred soldiers. In this case, particularly, it would be erroneous simply to attribute all principal causes to a nationalistic move against U.S. capital. Part of the friction originated between the domestic right and the Marxist left where the former feared President Eduardo Frei's Chileanization plans for copper would lead to broader reforms and Marxist political elements of the left who were busy maneuvering against the Christian Democrat party.

Nationalization

Gradually the governments of Peru and Chile became more responsive to the clamor of their peoples who increasingly insisted that nationals or the state should have greater control over the economy, especially the extractive industries. In Peru a military government took the lead to speed up nationalization of the oil industry, something that Mexico had done twenty-five years earlier. While in Chile two successive presidents, Frei and Salvador Allende, pushed the state to seize more and more control of copper. After nearly a half century of relatively secure development and high net profits, the Yankee entrepreneur was asked to take a back seat in both nations. To some people it might appear that a poetic justice was at work in Peru where the U.S. had long contributed to strengthening the Peruvian military establishment only to find a military junta seizing power illegally and then taking the initiative to replace foreign control over oil with local national control. Peacekeeping forces were keeping more than the peace—they were also trying to keep national control over what was left of the mineral wealth.

During the 1960s official Washington became less responsive to requests for direct intervention to protect the dollar, wherever it was, than it had been thirty or forty years earlier. Still the larger concerns expected protection even as that became more difficult. Fidel Castro's challenge had changed the alternatives for the U.S., and the Alliance for Progress introduced in 1961 had declared itself in favor of more independent reform in each nation. American airlines had a sound competitive position in Peru and Chile so there was not, as earlier, the concern that Germany or Italy might preempt these fields. The U.S. government through international banking channels or by means of grants and loans was still supporting, to varying degrees, the position of those who believed that trade would follow dollar loans. And through the U.S. governmental agency Overseas Private Investment Corporation (OPIC), private investors in foreign countries were provided considerable insurance protection against expropriation and revolutionary losses. In the meantime it had become passé over most of the world for any nation to try to protect its citizens' investments or collect on loans, private or public, by use of outright military force. But the Washington government, as all governments, continued to enter into negotiations to seek favorable compensatory terms when its citizens had property expropriated. In 1973 the negotiations in Chile and Peru were still taking place.

Ever since 1960 the thorny IPC dispute hinging on various economic and political problems has represented Peru's main thrust toward checking U.S. economic penetration there and in turn reflected the desire to assert the nation's economic independence. Back in 1932 a professor of law at the University of San Marcos had first challenged the legality of IPC claims to exploitation rights in the La Brea and Pariñas areas. When the moderate but progressive administration of Fernando Belaunde Terry (1967-1968) dallied in carrying out its campaign promises to expropriate IPC (he attempted to compromise), the opposition rose on a wide front. A revolutionary movement headed by army General Juan Velasco Alvarado took over the government in October 1968, claiming that Belaunde had harmed the country's interests. (In any event, Velasco used the IPC matter as one justification for his coup to oust Belaunde.) The alert nationalistic military junta then seized the disputed oil properties and refused to pay satisfactory compensation. Peru claimed that the oil company owed back taxes and also that IPC should pay $690,524,283, primarily on the basis that the company had been extracting oil illegally for forty-five years from the La Brea and Pariñas fields. IPC contested this. Washington suspended foreign-aid money which had been designated for Peru.

Other acts of both nationalization and expropriation have followed. Cerro and Grace felt the pressure first from a law by which the Lima government seized the larger agricultural holdings to convert them into farmers' cooperatives. For 600,000 acres of Cerro farm and ranch land some cash and government bonds were turned over in partial payment. When the Grace holdings were seized, Peru agreed to make compensation over a twenty-year period by using the profits from the newly created cooperatives. Some U.S. and other countries' mining interest concessions reverted to Peruvian government control as the new mining requirements became very difficult to meet. Italian as well as U.S. bank holdings in Peru have been affected by a law to nationalize banks so as to put the majority of stock in the hands of Peruvians. The case of the American ITT company subsidiary is a good example of the new stance taken by Peru's military junta. With nationalization in the air, ITT (October 1969) agreed to sell 69.1 percent of its subsidiary's stock to Peru for $17.9 million. ITT received $2.5 million cash with the rest of the payments to be made over a three-year period. In addition, ITT was committed to reinvest $8.2 million of the payments into an expansion program. While Peru was expropriating the rest of U.S. petroleum interests, it was signing contracts with foreigners (which included U.S. companies) for oil exploration in its Amazon region. In the meantime, the government of Peru announced that any company, in whatever business or industry, in which more than 49 percent was owned by foreign interests, would have to change to a majority Peruvian ownership before the end of 1972. The government announced development plans such as its intention to build a $21 million state-owned copper refinery near the southern port of Ilo. The Ministry of Energy and Mines was authorized by government decree (1970) to extend controls over the sale and refining of all existing operations, but the decree was not to be enforced for eighteen months. General Velasco insisted that his government was not Communist as some foreign and domestic sources charged, but rather that it was a revolutionary government bent on bringing about significant changes as it carried out "a real fight against injustice, hunger, exploitation." Large property interests, domestic as well as foreign were shaken, as the military junta celebrated its second year in power and Velasco announced that "the reactionary oligarchy must realize that its rule over Peru has ended forever."

In the area of world trade a new spirit was noted. The Peruvian and Soviet governments worked out in August 1970 a trade agreement whereby Russia would provide credits for Peru to purchase machinery and by which Russia would accept partial payment over a ten-year period in the form of Peruvian manufactured goods. By 1972 Peruvian agreements with China and Hungary called for economic and technical cooperation, and Lima restored diplomatic relations with Cuba. Other signs of Peruvian economic independence continued to crop up here and there as for example a $1.3 million fine of Plant Protection, a United States-owned industrial-security firm, which was alleged to have evaded taxes. Of course Peru has also seized private U.S. fishing vessels within the 200-mile limit and collected heavy fines in this way.

In Chile, President Frei, also preparing to move with the times, had a "Chileanization" plan for copper whereby the companies sold a 51 percent interest to the Chilean government. Plans were started in 1965 and by the fall of 1969, Kennecott officially turned over 51 percent of its shares in *El Teniente,* the world's largest underground copper mine. Frei soon announced an agreement for taking over Anaconda's largest mines, including the world's largest open-pit mine, but Anaconda's new mine, the *Exotica,* was not affected, since Chile already owned 25 percent there. Payments for the Chileanized mines were to be extended over a twelve-year period (1970-1981) during which time Chile would begin to participate in the profits. Anaconda agreed to the plan in order to avoid expropriation. (During the negotiations over Chileanization, two bills were introduced into the Chilean Congress which demanded outright expropriation.) Two newly established Chilean firms were created to take over the companies; they would hold 51 percent of the stock, while the Anaconda subsidiary would continue to own 49 percent. If the Christian Democrats had been able to hold onto power, the program of gradual nationalization of copper on a clearly cooperative basis with the U.S. owners might have succeeded. But the plan would have had to move rapidly if it was to have met the demands of the impatient masses many of whom had, justifiably or not, come to identify their poverty with foreign economic domination as well as with a combination of foreign and domestic monopolies.

It was no surprise that the Marxist (Socialist) Salvador Allende, September-October 1970, was elected and that this was received with considerable apprehension by the principal foreign interests as well as by official Washington. The U.S. government carelessly emphasized its skepticism by its failure to send a normal congratulatory message. Allende had won a plurality vote—then a congressional vote—with the support of a six-party coalition of leftist and either center or center-leftist groups. Even the Christian Democratic party supported constitutional reforms which made Allende's election in Congress almost certain. The first public statement by Washington expressed fear that "a Communist regime in Chile could threaten Argentina, Peru and Bolivia." Later, in March 1972, columnist Jack Anderson reported a memorandum allegedly written by two ITT employees in Chile which asserted that the State Department in 1970 had given the U.S. ambassador "maximum authority to do all possible—short of a Dominican Republic-type action—to keep Allende from taking power." Anderson alleged that ITT and the CIA had been in contact regarding this matter. Both the U.S. Senate Foreign Relations Committee and the Chilean Congress approved action calling for an inquiry into this alleged situation.

Before Allende had assumed office he pledged that his government would follow a multiparty, nationalist, popular, democratic, and revolutionary approach. On the surface it appeared to have much in common with the Velasco government next door. In an interview published in the *New York Times* on October 4, 1970, he stated that his government had no political agreement or understanding with the MIR (the Revolutionary Movement of the Left), and that he expected the Chilean right which was "linked to imperialist interests" to use "any means whatsoever" including violence and economic chaos to oppose him. Allende affirmed that the nation would "use the excess that our nation's economy produces" which as of the moment was leaving the country or staying in the hands of monopolies. He stated that Chileans must recover their basic resources "that are in the hands of foreign capital, essentially American—copper, iron, ore, nitrates, which are in your hands, the hands of American monopolies . . . . We are not going to imitate either the Soviet Union or Cuba or China. We are going to look for our own way . . . . We want to increase our cultural and commercial relations with the U.S., but we want to have the right to open relations with Cuba." This he called "Popular Unity."

Allende was installed on November 4, 1970, and in December of that year he submitted a constitutional amendment authorizing the government to nationalize the copper-mining industry. Compensation to the U.S. companies was to be made over a thirty-year period. The constitutional amendment of early 1971 nullified the previous agreements which Chile had made with the larger foreign copper companies. French and Russian mining experts were asked by the Chilean government to evaluate the past operation of the mines. The report, as interpreted by Chilean officials, claimed that among other shortcomings Anaconda had failed to remove rubble in its mines and thus had created a $20 million barrier. The Allende administration charged Anaconda and Kennecott with having taken excessive profits over the past years while practicing poor planning and inefficient operation with the use of inadequate equipment which was maintained in inadequate repair. Losses created by the machinery factor alone were estimated at $30 million. In effect, Chile charged that there had been a scramble to take out the best and most easily accessible ore while leaving great amounts of slag to jeopardize future operations of the mines. Members of the Chilean Socialist party recommended that compensation not be made to the former owners of the large copper interests. From then on confusion prevailed.

It may be years before a final determination of compensation for the nationalized mines will be made. But, in 1971, the Chilean government decided that the Office of Comptroller and the government would be authorized to deduct from its payments for the 51 percent being nationalized the amount of "excessive profits" for years between 1955 and 1970. It was determined that no compensation would be due Anaconda and Kennecott since the amount due the Chilean government was greater than the book value of their holdings. But since part of the Cerro Corporation interests were already jointly owned it appeared that Cerro had a claim for $14 million for the part of its interests which had been nationalized. Allende, who had stated earlier that he did not wish to provoke those long-time investors for he wanted good relations with the U.S., came out scoring the foreign copper concerns who had unduly exploited copper for years. He considered nationalization of copper to be similar to Peru's taking over foreign oil interests and he noted that compensation had not been made to IPC. He likewise commented that he believed the copper question was a matter which dealt with "private companies" and not with the U.S. government. Official Washington, in turn, expressed its discontent with Chilean reluctance to make "prompt and adequate compensation" for expropriated property. The U.S. was "deeply concerned" as there could be "serious implications"; there were suggestions that Chile's credit in international circles could be hurt. But Washington did not take an open offensive in an economic war, and the assistant secretary of state for inter-American affairs told a House subcommittee late in 1971 that although Chile's current plans did not provide for just compensation, it was best to wait and see what the final action would be. In the meantime the Chilean claims and the copper companies' counterclaims were heard before a tribunal in Santiago. Other foreign interests, especially where U.S. holdings were involved, were told to sell stock to Chile up to the controlling 51 percent figure. Smaller mineral interests and a variety of economic operations were also involved in Chilean plans to nationalize significant businesses and industries.

In January 1972 Kennecott requested payment of the $5.8 million due in December 1971 on the $92.9 million of notes held by Kennecott for the *El Teniente* mine. The Allende administration said that it had suspended payment while checking to see if proceeds of the notes were being "usefully invested" as called for by the "constitutional reform" under which the mine had been expropriated. In fact copper production was down 9 percent in 1971 compared with 1970, and in July 1971 Associated Press reported an additional lag. Strikes against the mines were still a serious problem, and there had also been a drop in the world price of copper. United States copper and other large investments were having similar difficulties with compensation as Chile sought to borrow from U.S. and European sources so that CODELCO (the Chilean Copper Corporation) could meet its most urgent debts.

A period of transition in investment and marketing was taking place. President Nixon said that the U.S. was not going to extend new bilateral economic benefits to a nation which expropriated U.S. interests without making "reasonable provision for . . . compensation." This appeared to be directed largely at Chile, Peru, Ecuador, and Bolivia. The U.S. Commerce Department reported that exports to Chile had dropped 26.8 percent in the first eleven months of 1971 as compared with the same period in 1970. While Chilean exports to the U.S. had dropped 37.8 percent for the same period, not all intercourse was on the decline. Chilean officials requested fifty more Peace Corps personnel—especially skilled specialists—and twenty-two of the then forty-four volunteers on two-year terms were requesting a third year by 1972. It seems that the Peace Corps work, mainly forestry, had been popular.

By February 1972 Kennecott Corporation had brought suit over the $5.8 million payment on the notes, and by March the New York Supreme Court had blocked funds in New York banks of the Chilean governmental corporations of CODELCO and CORFO. Chile, however, was able to refinance some of its debts with the aid of U.S. and European loans. When Kennecott received the bulk of its $5.9 million payment, the judge vacated the attachments which Kennecott had obtained on the Chilean bank accounts. Allende, however, felt that the two nations had been close to "economic war." For a time in February 1972 the Chilean National Airline (LAN) had suspended its flights to the U.S. for fear that Washington would seize planes as LAN's funds in a U.S. bank had already been frozen. About the same time as all this was going on, it was announced that China was making a loan to Chile of $70 million value to be extended over a four-year period for the building of small and medium-sized industries. A variety of other U.S.-owned holdings were being pressured to sell majority interests to Chile, these including smelting operations, motor-car assembly plants, and telecommunications. ITT officials claimed their part of the nationalized telephone company to be worth $153 million while Chilean officials placed its value at a figure much "closer to $25 million." ITT's

Annual Report (1971) reassured the stockholders that the company would be able to collect $89.6 million from OPIC. OPIC denied that a final decision had been made to that effect. While these developments had been taking place, some Chilean political elements proposed that their government simply confiscate the ITT property in Chile. But in this case, as in most, the policy seemed to be to negotiate with hard bargaining so as to make Chile more and more economically independent, without completely alienating foreign economic interests. Yet by August 1972 Washington was encouraging the Export-Import Bank and other U.S. lending agencies to hold back on Chile's credit until the Big Three were compensated. During the decade of almost continuous negotiations a reversal of economic pressures had occurred as U.S. economic intervention slowly gave way to Chilean nationalization and/or expropriation.

Consequences and Reflections

The governments of Chile and Peru have used their powers rather effectively to reverse economic intervention. In Chile the civil administrations of Frei and Allende have inched leftward into a more independent and nationalistic position, while in Peru a similar direction and stance has been established by a government which relied upon the military. Some of the domestic monopolies were losing control in both countries at the same time that the foreign giants were being reduced. It is not surprising that they should be shackled, for the two had aided each other in their rise to power and had supported each other in their heydays of "milk and clover." Regardless of what the future may hold, at this moment it seems that the economic centers, domestic and foreign, have been shaken in Chile and Peru to a point where they can never regain the same power positions they once had. But who can say with any certainty, for there are strange ways in the lands of the lower Andes.

In retrospect we see that the U.S. land frontier closed down late in the nineteenth century at the same time that the country demonstrated growth and modernization in technology, commerce, and finance. Then began a scouting for foreign fields of development. The Spanish-American War heralded the navy as the vanguard of U.S. entrance into the ranks of world powers. Then suddenly with the opening of the

Panama Canal, Chile and Peru were brought much closer in nautical miles to our eastern industrial and financial centers. They wanted capital and technology to match their resources and ready labor. During World War I England and Europe necessarily neglected their South American markets just as the U.S. was looking for areas of expansion. The combined forces of U.S. private and public enterprises carried economic intervention to the dominant foreign role. Again with World War II the almighty dollar strengthened its position over the two countries, and it was natural that such power was resented as nationalistic feelings developed in Peru and Chile. In the 1960s Washington expanded economic assistance programs both to develop the southern nations and to bolster Yankee investments, and some aspects of foreign aid were also considered to be intervention. There was no simple solution. If U.S. capital had been timid, other nations would have seized the opportunities for leadership in that part of the hemisphere and one can only speculate in what that would have resulted.

Hemispheric developments also seemed to cast a shadow in advance of major events following the close of World War II. By the 1950s the U.S. had about used up its trust and credibility which had accrued during the Good Neighbor days. With its return to interventionist actions military and proxy-military through machinations of the CIA—it further wasted its good will as with Colonel Castillo Armas and the invasion of Guatemala (1954) and again in the Bay of Pigs (1961). For a brief time the Alliance for Progress restored some of the credit only to have it badly depleted by the marine intervention in the Dominican Republic (1965). And since then, the U.S. activities in Southeast Asia have been widely criticized in Latin America which has an endemic distrust of Yankee intervention. The economic preponderance which had developed gradually was not something which the U.S. could suddenly drop. On the other hand, as Chile and Peru demanded greater control over their natural resources, the Department of State could have bowed politely to the inevitable while alerting its investors to the increasing risks and difficulties.

Along the way it had become apparent that official Washington could not stem the southern tide by the use of rational means. Very probably the large U.S. concerns could have benefited themselves by simply negotiating for either a much muted role or, if necessary, for their departure. Surely, in the late 1950s or even early 1960s they could have withdrawn in a manner which would have left better relations between Washington and these two countries. But it could hardly be expected that the economic giants would settle up and bow out graciously while official Washington was holding out hope of backing them up.

Powerful corporations have lobbied hard in Washington for help in dealing with Chile and Peru, but the hope born of talking has led to little more than wishful thinking as the dust settles on this facet of intervention. Although relations between the United States and Latin American nations usually shift according to the opportunistic winds of change, early 1973 saw even greater strain between Washington and the two South American capitals, especially with Santiago. Allende charged that a United States "virtual economic blockade" had been a factor in the sharp drop in foreign currency reserves and in this way a cause of Chile's economic difficulties. Peru's external finances reflected similar but less pressure, and a greater degree of compromise seemed possible as Minoperu (the state mining concern) and Petroperu (the state petroleum concern) have offered various foreign nations, including the United States, a contract role in the development of oil and the marketing of copper. But in the long view it appears that Peru as well as Chile has determined to maintain the basic control over its most valuable natural resources.

In closing I recognize that this brief, general treatment can not reflect all the many facets of the Chilean and Peruvian economic-political spectrum and its complexity of international relationships. Over the years to come there is apt to be much debate in Chile and some debate in the United States as to Washington's responsibility for Allende's downfall which came in September 1973. At various times in 1972 there were cabinet shufflings and reports of alleged assassination plots against high officials. Particularly disturbing to the economy, by July of 1973, was the widespread trucking strike. Finally the government fell, when on September 11, 1973, a military coup ousted the Allende administration. That same day Allende died amid rumors that he was assassinated or had committed suicide. Since then many opponents of the military junta have been executed or imprisoned. This was the first successful military coup against a Chilean civilian administration since 1927.

The established facts as of this writing (March 1974) are not adequate to make a firm decision as to the degree of outside interference or intervention in Chile. There is always a problem in sorting out the weight of evidence when treating with questions of both indirect as well as direct responsibility. But the United States Treasury Department as well as the State Department were involved in increasing the economic pressures which played a role in Allende's fall. It is noteworthy, also, that there is no evidence that the Russian government had particularly interested itself in economically bolstering the Chilean economy during the time that Washington was involved in weakening it. Only the future has the answer to the dividends to be lost or paid on the policies of these two nations. But twentieth-century history to date indicates a negative response to intervention, even if it is merely indirect intervention.

SUGGESTIONS FOR FURTHER RESEARCH

More extensive studies are needed of U.S. economic intervention in each of the Latin American countries if meaningful comparisons are to be made. Specialized work is being done, especially on loans, trade, and assistance programs. As yet, there remains to be done the more comprehensive analysis of the net effect of the dollar in all its forms. This will depend to a great extent upon the basic research which Chileans and Peruvians can do. Further studies should make it possible to evaluate better the long-term significance of the dollar in the individual nation as well as for the hemisphere and the entire world. And since the consequences of interventions in Chile and Peru are still emerging, it is important that this research be extended into the future.

It would be helpful if scholars could free themselves from the old cliché approaches which tend either to condemn or to condone U.S. economic penetration into the nations to the south. Space did not permit treatment of the implications of military missions for the economies of Chile and Peru; and the influences of AID programs were ignored in the main. Much research is still to be done on this latter point. It would be of great benefit to the researchers if the departments of the Treasury and of Commerce as well as the State Department would provide greater cooperation in making the basic economic facts available.

If the U.S. government is not aware of the conditions and arrangements under which our private concerns operate in Latin America it is time that such be known. The national interest is at stake in bringing this information to light. Congressional hearings were of great assistance to me in uncovering the facts surrounding private loans to Latin America in the 1920s. There appears to be a particular need for hearings that will delve into the activities of the dollar in Chile over recent years.

BIBLIOGRAPHIC NOTE

A good background study of Chilean-U.S. relations as of the year 1927 is that of Henry Clay Evans, *Chile and Its Relations with the United States* (Durham, N.C., 1927), and the most complete work in the overall span since 1880 is Frederick B. Pike's *Chile and the United States, 1880-1962* (South Bend, Ind., 1963). Claude C. Bowers, *Chile through Embassy Windows: 1939-1953* (New York, 1958), provides only surface treatment of most political and economic questions for that short interval. There was no serious treatment of twentieth-century Peruvian-U.S. relations until *Peru and the United States, 1900-1962* (South Bend, Ind., 1964) was prepared by James C. Carey. Of a more limited and specialized nature is *United States Foreign Policy and Peru,* ed. Daniel A. Sharp (Austin, Tex., 1972); two chapters were of considerable benefit: David C. Loring, "The Fisheries Dispute," with a critique by Admiral Luis E. Llosa, and Charles T. Goodsell, "Diplomatic Protection of United States Business in Peru."

General outlines (English language) of economic development and U.S. investments in Chile and Peru are traced in various broad studies: Jonathan V. Levin, *The Export Economies: Their Pattern of Development in Historical Perspective* (Cambridge, Mass., 1960); Nelson A. Rockefeller, *The Rockefeller Report on the Americas: The Official Report of a United States Presidential Mission for the Western Hemisphere* (New York, 1969); Markos Mamalakis and Clark W. Reynolds, *Essays on the Chilean Economy* (Homewood, Ill., 1965); and the United Nations publications *Analyses and Projections of Economic Development, VI, The Industrial Development of Peru* (Mexico, D.F., 1959), *Report of the Consultant Group Jointly Appointed by the Economic Commission for Latin America and the Organization of American States* (New York, 1961), *Boletín Económico de America Latina* (Santiago, Chile, 1962). For summary background of investments there is, of course, the U.S. Department of Commerce's *United States Investments in the Latin American Economy* (Washington, D.C., 1957), and *Investment in Peru: Basic Information for United States Businessmen* (Washington, D.C., 1957). Max Winkler early performed valuable studies of U.S. investments in Latin America with the two publications, *Investments of United States Capital in Latin America* (Boston, 1928), and *Foreign Bonds: An Autopsy* (Philadelphia, 1933). Winkler's 1928 work was one of the World Peace Foundation Pamphlets. There is also the careful study of Mario S. Zanartu and John J. Kennedy entitled *Overall Development of Chile* (South Bend, Ind., 1969) and Alan Angell's *Politics and the Labour Movement in Chile* (London, 1972).

Distrust for U.S. investment in Chile is strongly reflected in Jaime Eyzaguirre, *Elementos de la economía* (Santiago, Chile, 1954). In a somewhat similar vein is César Levano's *Por la nacionalización del petróleo* (Lima, Peru, 1960). Studies related to our subject which reflected Marxist and/or Communist points of view are found in the following: a collection of writings edited by Luis E. Aguilar and including essays of Blas Roca and Luis Carlos Prestes in *Marxism in Latin America* (New York, 1968); Ernst Halperin, *Nationalism and Communism in Chile* (Cambridge, Mass., 1965); and Anibal Quijano, *Nationalism and Capitalism in Peru: A Study in Neo-Imperialism* (New York, 1971).

The collected writings of other *Latinos* are available in Claudio Veliz, *Obstacles to Change in Latin America* (New York, 1965); on questions of nationalism see Samuel L. Bailey, *Nationalism in Latin America* (New York, 1971); Paul E. Sigmund's *Models of Political Change in Latin America* (New York, 1970) includes excerpts from the "Chileanization of Copper Law," and the "Decree of Expropriation of La Brea and Pariñas Oilfields and Refinery (October 9, 1968)."

It seems that there is no in-depth monograph dealing with U.S. economic intervention for either Peru or Chile. Various pamphlets and many newspaper articles have been done by Chilean and Peruvian writers (see Frederick B. Pike and James C. Carey). On general intervention matters see Marvin D. Bernstein, *Foreign Investment in Latin America: Cases and Attitudes* (New York, 1966); *Intervention in Latin America,* ed. C. Neale Ronning (New York, 1970); *How Latin America Views the United States Investor,* ed. Raymond Vernon (New York, 1966); and Quijano's perceptive Marxist treatment mentioned above carries through the Peruvian military reforms 1968-1971.

DOMESTIC PRESSURES FOR
ABSTENTION: VIETNAM

Ted Goertzel

Introduction

While America has had a long history of intervention in foreign wars, none has been so prolonged or has stimulated so much active and committed opposition as the Vietnam conflict. The social upheavals of the 1960s, following as they did the relative tranquillity of the 1950s, can be attributed in substantial part to the bitter controversy over Vietnam. The inability of the United States' vast military machine to subdue an ill-equipped and outnumbered peasant army has undermined confidence not only in the efficiency of the armed forces but also in the rightness of the cause and the enthusiasm of the Vietnamese themselves for American assistance. Indeed, the Vietnam debacle has undermined the prestige of the American power elite to an extent unprecedented at least since the Great Depression.

Perhaps the best thing which can come out of Vietnam is a profound reappraisal of America's role in foreign conflicts and, even more important, of the social institutions which led us to assume that our national interest required us to take the responsibility for imposing a non-Communist government on at least the southern part of Vietnam. American involvement in Vietnam cannot be understood as an isolated error in judgment. It was rather a logical outcome of the containment of communist doctrine which was deliberately adopted by the foreign policy establishment in the years immediately following the Second World War. The movement against American intervention in Vietnam necessarily became a movement against the ideology of the cold war and against the social groups which created and sustained it.

The Origins of Intervention

When Charles Edward Wilson, the General Electric president who became director of the Office of Defense Mobilization, called in a 1944 speech for the creation of a "permanent war economy . . . [which] must be initiated and administered by the executive branch . . . [with] the role of Congress limited to voting the needed funds," he spoke not only for himself but for a class of big businessmen who opposed any return to New Deal economic policies and preferred to use continued high military spending as a stimulus for the economy. The interests of these businessmen coincided with those of military leaders who sought a justification for maintaining the huge military establishment which had been built up for the struggle against fascism.

An expensive military machine can only be justified if it has a powerful and threatening enemy to confront. This was lacking in the period immediately following the Second World War since the allies had just succeeded in eliminating their enemies as military contenders. The alliance with the Soviet Union had always been a reluctant one, however, and the Soviet Union was readily cast once again in the role of enemy which it had played in 1917. When George F. Kennan argued in an article published anonymously in *Foreign Affairs* in 1947, but widely read earlier in government circles, that the Soviet Union was a devious and unrelenting enemy of American interests, he could not have anticipated how many powerful Americans would join him in expressing gratitude to "a Providence which, by providing the American people with this implacable challenge, has made their entire security as a nation dependent on their pulling themselves together and accepting the responsibilities of moral and political leadership that history plainly intended them to bear."

The moderate containment policy proposed by Kennan was transformed into a holy crusade by John Foster Dulles, Winston Churchill, and others of their persuasion. The Soviet threat was magnified and given almost supernatural powers to maintain a united worldwide conspiracy against all that was good in human existence. Limitations in Soviet aspirations and capabilities were ignored and divisions in the Communist world were glossed over in their eagerness to establish anti-communism as the top priority for the "free world." Domestic pressures for social reform could then be attacked as "Communist-inspired," and any questioning of military budgets and priorities was taboo for those who feared to run the risk of being labeled "soft-on-communism."

The Korean war came during the height of the anti-Communist sentiment with old heroes like General Douglas MacArthur still in power. It was not actively opposed by significant numbers of Americans, despite its unpopularity in the polls and the efforts of writers such as I. F. Stone to question the official explanation of its origins. American intervention in Indochina also began in the late 1940s and early 1950s, with the United States spending $2.6 billion to support the French effort to reestablish their imperial control of the area. This was done on the pretext of stopping "Soviet imperialism." President Eisenhower refused to send American forces to replace the French after their defeat in 1954. He did, however, plant the seeds for later American intervention by committing the United States to the support of the Diem regime in the south and by supporting Diem in his refusal to participate in the 1956 elections to choose a government for Vietnam.

Resistance to the repressive Diem regime grew slowly but steadily in southern Vietnam during the late 1950s and early 1960s, and Diem called for more and more American aid. Domestic preoccupation with anti-communism had declined in the United States, however, and the new generation which grew up after the Second World War was less accepting of the need to focus national efforts on a struggle against international communism. Intervention in Vietnam was escalated as quietly and with as little fanfare as possible because of doubts about public enthusiasm. The war seemed to grow spontaneously without the benefit of momentous decisions or definitive congressional action, precisely because it was planned secretly and because there was no serious debate about basic principles within the decision-making groups.

The *Pentagon Papers* and other selections of secret documents have filled in many of the gaps in our understanding of the process which led to intervention in Vietnam, although our knowledge of the historical record remains selective and shrouded in secrecy. The importance of the *Pentagon Papers*, however, is not in any new revelation of where the decision-making process went awry. Rather, the secret documents confirmed the critique of American policy and policy-making which had already been made by historians such as Gabriel Kolko. The documents verified that the insurgent movement began in South Vietnam. They showed that the South Vietnamese government, and indeed the very concept of South Vietnam as a separate nation, were deliberate creations of the United States designed to maintain American imperial power at the expense of political democracy and free elections in Vietnam. The documents show how the United States deliberately provoked North Vietnam in order to create incidents which could be used to win congressional approval for expanding the war.

Perhaps even more revealing is the evidence in the secret documents of the conscious manipulation of public opinion by the national security decision-makers. They led the public to believe that the war was being forced upon them. At each stage of the escalation, they told the public that they expected to win the war with a small increment in power. They further argued that bombing would be effective in ending the war. All these arguments were contradicted by Central Intelligence Agency reports that were available at the time the decisions were being made. The decision-makers had every reason to believe that the war would be long and costly, but they also realized that it would be better to wait until President Johnson was reelected before openly escalating it.

The secret documents do not reveal much that is new about the long-range goals and ideologies which shape American policy. One can learn more about these fundamental policy assumptions from the published works of men like George Kennan and Henry Kissinger than from secret documents. Yet it was the basic doctrine of containing communism, and not some error in the process of decision-making, which led the United States into Vietnam without significant public debate and without any serious consideration of the costs of such intervention and the benefits to be obtained.

The mentality of the decision-making elite has two key characteristics. First, it assumes that international relations are a contest, similar to a sporting event, in which each side is constantly struggling to win ground or points from the other. This first aspect of their world view is essentially similar to the classic balance-of-power assumptions of nineteenth-century European leaders, although it has been modernized with the trappings of game theory and systems analysis. The second key facet of their mentality is the assumption that communism is an overwhelming evil in the world and that any means used in stopping it are justified. Thus, the decision-makers reveal no qualms in supporting regimes such as that in Indonesia which, as documented by John

Hughes, slaughtered hundreds of thousands of people in a supposed attempt to stop communism. Yet they justified their continued intervention in Vietnam because withdrawal would, they argued, have caused a "bloodbath."

These two basic assumptions provide the ideological basis for the alliance of corporate and military power in the American power elite, although corporate power has generally maintained its supremacy in foreign-policy decision-making. For example, of the ninety-one individuals who held top positions as secretaries or undersecretaries of State and Defense, or as heads of the three military services, the Atomic Energy Commission, or the Central Intelligence Agency, during the period from 1940 to 1967, seventy came from major corporations and investment houses. This included eight of the ten secretaries of the air force, every secretary of the navy, eight of nine secretaries of the army, and every deputy secretary of defense. Civilian control of foreign policy was maintained during this era, but that control was exercised by a very limited segment of the civilian population.

Strategic and anti-Communist considerations are not always compatible. While the United States was forced by strategic considerations into an uncomfortable alliance with the Soviet Union in the Second World War, anti-Communism made it difficult for the United States to exploit the rivalry between China and the Soviet Union. Anti-communism led the United States to recognize the Nationalist regime on Taiwan as the legitimate government of China, while accepting the view that Mao and his colleagues were not truly Chinese at all but Russian agents. In an environment where Richard Nixon could attack John Kennedy in the famous 1960 televised debates for his reluctance to commit America to go to war over Quemoy and Matsu, two insignificant islands off the coast of China, it is not surprising that few political leaders had the courage to question American intervention in Vietnam.

The war in Vietnam made sense only from an anti-Communist viewpoint. As the *Pentagon Papers* reveal, the importance of the war for Washington was primarily symbolic. The older view of MacArthur that Asia was the first line of American defense was not accepted by the liberal policy-makers in the Johnson administration. They felt that Vietnam itself was "devoid of decisive military importance," but argued that intervention was justified in order to set an example that revolutionary movements would not be permitted in the "free world."

The reluctance of the military, and especially of the Central Intelligence Agency, to engage in guerrilla warfare in Asia reveals the dominance of corporate-anti-Communist considerations over military-strategic ones. It is important that the military not be made the scapegoat for Vietnam. It was the Kennedy administration which insisted that the military prepare for limited, "brush-fire" wars and created the Special Forces. On purely strategic grounds, nothing could be more foolish than to tie up American forces in Indochina, far from the scene of any potential conflict with the Soviet Union. The rewards for the military were limited to the opportunities which Vietnam provided to test equipment and to obtain combat experience needed for career advancement. Overall, the war in Vietnam was disastrous for the United States Army, leading to widespread breakdowns of morale and discipline and an alarmingly high frequency of killing ("fragging") of officers by enlisted men.

The decisions which led us into Vietnam were made by civilians, most of whom were wealthy businessmen. They disregarded the advice of intelligence officers who pointed out that Vietnam was of little strategic consequence. They overruled military officers who warned against getting engaged in a land war in Asia, and promoted those officers who agreed with their views. American intervention in Vietnam can only be explained in terms of the ideologies and class interests of the men who made the policies which led the United States into it.

Public Opinion and the Vietnam War

The most vocal and visible opponents of intervention in Vietnam were college and university students, and liberally educated professional people, who had skills and resources necessary to make their opposition dramatically known. Government spokesmen and other war supporters were eager to capitalize on this by labeling the dissenters as a group of effete eggheads, divorced from the hard-headed realities of life. While it is true that the most dramatic protest emerged from middle-class intellectual groups, it does not necessarily follow that the remainder of the population—the "silent majority"—supported American intervention in Vietnam.

Careful analysis of national surveys shows a pattern of opposition which is quite different from the conventional wisdom. While the

Vietnam war is often characterized as the least popular war in American history, the data show that the Korean intervention is a close contestant for this honor. Both were much less popular than the Second World War. Support for the Korean war declined markedly when China entered and the conflict appeared certain to escalate into a major war. Support for the Vietnamese war, similarly, declined rapidly as the war dragged on and American and South Vietnamese forces seemed to be doing badly. Support of the Vietnamese intervention declined from a high of 61 percent in August 1965 (with 24 percent opposed and 15 percent without an opinion) to lows of 32 percent in September 1969 and March 1970 (with 58 percent feeling that the United States made a mistake in sending troops to Vietnam and 10 percent without an opinion).

The most marked switch in opinion on Vietnam took place in March 1968 after the Tet offensive of that year. In the Gallup poll of early February 1968, 61 percent of the respondents indicated that they were "hawks" while 23 percent were "doves" and 16 percent had no opinion. In the March 1968 Gallup poll, 41 percent were "hawks" and 42 percent "doves." Doves increased to 55 percent by November 1969, with only 31 percent of the population classifying themselves as "hawks."

In both the Korean and the Vietnamese cases, early support for intervention seems to have resulted from a feeling among many citizens that it was their patriotic duty to rally-round-the-flag and support the president. Support waned when casualties mounted and little seemed to be accomplished. Those Americans who continued to support the president often did so out of feelings of loyalty and patriotic duty. George Gallup estimates that only about 20 percent of the population are hard-core hawks, supporting a hawkish policy under all conditions. Another 20 percent are hard-core doves. Many of the others support the president no matter what he does, or vary their opinion according to the circumstances.

More surprising are the data on the social characteristics of war supporters: for both the Korean and Vietnamese wars, supporters were most likely to be found among the wealthier, better educated, and younger respondents. This was especially true at the earlier stages of the Vietnam war, when support for intervention was almost universal in government and establishment circles. Wealthier, better educated people are generally more attuned to the opinion that is current in the most prestigious sectors of society. Young people also tend to be more responsive to the mood of the country at a given time because of their lack of time perspective. But the relationship between age and opinions about the war is not very strong.

By September 1969 survey results showed that dissatisfaction with the war was evenly distributed among all classes of the population. Of course, by this time getting out of Vietnam was a stated goal of the president, so many people felt that they could admit that the war was a mistake without concern about being in opposition to official government policy. Thus poll results often give seemingly contradictory results. In January 1971, for example, 72 percent of the respondents in the Gallup poll favored having their congressman vote to bring all troops out of Vietnam by the end of the year, with only 20 percent opposed. President Nixon opposed this resolution. Yet, in the February 1971 poll, 42 percent expressed approval for President Nixon's handling of the war, with only 45 percent disapproving. Many respondents' desire to see the conflict ended was contradicted by their feelings of loyalty to the president and their hope that his policies would in fact bring the war to a close. Many also felt an obligation to the American prisoners who were held in Vietnam, apparently accepting the president's argument that the only way to get them home was to continue the war. By February 1972 approval of Nixon's war policies had risen to 51 percent, with 39 percent disapproving, although all American troops had not been withdrawn.

This patriotic loyalty to the president is not, however, dependent on the policy option which a president chooses. After the attack on Pearl Harbor, it is likely that even a reluctant president would have been forced by public opinion to take action against Japan. The Vietnamese intervention was certainly not the result of any such public pressure. The United States entered gradually and surreptitiously in order to avoid arousing public opposition. Following the precedent set by President Wilson in 1916, Lyndon Johnson was elected in 1964 on a platform opposing American intervention. When President Johnson failed to keep his promise, approval of his handling of the war declined from 57 percent in July 1965 to 26 percent in March 1968 in the Gallup poll. In 1968 Richard Nixon was elected on the basis of a "secret plan" to end the war. His reelection in 1972, once again, was based on a promise of an early end to the conflict, even as plans were being made to return to the use of "civilian" advisers as during the Kennedy years.

Only a vigorous propaganda effort on the part of the government and the established news media won support for American intervention in Vietnam from even the wealthiest and best educated citizens. As the war dragged on, and the facts about the political and military situation in Vietnam became better known, public support declined rapidly. Finally, the government was forced by public opinion to begin withdrawing American troops while frantically developing even more sophisticated bombing devices to continue the killing without American ground troops. Public opinion cannot bear the responsibility for American involvement in Vietnam, although feelings of patriotism and loyalty to the president made it possible for the government to continue the war despite widespread public doubts about its wisdom.

The Movement against the War

While early opposition to the war, as expressed in the public opinion polls during the years from 1964 to 1966, was concentrated among the least educated and least affluent segments of the population, these citizens did not mount any organized social or political movement aimed at ending American intervention. The small pacifist and socialist movements were consistently opposed to American involvement in Vietnam, but these groups in and of themselves were able to launch only a small protest which, while it did not carry much political force, served to bring the issue before the American public. The anti-war movement has been able to exert a significant influence on policy only when it obtains support of a large number of people who become concerned about particular issues even though they are not consistent supporters of anti-war movements.

In the early 1960s, pacifist groups were successful in rallying considerable support for their campaigns against nuclear bomb testing and reliance on fallout shelters for protection against war. They won this support because a substantial segment of the population became convinced that bomb testing was a threat to their health and that the government was flirting with nuclear war by relying on brinksmanship and fallout shelters, the expense of which had no appeal and whose sale was tainted with political scandal. Once the atmospheric test ban treaty was signed in 1963, the government dropped compulsory air raid drills and deemphasized fallout shelters, and the large majority of liberal Americans lost interest in the anti-war movement and focused their attentions instead on the growing struggle over civil rights in the South.

Liberals were largely convinced by President Kennedy's American University speech in 1963, and President Johnson's campaign rhetoric in 1964, that the cold war was being thawed. The decisive defeat of Barry Goldwater at the polls seemed to close the anti-Communist chapter of American history. The anti-war movement reemerged when Johnson betrayed these promises and instituted Goldwater's foreign policy. Courageous journalists such as I. F. Stone uncovered many of the flaws and distortions in the arguments used by government spokesmen to justify escalation of the war. Prominent intellectuals, who had supported the Korean action in the belief that it was a necessary response to a Communist invasion, perceived that the situation in Vietnam was quite different and gave their signatures to advertisements in leading newspapers calling for an end to intervention.

The tactics of the anti-war movement in these early years were quite moderate. There were large peaceful demonstrations which aimed at dramatizing opposition to the war and raising the issue in the public consciousness. College students, threatened with the draft and with the possibility of college grades being used to determine draft deferments, were eager to hear what their professors had to say as the "teach-in" movement spread across the country. The importance of the draft as a stimulus to the anti-war movement should not be overemphasized, however. Opposition was concentrated largely among college students who had good prospects of being deferred, and as late as January 1969 the Gallup poll showed that 71 percent of Americans between twenty-one and twenty-nine years of age favored continuation of the draft after the Vietnam war was over (as compared to 67 percent of those in their thirties and forties and only 55 percent of those over fifty years of age).

Early anti-war speakers concentrated on factually refuting administration arguments. While Lyndon Johnson spoke frequently of supporting the Geneva Accords and of fighting for free elections in Vietnam, anti-war spokesmen pointed out that the Geneva Accords called for free elections in 1956 and that it was the United States-backed Diem regime which had refused to hold these elections because it knew Ho Chi Minh would have won. When the government published a "White Paper" alleging that there had been an invasion of the sovereign nation of South Vietnam by North Vietnam, anti-war speakers pointed out that the Geneva Accords specifically stated that Vietnam was one nation and that the temporary demarcation line dividing the northern and southern parts "should not in any way be interpreted as constituting a political or territorial boundary." The government "White Paper" gave case histories of typical "Vietcong" infiltrators who were supposedly part of an invading army, but a careful analysis of the appendixes of the document revealed that the large majority of these "foreign invaders" had been born in the southern part of Vietnam and were returning to their homeland. These arguments played a significant role in turning educated, middle-class Americans against the war.

The moderate nature of the early anti-war movement is often over-looked because of the degree of radicalism which emerged as the movement developed as part of the more general youth revolt of the 1960s. Most early war opponents did not go so far as to call for American withdrawal from Vietnam. Opposition was limited to the demand that the United States agree to negotiate. This tactic was effective in drawing attention to the fact that it was the Americans, and not the "Communists," who were refusing to negotiate. The risk inherent in making such moderate demands became apparent, however, when the American government finally did agree to negotiate but maintained a negotiating position which required the other side to give up and concede the establishment of South Vietnam as a separate nation under anti-Communist control before the fighting could come to a halt.

Even Students for a Democratic Society (SDS), which quickly evolved into one of the most radical and militant anti-war organizations, began its life as a moderate reformist group, in keeping with the upper middle-class backgrounds of its members. The early SDS conventions avoided using radical terms such as "socialist" in their literature. They aimed at forming a broad political coalition including the labor movement, liberal politicians, civil rights groups, liberal churches, students, and intellectuals. Their most ambitious goal was to convert the Democratic party into a party of liberal reform by excluding the dixiecrat elements and nominating more progressive candidates. They hoped to break the crust of public apathy and appeal to the goodwill of liberal-minded people throughout the society.

The early peace movement was clearly aimed at working within the system rather than overthrowing it. Even the most militant tactics such as sit-ins at draft boards and federal buildings, burning of draft cards, and even symbolic suicides were nonviolent and aimed at expressing individual conscience and at seeking public sympathy and support. Rather than engage in violence to force their opponents to change their behavior, the early anti-war activists engaged in symbolic acts which required that they suffer the consequences of any reprisals. Far from an expression of alienation and despair, a nonviolent movement requires a degree of confidence that the system and the people who run it will respond in a humane and considerate manner.

The early anti-war movement was also profoundly democratic and antitotalitarian in its organization and in the beliefs of its members. This fact is often obscured by the willingness of most anti-war groups to tolerate Communists, Maoists, and other more authoritarian groups in their ranks. The large demonstrations included traditional religious and philosophical pacifists, people who felt the Vietnam war was wrong but did not object to war on principle, as well as members of socialist groups who simply felt that the United States was fighting on the wrong side. The demonstrations reflected the widespread change of opinion among the educated middle classes about the war. The number of participants in demonstrations paralleled the rise of the percentage of the population which opposed the war in the polls. From 1965 to 1968, the percentage disapproving of the war rose from 21 percent to 56 percent in the Gallup poll, while the number participating in demonstrations rose from 25,000 to 300,000, according to data gathered for the National Commission on the Causes and Prevention of Violence.

Most anti-war activists remained in the mainstream political system, working, for example, in Eugene McCarthy's campaign in the 1968 primary elections, only to find that the party bosses in nonprimary states still controlled too many votes. The assassination of Robert Kennedy in June 1968 left the Democratic party with a candidate whose views on the war were scarcely distinguishable from those of the Republican candidate. It is not surprising that many of the early militants lost confidence in the possibilities of peaceful change through the electoral process. Students for a Democratic Society was destroyed as an effective organization when it split into the Progressive Labor faction, a doctrinaire Marxist-Leninist sect, and the more anarchic Weatherman faction which had given up on radical social change in America at least until the currently younger generation came into power. The Weathermen emphasized bombings and other violent tactics in support of revolutionary movements in third-world countries, but found that these actions also were more symbolic than effective.

It is ironic that it was the Nixon administration which finally took the steps which President Kennedy was afraid to take toward ending the cold war as the cornerstone of American foreign policy. Nixon moved to defuse Vietnam as a political issue by gradually withdrawing American ground combat troops (a policy which Lyndon Johnson would also have followed if it had been possible at an earlier stage of the war). Nixon also relied even more heavily on bombing raids, conducting by far the most intensive bombing campaign in human history even though bombing had been shown to be ineffective in the military goal of stopping the flow of supplies to the fighters in Vietnam. As Littauer and Uphoff and the American Friends Service Committee have documented, the air force and American corporations developed insidious antipersonnel weapons designed to increase the amount of pain and suffering to the point where the Vietnamese could no longer tolerate it. Plastic pellet bombs and tiny mines disguised as leaves or animal droppings were dropped indiscriminately over Vietnam, Laos, and Cambodia in an effort to drive the population from its homes so that the enemy forces would have no place to hide.

The Vietnamese do not vote in American elections, however, and Nixon's broader foreign policy steps toward a rapprochement with China and Russia won him tremendous popularity at home. The mood of the country was turning from anti-communism and ultranationalism to a focus on domestic priorities. Military appropriations for weapons such as the antiballistic missile were seriously questioned by Congress. This mood was expressed in the Democratic primaries of 1972, when the peace movement accomplished something that the SDS activists ten years earlier considered to be an almost impossible dream. Largely through the efforts of peace activists, the Democratic party nominated George McGovern, a peace and social-reform oriented candidate for the presidency.

The nomination of McGovern showed the success of the peace movement in mobilizing liberal middle-class opinion against the war. His dramatic defeat at the polls reflected the failure of the peace movement to extend its active support beyond these liberal middle-class groups. Nixon's popularity, however was based on his promise to end the Vietnam war soon after his reelection and on his abandonment of the containment doctrine with his trip to Peking. In order to live up to these promises, Nixon was forced to sign a cease-fire and withdraw American troops while leaving North Vietnamese troops stationed in southern Vietnam. From a long-term perspective, therefore, the 1972 elections can be seen as part of a movement away from the policies which led to American intervention in Vietnam.

If the United States were to dominate militarily in Vietnam and succeed in setting up South Vietnam as an independent anti-Communist nation, the benefit to America would be small. Even South Korea, the prototype of an Asian anti-Communist client state, is moving toward a rapprochement with North Korea and China. And America's own rapprochement with China undercuts any rationale for needing a ring of containment around that nation. China's military forces are primarily aimed at defense against the Soviet Union in any case. The fact that even Richard Nixon, with his militant anti-Communist background, was able to recognize the fact that the monolithic international Communist conspiracy no longer existed (if it ever did to the extent that was portrayed by those who used it as a rationale for American expansionism), and to realign American foreign policy on a more realistic appraisal of the balance of forces in the world, is a sign that the prospects are good for developing a more realistic, if not more humane, foreign policy. If Vietnam was never of decisive strategic importance, its symbolic value as a stand against international communism was also undermined. While the business elite which led America into Vietnam is still largely in control of foreign policy, we may hope that they have learned that domestic progress and tranquillity are at least as important to the security and well-being of the nation as imposing anti-Communist dictatorships on small nations around the world.

SUGGESTIONS FOR FURTHER RESEARCH

Researchers on American intervention in foreign conflicts must develop means of evaluating such efforts in terms of the goals that motivated involvement. Americans have placed great pride on never losing a war, yet this is relevant only from a limited military viewpoint. In terms of broader goals, it is easy to see today that the First World War was a failure as an effort to destroy German militarism and make the world safe for democracy. In this sense the American public views Vietnam also a failure: 68 percent of the respondents in a February 1972 Gallup poll felt that American participation in Vietnam had weakened our position throughout the world, while only 10 percent felt that it had been strengthened. In May 1971, 72 percent disagreed with President Nixon's statement that if we leave South Vietnam in a position to defend itself we will have peace in the next generation, while only 17 percent agreed. While the public may be reluctant to see America humiliated once our forces are engaged, it is clear that they also want to avoid a repetition of the Vietnam experience.

　　Much more research is needed on the formulation of American foreign policy and on the interests which influence and determine it. This research is impeded by the difficulties of gaining access to secret documents and by the reluctance of foundations and other agencies to finance studies of elite behavior. Yet it is at the top that foreign policy is made, and the tools of social science must be brought to bear on the establishment just as much as on ghetto residents or rebellious students if we are to understand, and change, the processes which led America into Vietnam.

　　Public opinion did not force the United States into Vietnam, but more research is needed on the factors which make the public so eager to follow the lead of government in foreign policy. Research is needed also on the ways in which public opinion is formed. The role of the news media, in particular, must be more fully evaluated. The media became quite critical of the intervention in Vietnam when this became fashionable in intellectual circles, but they must bear much of the responsibility for encouraging Americans to believe that our own nation is the force of goodness and light in the world while our opponents are evil incarnate.

　　Much of this simplistic thinking may be inherent in the language used by the media when they refer to Vietnamese guerrillas who launch a mortar attack as "terrorists," while they pass off massive antipersonnel bombing as simple "air strikes," regardless of the amount of terror which is caused in each case. The choice of terminology in supposedly objective news stories reveals the stereotypical biases with which we are led to view the world. The press refers to "Vietcong terrorists," not "National Liberation Front freedom-fighters"; to "allied troops," not "puppet troops"; to "the elected government of South Vietnam" (even if there was no opponent in the election), rather than to the "Thieu clique"; to "draft dodgers," rather than to "war resisters." The terms used in the Communist press seem obviously propagandistic to Americans, yet ours are little better. The word "Vietcong," for example, was made up by American and South Vietnamese psychological warfare specialists as a term of derision, yet it is used routinely in the American press.

Research is also needed on the means that can educate a population which is resistant to this type of propaganda. This may involve elimination of the sources of frustration in our society which give people the need to project their fears on those of another race or nation. Rather than focusing our efforts on anti-communism (or anti-semitism or even anti-fascism), we must develop positive goals which are capable of unifying the society. If our economic and political systems cannot survive without excessive military expenditures and client states around the world, then we must find ways of changing those systems. For the people of the smaller nations around the world cannot forever bear the brunt of American social problems.

BIBLIOGRAPHIC NOTE

The anti-Communist policies which led the United States into Vietnam were described well in advance of the events by Fred Cook in *The Warfare State* (New York, 1962). Cook followed the approach taken in *The Power Elite* (New York, 1956) by C. Wright Mills who stressed the increasing political strength of the military in American society. A more recent elaboration of this argument is Seymour Melman, *Pentagon Capitalism* (New York, 1970).

The role of the economic elite in shaping foreign policy is discussed in Richard Barnet, *The Economy of Death* (New York, 1972), and Gabriel Kolko, *The Roots of American Foreign Policy* (Boston, 1969). Further documentation is provided in Harry Magdoff, *The Age of Imperialism* (New York, 1969), and David Horowitz, *Corporations and the Cold War* (New York, 1970).

The numerous sources on the Vietnam intervention include a fine collection of public documents by Marvin Gettleman, *Vietnam: His-*

tory, Documents and Opinions on a Major World Crisis (New York, 1970). The more recent publication of the *Pentagon Papers* (New York, 1971) in an abridged edition edited by Neil Sheehan as well as in the complete edition introduced by Senator Mike Gravel (Boston, 1972) has made available many documents which were previously kept from the American public by military secrecy. Perhaps the best history of the secret decision-making processes, however, is provided by Ralph Stavins, Richard Barnet, and Marcus Raskin in *Washington Plans an Aggressive War* (New York, 1971).

The "bloodbath" which American officials welcomed as part of an anti-Communist terror campaign in Indonesia is described, albeit in a superficial journalistic style, in John Hughes, *Indonesian Upheaval* (New York, 1971). The ingenious ways in which barbarism has been automated are documented by Raphael Littauer and Norman Uphoff in *The Air War in Indochina* (Boston, 1972).

There is no comprehensive study of the role of public opinion in the Vietnam intervention, although Ralph White, *Nobody Wanted War* (New York, 1970), provides an often insightful psychological analysis of the various currents in American and Vietnamese opinion. Milton Rosenberg, Sidney Verba, and Philip Converse, *Vietnam and the Silent Majority: A Dove's Guide* (New York: 1970) is also useful although it was prepared with an immediate political purpose. George Gallup, "Public Opinion and the Vietnam War" *(Gallup Opinion Index,* Princeton, N.J., 1970), pulls together the results of Gallup polls during the Vietnam war. Other surveys are summarized in Hazel Erskine, "The Polls: Is the War a Mistake?" *(Public Opinion Quarterly,* Spring 1970).

A comparison of public opinion trends during the Korean and Vietnamese interventions is John Mueller, "Trends in Popular Support for the Wars in Korea and Vietnam" *(American Political Science Review,* 1971). The ways in which public opinion can be manipulated by presidential actions are analyzed in Seymour M. Lipset, "The President, the Polls, and Vietnam" *(Transaction,* 1966). The question of the relative support for intervention among different social classes is analyzed in Harlan Haha, "Dove Sentiment among Blue Collar Workers" *(Dissent,* 1970); Richard Hamilton, "Le Fondement populaire des solutions militaires dures" *(Revue Français de Sociologie,* 1969), and James Wright, "The Working Class, Authoritarianism and the War in Vietnam" *(Social Problems,* 1972).

The movement against intervention in Vietnam is analyzed in Irving L. Horowitz, *The Struggle Is the Message* (Berkeley, 1970). Some of the same material is more widely available in Jerome H. Skolnik, ed., *The*

Politics of Protest (New York, 1969). Richard Flacks provides interesting commentary on changes in the New Left during the Vietnam era in, "The New Left and American Politics after Ten Years" *(Journal of Social Issues,* 1971). Different sources of opposition to the war among activists and the public are analyzed in Howard Schuman, "Two Sources of Antiwar Sentiment" *(American Journal of Sociology,* 1972).

SURROGATE INTERVENTION: ALLIANCES & AIR POWER IN THE VIETNAM WAR

Donald J. Mrozek

IN THE UNITED STATES, it is common to think of the Vietnam War as dating from about 1965 to 1972—the period during which the nation's ground forces and air power were joined massively in battle against both the National Liberation Front and North Vietnam. American news media developed the idea, supported by many critics of the American commitment, that the Johnson and Nixon administrations had authorized independent air war against the North. Similarly, the notion has become widespread that United States air power is to substitute over the long-term for the use of ground forces.

This interpretation ignores several important facts. United States intervention in Southeast Asia since World War II has been a part of a global counterrevolutionary commitment. It has been grounded primarily on the exploitation of alliances, a customary American policy in twentieth-century wars and a replication of eighteenth-century British policy. Although high officials in Washington sought new applications for strategic air power and heavy bombing, they finally advocated their use only to control conditions in the ground war. The United States deterrent air force theoretically prevented the transformation of the Indochina War into World War III. But the proof that deterrence was effective lay in the fact that the retaliatory force was not used. This form of air power was of no practical value in meeting military problems in Indochina.

The unifying quality in the United States intervention in Southeast Asia has been a search for victory not through air power but through surrogates. In the cycle of American efforts, heavy bombing came late. Its roles were to sever North Vietnamese ties to the Vietcong and to strengthen Washington's ally in Saigon. It was never to substitute for ground forces.

After World War II, United States policy toward Indochina could be described largely as one of "watchful waiting," of seeing what the French could do to reestablish control over their old colonies. Franklin Roosevelt had been especially unsympathetic to French imperial resurgence; and Truman and his advisers regarded the French effort as a remnant of nineteenth-century Western expansionism. But by 1946 Washington wanted a force in Indochina which would forestall a Vietminh victory and, presumably, an extension of Communist power. Delay in adopting a firm course of action was possible because Indochina, while significant, was not central among the concerns of policymakers troubling over the future of Japan and working for the consolidation of China.

As long as it remained possible that Chiang Kai-shek might take hold in China and that the United States would be able to develop a Sino-American alliance as the basis for order in East Asia and the Western Pacific, the status of both Indochina and Japan remained equivocal. After the victory of the Communists in 1949 put an end to the pretensions of Chiang, the Truman administration moved to create an American situation of strength in Japan. By this approach, Southeast Asia assumed a vastly greater significance. If for political reasons Japan were to be denied its "natural" trading partner, China, it must be assured substitutes. Therefore the Communists must not be permitted to control Indochina, which was to be integrated into the Japanese trading system. This policy acquired greater urgency after the outbreak of the Korean War; and the United States accepted the somewhat anomalous role of supporting the French, who were fighting the Vietminh to secure their own imperial advantages, in order to save Indochina for the Japanese. In this way the Korean War served as a chrysalis for the clarification of American policy, enabling Truman to sort out national priorities in the midst of crisis.

The Truman administration saw local conflicts only as a part of a dualistic global confrontation with the Soviet Union in which Moscow was the capital of an international revolutionary conspiracy. White House staff members close to the president had predicted friction and possible military engagements until the world had finally been divided into two camps with no "undecided" areas. Then a new phase was to begin—either a period of accommodation or a general war. Because of this belief, the Truman administration considered the Korean War a triumph of their policy of deterrence and massive retaliation. The conflict had remained limited instead of escalating swiftly into the general war which they had been expecting. In this context, the very failure to discriminate between Soviet and Chinese activity underscored the impression of effective deterrence. Moreover Truman and his staff successfully transformed the United States' position on Korea into the United Nations' position, and thus a major American intervention was internationally sanctioned and formally "allied."

The Eisenhower administration's alienation from the war derived more from what they considered mismanagement of defense budgets than from misconceptions about policy, except with respect to the commitment of United States ground forces. Annual military spending quadrupled during the conflict, and Eisenhower's advisers suggested that no bureaucracy could expand by that multiple in only a few months and retain any pretense to efficiency. They accused Truman of accepting a "boom and bust" cycle in military procurement and preparedness and demanded a rejection of the psychology of crisis which justified training United States defenses against specific but theoretical periods of maximum threat.

The Eisenhower critique of Truman policy was largely an attack on a "straw man." At least as much as his successor, Truman had worked to smooth defense procurement curves to protect the nation from economic imbalance and to continue its military machine in good repair. This was the import of the president's Air Policy Commission (the 1947-1948 Finletter Report) whose recommendations included a virtual integration of commercial and military planning in the context of which the nation could use reliable, regular production as a factor in defense calculations. It was, moreover, the leading consideration behind his effort to limit the defense budget to $15 billion annually. This was the maximum figure which he had decided the United States could spend indefinitely without creating economic chaos. Although the Korean military build-up seriously distorted this effort, it was unfair to claim that Truman had never made it, particularly since Eisenhower had associated himself with his predecessor's program while it was being pursued.

In the area of manpower, however, the Eisenhower critique was more pertinent. Although Truman and his staff had worked vigorously for the development of international alliances under United States hegemony (and although they used the Korean crisis to press these programs forward among reluctant nations), the UN force in Korea remained overwhelmingly American. Truman's swift commitment of United States forces to stem the North Korean advance was ultimately unilateral; and the "alliance" was largely token. Here was a substantive failure, for such unilateral commitment made American manpower the hostage of foreign states. In this respect, Truman lost opportunities to assume diplomatic and military initiatives. He had begun to seek foreign assistance instead of providing it to others.

In adopting a policy of "never again" with respect to limited warfare, the Eisenhower administration rejected not the small war *per se* but the small *unilateral* war. For it was the specter of dispersing United States strength into "obscure, far distant" corners of the world which was appalling to Washington and presumably attractive to Moscow (although in fact the Soviet Union found dispersal of its own energies a less than happy prospect). On the other hand, if effective alliances could be established so that any probe by Communist forces triggered an automatic and truly international defensive response, the benefits of such probes would diminish radically and immediately because they would achieve little more than the perfection of an anti-Communist world-in-arms. While the United States maintained its air-atomic deterrent to general war, it would also develop and dominate a network of alliances which would make limited war vastly less profitable to a hostile major power.

But for such a policy to function successfully the Eisenhower administration had to do more than meet perceived threats from a presumably conspiratorial enemy. It had to overcome the lassitude of its reluctant allies, many of which, such as France, had interests inconsistent with those of the United States (as in the example of American concern for Indochina as a Japanese trading area while the French worked to retain control in their own interest). If the outbreak of the Korean War provided Truman and Secretary of State Dean Acheson a golden opportunity to win acceptance for their alliance of the Western powers (especially NATO), the Korean truce created conditions which placed more of the burdens of the Western presence in Asia on the shoulders of the French. The assumption was widespread that a cease-fire in Korea would mean an intensification of fighting in Indochina—an assumption that seemed logical and proved correct. Already committed to the protection of their Asian empire, now formed as the Associated States, the French were thus made the main source of manpower in the effort to "contain" Communist activity. Their national interest in maintaining this empire pressed them into a role which largely resembled that which the United States administrations hoped they would perform in the international anti-Communist alliance. In this context, the American acceptance of the Korean truce—hardly less of a unilateral action than the 1950 decision to intervene militarily—represents their acceptance of relocating the theater of engagement. But now the United States preferred the role of critic, if not director, while the French played the major role.

The Eisenhower administration thereupon entered a new phase in this first cycle of intervention in Southeast Asia. It provided aid and advice to the French, but not ground forces. In this phase, air power had a theoretically critical but practically marginal function: to deter possible attack by the Soviet Union. This represented another step away from the hostility of Roosevelt to nineteenth-century colonialism. For Truman and Eisenhower both decided to support France in its colonialist venture in order to achieve stability in Indochina which could destroy the Vietminh. But Eisenhower hoped to remain circumspect. He was willing to send money, but not men or even United States aircraft. Even in the crisis of Dien Bien Phu, he was reluctant to commit American ground forces or air power and would not even consider it except in the context of a real alliance.

American observers had assumed that the French would hold Dien Bien Phu—a conviction reflected in proposals that aircraft be transferred to the French and flown by their own pilots (surely not the speediest way to meet an emergency). Washington foresaw no strict military reason for complete French withdrawal from Indochina even in the event of defeat. This view—which disregarded French domestic politics, the psychological significance of a major loss to the Vietminh, and what must have been a growing distrust of United States intentions and actions—did little to prepare the Eisenhower administration to assume direct responsibility for the status of Indochina when the French at last yielded. But the American government was not at a loss for a course of action. Some high officials, such as Secretary of Defense Charles E. Wilson (former chairman of General Motors), had warned that the United States would consider intervening with ground forces if it saw its interests threatened. Moreover the refusal of Walter Bedell Smith, the United States delegate to the Geneva Conference of 1954, to ratify the peace agreements suggested clearly that Eisenhower and his advisers were not prepared to be stampeded into an uncomfortable settlement by a declining ally.

But the Geneva Accords did bring an end to another phase of United States intervention. The French who had served as the main force for the achievement of American objectives now withdrew. American aid in Indochina had failed. But the Geneva Conference and the agreements it produced permitted a brief breathing spell during which the United States could work to activate new tactics to achieve its broad aim of a non-Communist Vietnam.

With the French gone, the United States accepted the role of bolstering an indigenous South Vietnamese ally, taking advantage of the delay before the projected national elections. Some high officials, such as General J. Lawton Collins, doubted the United States could find a suitable ally. But others—a dominant group led by Secretary of State John Foster Dulles—foresaw no alternative to support of Ngo Dinh Diem except total victory for the Vietminh. American advisers were to guide this Saigon regime toward the creation of a national army which would be proof against the Communists and would negate the Geneva Accords in the bargain. But the United States would avoid committing combat troops. It would provide military aid; and, through special protocols concerning the former French "Associated States," Washington's new SEATO alliances would include South Vietnam under the protection of United States air-atomic deterrence. After the Geneva Conference, then, the United States entered into support of surrogate forces in Southeast Asia. But now the surrogates were Vietnamese, not French. Ultimately, therefore, it was no longer "Western" but American prestige which had been added to the stakes of the contest.

While there were signs of trouble in Southeast Asia during the Eisenhower administration, such as the deterioration of conditions in Laos, official United States opinion of the Diem regime remained high. It was widely understood that the insurgent activity in Vietnam must be considered primarily political and that any military measure to counteract initiatives was also largely political in impact. Thus while the National Liberation Front (Vietcong) engaged in irregular military operations against the Saigon regime, the appropriate response was to strengthen the government in *all* respects—social, economic, and political, as well as military. The weapon with which to counter insurgency was national stability.

It is also important to realize that the Eisenhower administration was not expecting a simple replay of the Korean War. The versatility of government officials was represented in the successful subversion of the Huk guerrilla movement in the Philippines by means of moderate social reform; and the acceptance of the social reform model to counter the Vietminh and the Vietcong was symbolized by plans for Vietnam inspired by Major General Edward Lansdale, a leading American architect of anti-Huk operations. But Vietcong activity increased while the Diem regime was presumably strengthening its hold on South Vietnam; and the Washington of the "New Frontier" considered some action necessary, even though the situation did not justify sudden and unrestricted commitment. General Lyman Lemnitzer, the chairman of the Joint Chiefs of Staff, warned President John Kennedy that the loss of Laos and Vietnam would mean losing "Asia all the way to Singapore." Vice President Lyndon Johnson, returning from a 1961 tour of the Pacific, advised that the United States provide aid or else "throw in the towel" and "pull back our defenses to San Francisco."

Nonetheless Kennedy and his advisers continued to believe that Diem was well in command and that more aid and a larger (although modest compared to later figures) number of advisers and support units would enable the Saigon regime to destroy the Vietcong. General Maxwell Taylor, the president's choice as new chairman of the Joint Chiefs, recommended sending between 6,000 and 8,000 men to South Vietnam under the cover of a flood relief task force. Meanwhile Secretary of State Dean Rusk stressed the need for political reforms in South Vietnam, demonstrating again that local forces must carry the main burden and that political loyalty was prerequisite to success. Only the prevailing assumption that the Diem regime was fundamentally sound permitted confidence that so small an American force could achieve such broad United States objectives. This optimistic assessment survived through 1962 and into early 1963 (unbroken even by the Laos settlement which proved to be an "agreement to disagree"). Characteristic were the calls of Secretary of Defense Robert McNamara for plans to withdraw American forces because of "our tremendous success."

Several assumptions of high significance for later developments included: that the Diem regime was sound, that the United States would therefore be able to commit a limited number of troops without excessive risk (either of loss or escalation), that with little assistance the Diem regime could root out the Vietcong, and that North Vietnam would abstain from fighting. In 1961 General Taylor told the president that a major war in Asia was unlikely since North Vietnam was "extremely vulnerable to conventional bombing." United States officials, moreover, assumed that their own commitment to the Diem regime was an integrated element in the authentic destiny of South Vietnam—not a foreign intrusion. They judged further that any activity by the North Vietnamese would constitute aggression by a foreign invader and a transformation of the status quo, in which the Saigon regime with its American aid and advisers worked to counter a local Vietcong insurgency. Taylor believed that the North would abstain for fear of United States bombing; and thus he set out for the United States Air Force the task of controlling the character of the ground war.

These assumptions and beliefs proved disastrously erroneous. The Buddhist uprisings in South Vietnam (particularly in Hué) exposed the weaknesses of Saigon's political posture. Even more serious, perhaps, was the forceful reaction of the Diem regime which raised the specter of a civil war within the areas officially under government control. In August 1963 the Diem government further angered Washington by raiding Buddhist pagodas, aggravating Vietnamese politics and—far more serious—violating a pledge to the United States government and indicating that Saigon might attempt to pursue an independent course. Under Secretary of State George Ball told Ambassador Henry Cabot Lodge that Diem must remove his brother-in-law Ngo Dinh Nhu from power in the Saigon regime if he wanted continued American support. But Lodge recommended direct United States contact with dissident Vietnamese generals, arguing that Diem would never accede to Ball's demand. The National Security Council advised the president to accept and support a coup d'etat in South Vietnam provided it had a strong chance for success. For several months, Diem's future remained unclear. But Lodge continued to report that his regime was intransigent. In

November 1963 Diem's regime was overthrown; and Diem and Nhu were killed.

The extinction of the Diem regime produced consequences in the structure of American policy roughly comparable in kind to the loss of its French ally after Dien Bien Phu. The United States government had believed the French position fundamentally sound; but this had proved wrong. Then it believed that Diem was secure; this too proved incorrect. Thus the United States experienced once again the loss of an ally and faced the prospect of raising the level of its own commitments. From the time of the 1963 coup, Washington assumed increasing responsibility for the control of conditions in South Vietnam, both to prevent the consolidation of the Vietnams under Communist control (now denying any independence of action among the Vietcong) and again to buy time to build an indigenous force to achieve American objectives.

Early actions to support the generals' junta (officially headed by General Nguyen Khanh) were consistent with past assumptions and precursive of future involvement: Operations Plan 34 A, initiated in February 1964 called for clandestine military action against North Vietnam; in March, Secretary Robert McNamara agreed that new pressure should be brought to bear on the North to strengthen the morale of the Khanh regime; and in April, the Joint Chiefs of Staff recommended ninety-four potential bombing targets in North Vietnam. General Khanh told Lodge in May that he wanted to declare war on North Vietnam and asked the United States to approve and join the attack. Significantly, McNamara reminded them that bombing could only assist by limiting aid to the Vietcong and was no substitute for defeating the Vietcong on the ground. But Lodge agreed that something had to be done. At a meeting in Honolulu during the following month, he advised the president, Lyndon Johnson, that selective bombing of the North could avert the collapse of the Saigon government. The consensus of the meeting, despite Lodge's objections, was that congressional approval of broader action was desirable.

While Khanh propagandized about a "march north" (indulging himself in dreams of the offensive), the South Vietnamese staged raids on North Vietnamese islands in the Gulf of Tonkin. In August 1964 the U.S.S. *Maddox* was attacked by North Vietnamese patrol boats, apparently attempting to forestall repeated raids. Within twelve hours, American officials authorized "retaliatory" air raids on North Vietnam. A resolution meeting the purposes outlined by Rusk, McNamara, and John McCone at Honolulu was hurried through Congress (aided by McNamara's denial of all knowledge of South Vietnamese attacks and by the consent of Senator J. William Fulbright); and the president received what he interpreted as a blank check for future operations in Vietnam.

After the Tonkin incident, recommendations to use air power to govern the character of the South Vietnamese war increased in number and significance. In August General Taylor, now ambassador in Saigon, repeated his thesis of 1961: that bombing could prevent the collapse of the South and control the terms of the war by "punishing" the North. In September Assistant Secretary of Defense John T. McNaughton outlined a so-called provocation plan calling for bombing Laotian infiltration routes and coastal raids in the North, as well as continued destroyer patrols in the Gulf of Tonkin. President Johnson authorized patrols and air strikes; and in October the air war in Laos began in earnest. This extension of the war into neighboring territory was expected to improve the situation in the South. Moreover it established circumstances tending to even greater involvement. When the Vietcong attacked the American airfield at Bien Hoa (itself a form of retaliatory raid), the Joint Chiefs immediately urged air strikes against the North. Taylor recommended the bombing of selected targets. Johnson delayed, waiting for a report from a special study group headed by William Bundy. All options that were suggested to the president were variants of air power pressure: selected air strikes, total conventional air war, and graduated air war. In December Johnson adopted the selected strike option, to be followed by graduated air war. The policy of incremental escalation (widely taken in North Vietnam as a sign of weakness in the United States position) aimed at providing Hanoi opportunities to cut loose from the Vietcong while also characterizing United States operations as defensive responses to Northern aggression.

The Kennedy administration had confined its efforts largely to ground operations. But the Johnson administration expanded the uses of air power in both North and South. The context of this shift was the reported increase in Hanoi's aid to the Vietcong—presumably indigenous rebels, even if they were supported by the North or received guidance and direction from Hanoi. But Maxwell Taylor reported that

North Vietnamese regular troops were moving into the South and were largely responsible for the National Liberation Front's gaining control of most of South Vietnam. The thesis was simple: while the United States loftily observed a coup d'etat, the North Vietnamese were presumably moving in to deliver the coup de grace to the moribund Saigon regime.

Washington policy-makers insisted that this called for a new and strenuous effort. First, Hanoi must be made to feel vulnerable and to understand that aid to the Vietcong could mean attack in the North. Second, they must withdraw their forces and permit hostilities to return to the level prior to introduction of North Vietnamese regulars. Against this background, the Vietcong attacked the American base at Pleiku on February 7, 1965. The United States responded immediately with air strikes against North Vietnam. In a now famous simile, William Bundy commented that "Pleikus are like streetcars"—if one remains patient, they will come along sooner or later. By depicting the Pleiku attack as outside the norms which the United States had somehow accepted for the war, administration officials seized an opportunity to begin the retaliatory strikes which were soon reorganized into full-scale, planned bombing of the North in Operation Rolling Thunder. This transformation was neither accidental nor incidental to American interests. For the Johnson administration wished to establish a relationship between United States bombing and North Vietnamese ground support—the bombing was justified while the aid continued (a formula maintained in the United States reading of the 1968 bombing pause and in the Nixon administration's use of "protective reaction" strikes that were basically variants of the Pleiku scenario). As an added benefit, the bombing program guaranteed action and funds for the U.S. Air Force.

But air power was not enough. Taylor, who had urged bombing the North, at first hesitated to support a large troop commitment. Under Secretary Ball opposed it. But from mid-1965 Johnson authorized increasing force levels. The arrival of new United States troops added still another rationale for the employment of air power—the protection of American forces. By the end of 1965 when General William Westmoreland projected his requirements at about 450,000 men, it was clear that the existing bombing program was not producing adequate results. In a January 1966 memorandum for the president, McNamara described the situation as an escalating military stalemate.

At first, after urging from military men such as Admiral U. S. Grant Sharp who believed that escalated air attacks would drive Hanoi to peace talks, McNamara recommended more and greater attacks, such as destruction of North Vietnamese petrol, oil, and lubricant (POL) storage areas. Disregarding Ball's advice to cut American losses in the air war, Johnson authorized the POL attacks; and the strikes on these facilities began in June 1966. Although all major POL sites were destroyed by August, reports indicated that the flow of aid to the Vietcong remained unchanged. In September a study directed to McNamara concluded that Operation Rolling Thunder had "no measurable direct effect" on North Vietnam's capability in the South. Impressed by this report and by his own observation that the "pacification" program through which Saigon hoped to gain control of its own population was a failure, the secretary of defense suggested withdrawal.

As 1966 ended, disaffection for the war mounted within the administration itself as well as among the American people (manifest not only in left-oriented politics but in the rightist slogan "Why Wait 'Til '68?" used by some Republicans during the 1966 elections). McNamara had questioned not only the usefulness of the bombing but also further increases in troop levels. The Joint Chiefs opposed him on both counts: they regarded air power as their "trump card," and they urged authorization of more ground forces. Throughout 1967 this divergence became more pronounced. The Joint Chiefs pressed successfully for continued operations, such as the "spring air offensive" which Johnson approved in February. But McNamara remained cautious. In April the Joint Chiefs recommended expanding the air and ground war through Cambodia and Laos, and possibly even into North Vietnam. Johnson himself was becoming hesitant, however; and he speculated that if United States escalation were met with increases in enemy forces, he would be confronted with a military stalemate.

The growing disenchantment of both government officials (excluding the Joint Chiefs) and the American people created a situation roughly comparable to that of the French on the eve of defeat at Dien Bien Phu. When the Vietcong began their important Tet offensive of 1968, challenging Saigon's control even in the major cities in January and February of that year, Johnson's fears of an escalating but unresolvable war appeared justified. The Tet offensive did not amount to a total defeat of American objectives. But it forced reconsideration of

United States tactics. Although the Joint Chiefs recommended mobilizing the reserves and raising ground forces in South Vietnam by about 200,000, McNamara rejected the proposals. By this time, McNamara was being edged out of the administration because of his disaffection with the war and a consequent apparent defection from the camp loyal to Johnson. The secretary-designate of defense, Clark M. Clifford, authorized a policy review which advocated a "population security" strategy consistent with the bombing in the South which had effects conforming to Samuel P. Huntington's model of "forced draft urbanization." This strategy involved compelling civilians to move from rural to urban areas through a bombing and scorched-earth policy under the rubric of "anti-Maoist urban revolution." Edward M. Opton, Jr., has described this as "one of the most Panglossian rationalizations of the murder of civilians since Adolph Eichmann described himself as a coordinator of railroad timetables." Within the historical context of the ground engagement, Johnson's decision to limit and then halt the bombing of the North represented an effort to readjust American involvement and buy time to restore order in the South. Although the president's bombing pause of March 31, 1968, was as unilateral as his initiation of the bombing years earlier, he (and his successor) claimed that it was based on an "international understanding" in order to create diplomatic pressure for restraint in Hanoi.

The bombing pause and the termination of the United States ground force build-up signaled the end of another phase in the cycle of American intervention. The policy of using American ground troops to control conditions in the South had proved ineffectual and indeterminate. But it was left to Richard Nixon to activate new programs implicit in Johnson's decisions. First, "Vietnamization" of the war would permit the stage-by-stage withdrawal of Western (in this case American) troops. Gradualism would presumably enable the South Vietnamese, in association with neighboring states, to gain sufficient strength and skill to work as an indigenous anti-Communist force. Second, the "internationalization" of the war (so that it was publicly as well as actually a war throughout Indochina rather than one officially restricted to South Vietnam) would therefore continue, gaining force from United States air intervention and from specific land "incursions" such as the invasion of Cambodia in 1970. Third, the United States would depart from the Kennedy-Johnson tactic of gradual escalation and pursue a bolder course permitting resumption of bombing, mining Haiphong harbor, preparing clandestine ground forces, and engaging in ground operations such as the Cambodian invasion. The effect of this approach would presumably be to regain flexibility in policy-formation, to reduce restraints from either public or congressional sectors, and to suggest to Hanoi that a qualitatively different diplomacy from that of the Johnson years was in the ascendant in Washington.

As the Nixon administration began to execute this new phase in the Indochina intervention, the relationship of its policies to those of the Kennedy-Johnson years broadly resembled that of Eisenhower's to Truman's. Nixon and Eisenhower had both attained the presidency amid popular disaffection over an indeterminate war, a progressing stalemate. The Kennedy-Johnson and Truman administrations had taken high-risk courses of action involving commitment of United States forces (and other Western forces). The unsuccessful efforts of Johnson to win allies in Europe for the Indochina war had much in common with Truman's experience in Korea. Their successors determined to pursue less visible interventions, to depend more heavily on local forces, to use periods of truce and tenuous agreement to permit the development of new surrogates, and to stave off failure by allowing or accelerating the internationalization of the conflict. The Johnson Doctrine pronounced the United States willing to intervene unilaterally anywhere in the world where it identified threats to its national interest. The Nixon Doctrine claimed the right to intervene on an equally wide scale but to do so using soldiers from other countries.

United States policy in Indochina has been a planners' war between theory and reality. If one accepts a narrow, arbitrary, or inaccurate premise, all excesses and bizarre deviations from what seems to be common sense follow with the inevitability of logic. As G. K. Chesterton has suggested, a madman is one who has lost everything except his reason. In this case, the practical interests of the United States in avoiding the loss of American lives, creating stability in Indochina, and preventing an exclusionist order in Asia were converted into policies based on seriously flawed observations and premises.

Incorrect assumptions concerning the Vietminh, the French, the Diem regime, and the North Vietnamese (as well as about the American people) permitted the adoption of successive tactics of commitment.

Alienation from the Vietminh led to acceptance of French colonialist efforts as the vehicle for consolidating the Western position in Indochina. Generalizing anti-Communist conflict in Asia so that the Korean War was viewed in tandem with that in Indochina terminated in active support of the French during and after Korea. The development of the Diem regime as a surrogate after the French collapse ultimately required the use of United States ground forces, on the assumption that his government was basically secure. The failure of this ally sparked the build-up of United States troops and a massive air war to control conditions in the South, as well as the extension of the war through Indochina.

Within this network of premises and practices, United States air power was an instrument for developing the anti-Communist alliance. It served primarily as the device whereby Washington would control conditions on the ground in Vietnam and thereby strengthen its surrogate. The bombing of the North, the ventures into Laos and Cambodia, the bombing generally through Indochina, and the bombing in South Vietnam itself were efforts to force disengagement by the North Vietnamese and to compel loyalty in the South.

But it is ironic that a government which can think in megadeaths and can contemplate the loss of 50 to 100 million United States citizens in possible thermonuclear war would presume that the mere thought of air war would "deter" North Vietnam. It is also ironic that it achieved an increasing forced urbanization of South Vietnam by disrupting life outside the cities even though the existing regimes in Saigon were incompetent to manage the areas already under official control. But these questions ultimately had marginal impact. In the American experience in Indochina, such departures from practicality were the perfection of logic and the price of alliance.

SUGGESTIONS FOR FURTHER RESEARCH

With the publication of the *Pentagon Papers* and with the retirement from service of an increasing number of United States officers, the Indochina War is fast becoming well documented. Because of the newness of so much material and also because so much writing on the subject has been highly partisan, profitable areas for research are plentiful.

Our understanding of the United States involvement would improve greatly if historians considered the *structure* of events in Indochina as well as what policy-makers hoped to achieve. Thus, the commentaries on the ecological war, which frequently (and understandably) develop into fervent moral tracts, suggest an important line of exploration: the military logic of defoliation and the political virtues of making much of South Vietnam uninhabitable. This might help the researcher escape the inadequate framework of analysis which classifies operations as imperialist or freedom-serving, depending on political preference, and accept one that enables him to discover the concrete structure of the experience.

It is also important to have intellectual histories of the United States intervention. The fascination of Americans for machinery, specifically for air power but also for ground force technology, has been critical in granting credence to the premises of the bombing program. Moreover the dualistic vision of world politics, which had so much to do with United States alienation from the Vietminh, must be integrated into comprehensive studies of the war. The whole process of abstracting experience, so that a hut is classified as an "enemy structure" as easily as a factory, has also been basic to America's experience in Vietnam; and the "remoteness of mind" is a logical parallel to a remote-control war with allies frequently enlisted as players.

Such explorations of the structural and intellectual history of America in Vietnam will likely permit consideration of a number of important propositions: that United States commitment of ground forces was never anything but a stopgap, that United States use of air power was only an interim measure to prevent the collapse of allies, and that the *idée fixe* of American policy has been the internationalization of force to meet even local military and political emergencies.

BIBLIOGRAPHIC NOTE

A good starting point for studies of the Indochina war is the insightful work of Bernard Fall, including *Viet Nam Witness* (New York, 1966) and *The Two Viet-Nams* (New York, 1967). The basic source for information on the United States involvement is the "Pentagon Papers," easily available in the highly condensed *New York Times* edition (Neil Sheehan et al., eds., New York, 1971), in the more thorough Gravel edition, or in the twelve-volume Department of Defense version, *United States-Vietnam Relations 1945-1967* (Washington, D.C., 1971). See also Noam Chomsky,

American Power and the New Mandarins (New York, 1969) and *At War with Asia* (New York, 1970), polemics rich in information.

On the significance of alliances and links between the Korean and Southeast Asian conflicts, see Fall, *Last Reflections on a War* (New York, 1967). Also see Gabriel Kolko, *The Limits of Power* (New York, 1972) and, for the sake of clever speculation from media reports, I. F. Stone, *The Hidden History of the Korean War* (New York, 1952; reissued, 1969). Harry S. Truman, *Memoirs,* 2 vols. (New York, 1955-1956), and Dean Acheson, *Present at the Creation* (New York, 1969), provide important, if biased, perspectives on the Asian conflict through the end of their tenure. For an example of quasi-official thinking about air power in the Korean War and its future possible uses, see R[obert] F[rank] Futrell, *The United States Air Force in Korea 1950-1953* (New York, 1961), which argues that the Korean air war was a major success politically and militarily.

An important record of the deterioration of the French position in Indochina is Fall, *Street without Joy: Insurgency in Indochina,* 3d ed. (Harrisburg, Pa., 1963). For interesting information on the American impression of the status of the French at the time of Dien Bien Phu, see the same author's *Hell in a Very Small Place* (Philadelphia, 1966), which also comments on United States consideration of intervention through air power before the fall of that bastion.

The North Vietnamese perspective on politics and military tactics is considered in Patrick J. McGarvey, *Visions of Victory: Selected Vietnamese Communist Military Writings, 1964-1968* (Stanford, Calif., 1969). Jean Lacouture, *Ho Chi Minh* (London, 1968), is a fine biography with useful insights into the military and political dynamics of North Vietnam. Similarly, for a broad view, see G. K. Tanham, *Communist Revolutionary Warfare* (New York, 1961), and Jack Woodis, ed., *Ho Chi Minh: Selected Articles and Speeches, 1920-1967.* These works provide not only a survey of the military thinking of the North Vietnamese but also Hanoi's view of the increasing United States ground and air intervention.

Interesting studies dealing with the United States understanding of the war as a political problem include Robert Shaplen, *The Lost Revolution* (New York, 1966), and Milton Osborne, *Strategic Hamlets in South Vietnam* (Ithaca, N.Y., 1965), the latter of which explores the reasons for the failure of counterinsurgency. Of interest for a study of the deterioration of social and political conditions in South Vietnam is Thich Nhat Hahn, *Lotus in a Sea of Fire: Vietnam* (New York, 1967), providing a Buddhist commentary on the war and its impact. An important example of government studies recording the decline in

Saigon's control of the countryside is Ray E. Davis, *An Analysis of Property Tax Compliance in Vietnam* (Saigon, 1965). See also General William C. Westmoreland and Admiral U.S. Grant Sharp, "Report on the War in Vietnam" (Washington, D.C., 1968).

Attempts at documenting United States "ecological warfare," significant in evaluating the question of forced-draft urbanization, include John Lewallen, *The Ecology of Devastation: Indochina* (Baltimore, Md., 1971), Barry Weisberg, ed., *Ecocide in Indochina* (San Francisco, 1970), and especially Frances Fitzgerald, *Fire in the Lake* (Boston, 1972). The reader may wish to consider such works not only from an ethical or ecological premise but also for their implications concerning the concrete results of the structure of American policy.

The reports of congressional committees investigating the origins and character of the United States war effort are readily available. Particularly instructive are those of the Senate Foreign Relations and Armed Services committees, including the latter's 1967 investigation of *Air War against North Vietnam*. Frank Harvey, *Air War–Vietnam* (New York, 1967), is impressionistic but offers occasional insights. Colonel Jack Broughton, *Thud Ridge* (Philadelphia, 1969), is more useful for information on fighter-bomber raids on North Vietnam. The *Pentagon Papers* are rich in material concerning the rise and decline of United States bombing policy between 1965 and 1968. The reader may also wish to see Townsend Hoopes, *The Limits of Intervention* (New York, 1969), for a former insider's thoughts on the bombing. Perhaps the best available study describing the nature and scope of the American bombing program is the revised edition of Ralph Littauer and Norman Uphoff, eds., *The Air War in Indochina* (Boston, 1972).

RELATIVE ABSTENTION:
INDIA & PAKISTAN

William L. Richter

AMERICAN POLICY toward South Asia during the quarter-century since India and Pakistan became independent states (August 1947) has been based upon global, strategic, cold-war-related considerations while all the several wars of the region during this period have been distinctively regional in character. The conflicts between India and Pakistan over the status of the former princely state of Jammu and Kashmir (1948-1949, 1965, 1971), between India and China over disputed Himalayan border territories (1962), between Pakistan and the combined forces of India and the Bangladesh independence movement (1971), and a host of lesser outbreaks over Hyderabad, Goa, the Rann of Kutch, and other territories all derive more from the contours of British colonialism in India and the problems of decolonization, than from the worldwide ideological and strategic contest which motivated most United States foreign policy during the 1950s and 1960s. This disjuncture between global and regional issues and perspectives has posed foreign policy dilemmas for the United States as well as for other major powers. All three "global" powers have vacillated in the extent and direction of their subcontinental involvement.

American policy toward South Asia has been both moderated and complicated by the fact that the United States has no direct economic or political interest in the region. The factors of oil and Zionist nationalism which involve the United States in the Middle East have no corollary in South Asia.

In one sense, this absence of material interest has helped to limit American involvement in the subcontinent, but it has also meant that American policy toward South Asia has been determined largely by factors extraneous to the region. The United States has been guided in its South Asian policy by its global interests and has therefore tended to view regional conflicts largely from a global perspective. It has thus failed to recognize the local consequences of some of its more broadly conceived political actions. For instance, when American arms were given to Pakistan after 1954 to contain Communist expansion, or to India in 1962 to fight the Chinese, the United States was not, by its own standards, intervening in any Indo-Pakistani conflicts. From India's point of view in the first instance and Pakistan's in the second, however, the American aid was very clearly an intervention which unfavorably tipped the precarious military balance in the subcontinent. From such regional perspectives, even the American decision to terminate military aid to both India and Pakistan at the time of the 1965 Kashmir war was not considered by either side to constitute American subcontinental involvement. Pakistan saw the cessation as favoring India (in which a munitions industry had been developed), and Indians argued that American policy unfairly equated Pakistan and India and sought to balance the former against the latter.

Other forms of American aid have at various times been considered interventionist by their South Asian recipients—PL 480 food shipments, Peace Corps, even cultural missions—but these have more frequently been interpreted as intruding upon domestic rather than regional politics. An inquiry into the nature, extent, and consequences of American intervention can therefore be limited for practical purposes to military aid and other actions which have affected relations between the major countries of the region: India and Pakistan.

Military Aid and Its Political Consequences

The United States cannot be said to have intervened fully in any conflict between India and Pakistan. American combat troops, for instance, have not seen action in South Asia as they have in Vietnam and Thailand in the last decade or as they did in Lebanon in 1958. On the other hand, the United States has not fully abstained from intervention in Indo-Pakistani affairs. At the very least American presidents have used diplomatic channels to bring pressure upon both countries, and United States delegates to the United Nations have sponsored resolutions concerning subcontinent affairs. On the continuum between these two extremes, the giving of military aid has been the most potent, if not the most intentional, form of intervention.

The global context within which United States arms were given to both India and Pakistan was one in which American policy-makers perceived Communist military expansion to be a real and powerful threat both to post-1945 world order and to American and West European interests in Asia. The policy of containment had been formulated in 1947 as a counter to this threat and had been implemented in NATO, the Truman Doctrine, Point Four, and other programs. The extension of containment to the Middle East and to Southeast Asia provided the rationale for the creation of two additional treaty organizations (or alliances) patterned upon NATO: the Baghdad Pact (1955, later renamed CENTO) and the South East Asia Treaty Organization (SEATO, 1954).

The regional context within which arms were given to Pakistan in 1954 and afterward was one in which that militarily weak and geographically divided country felt severely threatened by its mammoth neighbor, India. Created as an independent homeland for Indian Muslims in 1947, Pakistan was perceived to be extremely vulnerable to attack along its two extensive borders with India, even to total reabsorption, as some militant Hindu spokesmen advocated during the early years of independence. Pakistan's fears of India were reinforced by the latter's political and military action in various princely state areas in which both countries had interests: Junagadh, Hyderabad, and most importantly, Kashmir.

The Kashmir conflict has been central to Indo-Pakistani relations since the two countries became independent. Lying adjacent to both India and Pakistan, Kashmir was the largest princely state (85,000 square miles), with a predominantly Muslim population under the rule of a Hindu Maharaja. When, at the time of partition, Maharaja Hari Singh delayed taking a decision on the merger of his state with India or Pakistan, armed tribesmen from Pakistan invaded the state. In return for the state's accession to India, Indian troops were flown into Kashmir and effectively stopped the rebel advance, but were unable to expel them from areas they had captured. From Pakistan's perspective, India's actions in Kashmir not only denied self-determination to a predominantly Muslim population but also denied to Pakistan a large piece of strategically valuable territory.

Unable by itself to match India's greater resources and power (originally a ratio of approximately 4 to 1), Pakistan sought outside support to bolster its security. In accordance with its predominant ideology, it turned first to the Muslim states of the Middle East, but found little support there. The United States, with both its material resources and its interest in bolstering weaker countries against perceived threats of communist advance, appeared a logical ally.

Despite American assurances that her arms would not be used against India and offers to include India in the United States-sponsored defense pacts, the supply of arms to Pakistan worsened Indo-American relations and facilitated warmer ties between India and the two major Communist states. Soviet and Chinese leaders were warmly received in India in 1955 and 1956, the Chinese visits hailed widely with the slogan, *"Hindi Chini bhai-bhai"* and "Indians and Chinese are brothers."

This spirit of Sino-Indian fellowship deteriorated rapidly, however, as clashes occurred between the two Asian giants over Himalayan territories to which they both laid claim. Responding to such conflict, some American spokesmen argued for a reconsideration of American policy in the subcontinent. Most notably, Senator John F. Kennedy urged in 1959 that United States interest lay in strengthening India, "the world's largest democracy," against its major competitor in Asia, China. After Kennedy's accession to the presidency in 1961, steps were taken to implement this policy by improving relations with India. Despite adverse American reactions to India's "liberation" of Goa in late 1961 (in part because of American ties to Portugal, Goa's previous colonial master), the United States responded strongly to the outbreak of Sino-Indian war in October 1962 with the supply of arms and other assistance to India.

United States military support to India in 1962 and later was small compared to that given Pakistan since 1954, but it was sufficient to cause Pakistan to feel betrayed by its former ally. The United States-Pakistani relationship had already been weakened by the embarrassment of a 1960 incident involving Soviet exposure of a downed American U-2 spy plane which had taken off from a West Pakistani military airfield. American assistance to India led Pakistan to question the peculiar assets of its relationship with the United States. Without abandoning formal membership in SEATO and CENTO, Pakistan again sought new friends and allies and again a logical choice presented itself—its "enemy's enemy," China.

In 1965 war again erupted between India and Pakistan. In response to India's moves to alter Kashmir's special constitutional status within the Indian Union, Pakistan infiltrated irregulars into Kashmir to foment discontent and keep alive Pakistani claims to Kashmir. India responded with full-scale military attacks into Pakistani-held Kashmir and into West Pakistan proper. During the three weeks before a UN cease-fire was implemented, the major powers' actions reflected their new alignments. China blamed India for the conflict and threatened to precipitate renewal of hostilities on the Himalayan front. The United States, embarrassed by the use of American arms on both sides, took a neutral stance and cut off military aid to both countries, a move that hurt Pakistan more than India. The Soviet Union, eager to improve its ties with Pakistan, but not to alienate India, played an active neutral role by hosting an Indo-Pakistani peace conference at Tashkent in early January 1966.

The American embargo on arms aid to India and Pakistan represented both a realization that previous aid to one country, regardless of its objectives, had produced adverse political reaction in the other. It also reflected the declining importance of the cold war. Whether or not the objective of containment had been achieved, the military aid used to achieve that objective had in at least two instances disturbed the power relationship between India and Pakistan in the subcontinent. Formal abstention from involvement in the Kashmir conflict and other Indo-Pakistani issues notwithstanding, the political effect was one of unwitting intervention.

The Bangladesh Crisis and American Response

The greatest challenges to American neutrality in South Asian regional problems occurred during the 1971 Bangladesh crisis. The American response displayed the familiar tendency of letting global objectives dictate policy toward the South Asian region. It also, strikingly, demonstrated a shift of American support back to Pakistan and a subsequent worsening of Indo-American relations which reached their lowest point in at least a decade. The most crucial fact for this inquiry, however, is that the United States abstained from involvement in the conflict early in 1971, when it might have had some effect, yet threatened interven-tion in support of the losing Pakistanis in the December war, when such a move was almost certain to be futile.

Part of the complexity of the Bangladesh crisis lay in the fact that it was not just one conflict, but at least three, inextricably interwoven conflicts. The most obvious and deep-seated conflict was that between the two wings of Pakistan. Though East Pakistan contained roughly 55 percent of the country's population, West Pakistan continuously held a dominant position politically, culturally, economically, and in coveted military and bureaucratic positions. Foreign exchange from the sale of East Pakistan's jute had been used to finance the development of West Pakistani industry. It was only after prolonged agitation that the East Pakistanis had succeeded in having their Bengali language named as a national language coequal with Urdu, the dominant high-language of the West.

Augmenting the regional disparities and disagreements between East and West was a second political conflict between supporters of popular, representative institutions and those favoring authoritarian-bureaucratic ones. From its creation in 1947 until late 1970, Pakistan did not hold a single nationwide election based on direct popular franchise. Martial law was imposed from 1958 to 1962 and again in early 1969. During the six and a half years of the Second Republic, 1962-1969, the "Basic Democracy" system used indirect elections, curtailment of political parties, and disqualification of leading politicians to hold popular participation within limits and avoid the factional and "corrupt" poli-tics which preceded the 1958 military takeover.

The political conflict overlapped the regional one to a significant degree. Popular political pressures were stronger and political parties more coherent in the East, while both the military and the bureaucracy were drawn more heavily from the West. Most importantly, the East, with its slight majority, had the most to gain politically from a fully representative political system.

The third relevant conflict, interwoven with the other two, was the international one between India and Pakistan. West Pakistanis suspected Indian collusion in disturbances which occurred in the East and the sizable Hindu minority in Bengal was frequently characterized as an Indian fifth column. Bengalis, on the other hand, regarded the perpet-ual Pakistani confrontation with India over Kashmir as an issue which unnecessarily endangered their security for the benefit of the West and the military. India, in turn, tended to sympathize with the aspirations of Bengalis and many West Pakistanis for popular representative government and reduction of regional disparities and inequities. In 1968 Pakistan charged Bengali leader Sheikh Mujibur Rahman and others with conspiring with the Indians to dismember Pakistan.

All three of these conflicts converged in 1971. In early December 1970 Pakistan's first general elections were held peacefully and effectively preparatory to return to a parliamentary political system. The Awami League, led by Sheikh Mujib, captured a phenomenal 72 percent of the vote and all but two of the 169 seats accorded East Bengal in the national constituent assembly. With East Pakistan's slight numerical majority, the Awami League thus had an absolute majority in the Assembly and promised to implement in the constitution the six-point program on which it had fought the elections—a program which generally called for regional autonomy and decentralization of governmental powers.

Zulfiqar Ali Bhutto, whose Pakistan People's party had won a majority of the West Pakistani seats, anticipated the potential shift of power from West to East which Awami League domination of the Assembly would entail and refused to participate until ground rules could be worked out between the two major party leaders. The martial-law president, General Yahya Khan, was sympathetic to Bhutto's position and opposed the establishment of a constitution that would "destroy the unity of Pakistan." When he postponed the opening of the Assembly, Sheikh Mujib called a general strike throughout East Bengal. Negotiations broke down and, on the night of March 25, 1971, federal troops from West Pakistan moved to annihilate the Bengali resistance. In ensuing months the Bengalis proclaimed themselves the independent state of Bangladesh and fought a hard guerrilla war against vastly better-trained and better-armed Pakistani troops.

Around ten million refugees, the largest exodus in modern history, escaped to India and countless other Bengalis were uprooted from their homes, murdered, raped, and mutilated. India provided clandestine training and weapons for rebel troops but held back on more active involvement or even on recognition of the Bangladesh regime for fear of confirming the Pakistani charge that the rebellion was Indian-inspired. Meanwhile, Indian and Bangladesh spokesmen sought to publicize the crisis and to gain international support for the refugee effort.

The responses of the Soviet Union and China were clear but restrained. China gave verbal support to Pakistan, but was noticeably slow in providing arms. The Soviet Union signed a defense treaty with India in August 1971, the effect of which was to neutralize any threat of Chinese intervention. Meanwhile, Soviet arms shipments to India continued in large numbers.

The United States attempted to abstain from involvement in the conflict in order not to alienate either India or Pakistan. Top leaders from both countries were received in Washington and President Nixon followed a visit by India's prime minister, Indira Gandhi, with an announcement that arms aid to Pakistan—which had been resumed on a limited "one-time-only" basis after the 1965 ban—would be terminated entirely. Subsequent discovery that shipments were still continuing (explained by administration officials as merely delivery of sales which had already been made) undercut the administration's *bona fides* and heightened Indian suspicion.

During this period the United States provided assistance for refugee relief, attempted to persuade India not to escalate the conflict by becoming an active belligerent, and, at the same time, privately urged President Yahya Khan to take steps which might facilitate a "political settlement" of the civil war. But it is questionable whether any political solution could have been found to mend the East-West split after the massacres of March 25 and later. Whether administration failure to realize the inevitable alternatives was simple misjudgment or wishful self-delusion is difficult to determine, but the United States did have several reasons, both traditional and strategic, to oppose the break-up of Pakistan. The most obvious is the tendency of established governments to support established governments, regardless of the merits of the rebellion against them. Strategically, the United States had come to view Pakistan as an important factor in the South Asian "balance of power." Division of the country would upset that balance and leave India "unchecked" to impose her will upon the other countries of the region. Moreover, a dominant India allied to the Soviet would only more greatly upset big power relations in Asia. Finally, Pakistan was a key link in the Nixon administration's moves to improve relations with the People's Republic of China, including the secret arrangements for presidential adviser Henry Kissinger's first visit to Peking via Pakistan in

1971. Again, global considerations outweighed regional ones in strategic planning.

The United States action most damaging to its relations with India, however, came during the last five weeks of 1971. Indian involvement in the war escalated, Pakistani planes bombed Indian airports, Indian troops entered East Bengal in massive force, and fighting began at many points on the Western front. President Nixon dispatched a task force of the Seventh Fleet from the Tonkin Gulf to the Bay of Bengal, ostensibly to evacuate United States civilians in East Bengal, but more accurately to counter an increased Soviet naval presence in the Indian Ocean. The Pakistanis mistakenly interpreted the approach of the carrier U.S.S. *Enterprise* and its task force as impending support, while the Indians indignantly described it as an unsuccessful exercise in gunboat diplomacy. Though American spokesmen publicly proclaimed that the United States wished to maintain an even-handed approach to India and Pakistan, the president privately (as revealed by columnist Jack Anderson) sought means to "tilt the balance in favor of Pakistan." United Nations Ambassador George Bush did just that, in a resolution (vetoed by the USSR in the Security Council but passed 104-11 in the General Assembly) and speeches which condemned India's "massive aggression" in Pakistan's civil war.

Deputy Defense Secretary David Packard warned (in a meeting of the National Security Council's Washington Special Action Group [WSAG] on December 8) that "the overriding consideration is the practical problem of either doing something effective or doing nothing. If you don't win, don't get involved. If we were to attempt something it would have to be with a certainty that it would affect the outcome. Let's not get in if we know we are going to lose. Find some way to stay out."

Despite such a clear statement of the fundamental considerations underlying the choice between intervention and abstention, the United States in the following week took moves which alienated India, perhaps irreparably, but did not substantially affect the outcome of the conflict or bolster Pakistan's performance in it. In addition to the United Nations speeches and the Seventh Fleet maneuvers, the proposal to supply arms to Pakistan through third countries, particularly Jordan, when made public (by Jack Anderson's revelations) further worsened Indo-American relations without helping Pakistan. Though the proposal to permit the transfer of Jordanian weapons to Pakistan was rejected in the WSAG meetings—on the legal ground that a country ineligible to receive direct United States military aid could not receive such third-country transfers—Jordan did "loan" ten United States-supplied fighter aircraft (F-104s) to Pakistan for the duration of the war. Libya also supplied five F-5 fighters and Iran a wide range of military supplies, much of it presumably American in origin.

Various explanations have been offered for President Nixon's notable bias for Pakistan in the 1971 conflict and the near-intervention or half-hearted intervention which resulted from it: the relative courtesy shown Nixon on previous visits to India and Pakistan; the traditional bias of Republicans toward Pakistan and Democrats toward India; Nixon's great respect for military leaders like General Yahya Khan; the desire of the administration not to alienate Pakistan's other ally, China. President Nixon's own explanation, embodied in his report to Congress in February 1972, stressed that the outbreak of the war (for which the blame was laid almost entirely on India) had destroyed the efforts which the United States had exerted throughout 1971 to effect a political settlement between East and West Pakistan. He also argued that the threat of Indian occupation of Pakistani-held Kashmir and destruction of Pakistan's military forces in the West was a real possibility and was averted by United States actions: "If we had not taken a stand against the war, it would have been prolonged and the likelihood of an attack in the West greatly increased." Finally, he argued, failure of the United States to act would have encouraged separatism in other multiethnic states, together with big-power support such as the Indo-Soviet treaty. He summarized interpretation of the choice between intervention and abstention as follows:

> The U.S. had two choices when the war broke out. We could take a stand against the war and try to stop it, or we could maintain a "neutral" position and acquiesce in it. The former course meant strains in our relations with India, as well as the risk of failure. But the latter course, I concluded, ran even greater risks. Acquiescence had ominous implications for the survival of Pakistan, for the stability of many other countries in the world, for the integrity of international processes for keeping the peace, and for relations among the great powers. These risks were unacceptable.

These arguments appear to be consistent both with Nixon's actions during the crisis and with the overall global strategy of the Nixon administration. Big-power negotiation based upon national interest has largely replaced containment and confrontation as cornerstones of United States policy. Just as Peking and Moscow have been integral to Nixon's Vietnam strategy, great-power relations—both the mitigation of Soviet diplomatic advances and the forging of closer relations with China—appeared to be particularly overriding concerns behind Nixon's South Asia moves. More than simply an apology, the president's arguments are a better key to his actions in the crisis than some of the semi-psychoanalytic explanations noted earlier.

The crucial question is whether these perceptions, even if sincere and genuine, were accurate. The Yahya Khan regime did restore a semblance of civilian rule in East Bengal in August 1971, but the move appeared to be little more than window dressing designed, among other things, to mollify United States pressure and world public opinion. Though some Indians militantly cried for a final "solution" to the Kashmir question and for elimination of Pakistan as an antagonist, there also seems to be little support for the argument that the Indian government held these views. To assume that the United States' gestures during the conflict had anything to do with India's termination of military action when her limited objectives were accomplished is an exercise in *post hoc ergo propter hoc* reasoning. Finally, it is extremely difficult to argue that India's two-week military action, followed by the speedy repatriation of the ten million Bengali refugees, constituted any prolongation of the human tragedy in South Asia.

That the United States chose sides in the December war was not so damaging to its reputation as the fact that it did so while proclaiming its "even-handed" position. That it intervened, or at least threatened to, was not nearly so disastrous as the fact that it did so ineffectively, on doubtful premises, and in support of a cause which was not only admittedly doomed but also at variance with predominant opinion both within the State Department and in the American public at large.

The Future United States Role in South Asia

"The crisis of 1971," President Nixon noted in his January address, "transformed South Asia." The role that the United States will play in the region in the near future will be determined by the new political configuration and constrained by the legacy of its actions in 1971. In the place of two large nations, surrounded by a handful of smaller countries, South Asia now consists of one overwhelmingly large and regionally powerful nation, two relatively large but much weaker countries, and a handful of peripheral states. The task of reconstruction is formidable in both Pakistan and Bangladesh and both countries have welcomed American aid in the wake of the war.

India's predominance in the subcontinent is an undisputable fact, with which Pakistan, Bangladesh, and outside powers have come to terms. The response of Pakistan's postwar civilian government, headed by Zulfiqar Ali Bhutto, has been to seek accommodation with India on a bilateral basis. Talks between Bhutto and Gandhi at Simla (in the Indian Himalayas north of Delhi) in early July 1972 and later negotiations have led to some limited agreements on outstanding issues and, perhaps more importantly, to a noticeable reduction in animosity between the two countries.

For Bangladesh, the situation and response to India's dominant position are quite different. Emerging from a year of strife heavily indebted to India for moral and material support, Bangladesh has become increasingly mindful of the need to maintain its own identity vis-à-vis its giant neighbor and benefactor. The ties between the two countries are likely to remain strong for some time, but Bangladesh can be expected in the long run to attempt to balance these with outside diplomatic and economic linkages.

Any outside power must recognize India's emergent hegemony in the subcontinent. Any attempt to rebuild Pakistan's military capacity to the point of again challenging Indian hegemony would be both futile and rightly interpreted as an attempt to intimidate India.

In this context there is little scope for positive United States initiative beyond the provision of economic aid for reconstruction and development. The United States continues to have no material interest in the subcontinent. Despite the decline in the cold war and the diminishing of containment as a global strategy, South Asia is still seen to have some strategic importance, both with respect to the maintenance of some balance between Soviet and Chinese interests in Asia and with some respect to the protection of Middle Eastern oil resources. Neither of these considerations would seem to justify the resumption of extensive arms aid to Pakistan or to any other South Asian country, but the increased military aid to Iran and American naval activity in the Indian Ocean occasioned by these twin concerns are regarded with some alarm by Indian military and political analysts.

For most of the quarter-century of Indian and Pakistani independence, global politics have infected and interfered with South Asian regional politics. Great-power rivalry in the Indian Ocean is far from ending, but recent United States diplomatic moves make any return to the polarized arms race of the cold war appear unlikely.

Future United States policy toward South Asia depends heavily on the willingness of India and Pakistan to seek bilateral peaceful solutions to their differences without the interference of outside powers. If regional problems and the search for their solution can thus be isolated from global politics and great-power competition, it may be possible for the United States and other outside powers to avoid future troublesome choices between intervention and abstention in South Asian affairs.

SUGGESTIONS FOR FURTHER RESEARCH

Though commentators have often alluded to the relationship between heavy U.S. aid and subsequent military takeover in Pakistan, Vietnam, Greece, Turkey, and various Latin American countries, little systematic research has been conducted to confirm or refute the existence of such a relationship. The question could be approached either within a single country, like Pakistan between 1954 and 1958, or as a comparison of two or more countries.

Similarly, commentators have argued that fluctuations in U.S. arms aid have upset regional power balances by encouraging aggressive action by the recipient of an arms increase or by the opponent of a country receiving an arms cutback. Frequently the support for such an assessment is circumstantial and inferential. Might more precise support or refutation of such inferences be made by investigation of military and political memoirs, public documents, and the public statements of political leaders?

Indo-American relations suffered in two separate instances where India "liberated" territory from an American ally: Goa (1961) and Bangladesh (1971). Further comparison of these two incidents, and the American response to them, would be instructive.

What is the composition of the "India lobby" and of the "Pakistan lobby" in the United States? Is the India lobby predominantly Democratic and the Pakistan lobby predominantly Republican? Were the groups and individuals who supported the Bangladesh cause the same as (or similar to) those who earlier supported the independence of Biafra from Nigeria? Some of these questions might be answered by analysis of congressional speeches and other material in the *Congressional Record,* or of letters to the editor in major U.S. newspapers.

BIBLIOGRAPHIC NOTE

A general background of United States policy toward the countries of South Asia may be obtained from Norman D. Palmer, *South Asia and United States Foreign Policy* (New York: Houghton Mifflin, 1966), which is now somewhat out of date and W. Norman Brown, *The United States and India, Pakistan, Bangladesh,* 3d ed. (Cambridge: Harvard University Press, 1972), which is current but somewhat more general in approach. Two additional works that extend in scope beyond South Asia but nevertheless provide stimulating insights are Michael Brecher, *The New States of Asia* (New York: Oxford University Press, 1966), and Werner Levi, *The Challenge of World Politics in South and Southeast Asia* (Englewood Cliffs, N.J.: Prentice-Hall, 1968). A collection of articles edited by S. P. Varma and K. P. Misra, *Foreign Policies in South Asia* (Bombay: Orient Longmans, 1969), includes discussion of the role of outside powers and provides a South Asian (predominantly Indian) discussion of related issues. By far the most thorough discussion of big-power involvement in South Asian affairs is William J. Barnds, *India, Pakistan, and the Great Powers* (New York: Praeger, 1972).

The best treatment of the Bangladesh war itself and the events leading up to it is Mohammed Ayoob and K. Subrahmanyam, *The Liberation War* (New Delhi: S. Chand, 1972). Useful commentary and documents concerning the conflict are provided in *Bangladesh: The Birth of a Nation,* compiled by Marta R. Nicholas and Philip Oldenburg (Madras: M. Seshachlan & Co., 1972). A larger selection of documents and articles, similarly sympathetic to the Bangladesh cause, may be found in *Bangladesh Documents* (New Delhi: Ministry of External Affairs, 1971). Other studies published in India in 1971 reflect the ongoing debate in that country over policy alternatives. Among these, the best is Pran Chopra, ed., *The Challenge of Bangla Desh* (New York: Humanities Press, 1971), but see also Subhash C. Kashyap, ed., *Bangladesh:*

Background and Perspectives (New Delhi: Institute of Constitutional and Parliamentary Studies, 1971); D. R. Mankekar, *Pak Colonialism in East Bengal* (Bombay: Somaiya Publications, 1971); and Dom Moraes, *The Tempest Within* (Delhi: Vikas Publications, 1971). A very insightful analysis which focuses upon India's developing relationship with the Soviet Union during this same period is found in Pran Chopra, *Before and After the Indo-Soviet Treaty* (New Delhi: S. Chand, 1971). Data concerning U.S. and Soviet arms aid to South Asian countries prior to the war may be found in *The Arms Trade with the Third World* (Stockholm: Stockholm International Peace Research Institute, 1971).

Numerous journalistic "instant histories" emerged in India immediately following the war, such as S. S. Sethi, *The Decisive War: Emergence of a New Nation* (New Delhi: Sagar Publications, 1972), and Major-General D. K. Palit, *The Lighting Campaign: The Indo-Pakistan War 1971* (New Delhi: Thomson Press, 1972), the latter of which includes a detailed account of the fighting, supported by photos and maps. More scholarly in approach and useful because it includes a discussion of the role of U.S. aid to Pakistan is Subrata Roy Chowdhury, *The Genesis of Bangladesh* (New York: Asia Publishing House, 1972).

Pakistani accounts of the war and its origins are more difficult to come by. One such treatment is Kalim Siddiqui, *Conflict, Crisis and War in Pakistan* (New York: Praeger, 1972), but more insight into the internal events leading to the crisis may be gained by consulting two earlier studies: Rounaq Jahan, *Pakistan: Failure in National Integration* (New York: Columbia University Press, 1972), and the forthrightly Marxist account by Tariq Ali, *Pakistan: Military Rule or People's Power* (New York: William Morrow, 1970). An additional source of leftist and critical Pakistani opinion on the war may be found in the several issues of the monthly journal *Pakistan Forum* (Sault Ste. Marie, Canada) which appeared during 1971 and 1972.

It is valuable at many points to refer to the speeches and public statements of national leaders: Sheikh Mujibur Rahman, *Bangladesh, My Bangladesh* (Selected Speeches and Statements, October 28, 1970, to March 26, 1971) (New Delhi: Orient Longmans, 1972); Indira Gandhi, *India and Bangla Desh* (Selected Speeches and Statements, March to December 1971) (Delhi: Orient Longmans, 1972); and Swaran Singh and S. Sen, *Bangla Desh and Indo-Pak War: India Speaks at the U.N.* (New Delhi: Publications Division, Ministry of Information and Broadcasting, Government of India, 1972). The Pakistani position on the war is detailed in its *White Paper on the Crisis in East Pakistan*

(Islamabad: Ministry of Information and National Affairs, 5 August 1971) and in a series of background reports published by the Pakistan embassy in Washington, D.C., during 1971. Zulfiqar Ali Bhutto's account of events during the early part of that year is published under the title *The Great Tragedy* (Karachi: Pakistan People's Party, 1971).

Few episodes in foreign-policy making have been subjected to as much immediate publicity as the American actions of December 1971. Columnist Jack Anderson secured and published minutes of the meetings of the Washington Special Action Group and National Security Council which revealed high-level policy planning during the crisis. Besides the syndicated publication of these revealing materials in the *Washington Post* and other newspapers at the time, they have also been reprinted and analyzed in Vinod Gupta, *The Anderson Papers* (Delhi: Vikas, 1972). Several congressional hearings and reports also throw light on the conflict and American reaction to it. See Edward M. Kennedy, *Crisis in South Asia: A Report to the Subcommittee to Investigate Problems Connected with Refugees and Escapees of the Committee on the Judiciary, United States Senate,* November 1, 1971 (Washington, D.C.: Government Printing Office, 1971); *Foreign Assistance Act of 1972: Hearings before the Committee on Foreign Relations, United States Senate,* April 17, 18, and 19, 1972 (Washington, D.C.: Government Printing Office, 1972); *United States Interests in and Policies toward South Asia: Hearings before the Subcommittee on the Near East and South Asia of the Committee on Foreign Affairs, House of Representatives,* March 12, 15, 20, and 27, 1973 (Washington, D.C.: Government Printing Office, 1973); *The United States and South Asia: Report of the Subcommittee on the Near East and South Asia of the Committee on Foreign Affairs, House of Representatives,* May 26, 1973 (Washington, D.C.: Government Printing Office, 1973); and Dorfman, Mason, & Marglin, "Conflict in East Pakistan: Background and Prospects," *Congressional Record,* 92d Cong., 1st sess., Vol. 117, part 8, April 7, 1971 pp. 10132-34. The best statement of President Nixon's own position, albeit in retrospect, is given in his foreign policy report to the Congress, *United States Foreign Policy for the 1970's: The Emerging Structure of Peace,* February 9, 1972 (Washington, D.C.: Government Printing Office, 1972), pp. 141-52.

Finally, since the Bangladesh conflict is still a relatively recent event, good treatment of various aspects of it may be found in journals such as *Asian Survey, Pacific Affairs,* and *Foreign Affairs.*

THE CONTRIBUTORS

James C. Carey, professor of history at Kansas State University, from 1948 to the present, has resided in Latin America for ten years with five years of this period being in Peru. He is the author of *Peru and the United States, 1900-1962.* In 1945 he served as a member of the city and provincial government for Callao, Peru.

Theodore A. Couloumbis was born in Athens, educated in Connecticut, and holds a Ph.D. from the American University, Washington, D.C. After service in the United States Army, he spent five years as an operations research analyst in the Department of Defense. At present he is associate professor of international relations at the American University. He is the author of *Greek Political Reaction to American and NATO Influences* (1966) and of numerous recent articles and congressional briefs.

Dennis Deutsch is a graduate of the University of Pittsburgh, 1971, cum laude with distinction in history. During the academic year 1971-1972 he attended the University of Pittsburgh, Graduate Department of History as a teaching assistant in Modern Israeli and Jewish history and received his M.A. degree, June 1972.

Ted Goertzel received his Ph.D. in sociology from Washington University in St. Louis in 1970 and is currently associate professor at Rutgers University. He is actively interested in group dynamics with special emphasis on student activism in the United States and Latin America. He has a textbook on political society.

Norman A. Graebner holds the Edward R. Stettinius Professorship in Modern American History at the University of Virginia. Among his many books the most recent have been *Manifest Destiny* (1968) and, with Gilbert Fite, *Recent United States History* (1972). He was educated at the University of Wisconsin—Milwaukee, at the University of Oklahoma and holds a Ph.D. from the University of Chicago.

Kenneth J. Hagan holds a doctorate from Claremont Graduate School and the bachelor's and master's degrees from the University of California at Berkeley. He is an assistant professor of history at the United States Naval Academy and previously taught at Claremont Men's College. He is the author of *American Gunboat Diplomacy and the Old Navy, 1877-1889* (1973) and a contributor to *Makers of American Diplomacy* (1973).

P. Edward Haley was educated at Stanford University and received his Ph.D. in international relations from the Johns Hopkins University in 1968. The author of *Revolution and Intervention: The Diplomacy of Taft and Wilson, 1910-1917* (1970) he received the *Premio Sahagun* award of the National Institute of Anthropology and History, Mexico, in 1970. He is on the faculty of the Claremont Graduate School.

Robin Higham received his Ph.D. from Harvard in 1957. Editor of *Military Affairs* and of *Aerospace Historian* and the author of *Air Power: A Concise History* (1972), he is professor of history at Kansas State University.

P. Wesley Kriebel, a native of Philadelphia, has been a commissioned officer in the Foreign Service of the United States since 1954. His assignments have taken him to the United Kingdom, Canada, and, most recently, two years of temporary duty on the Navy Staff in the Department of Defense and as First Secretary of the Political Section in the American Embassy at Seoul. At present he is assigned to the Office of Korean Affairs at the Department of State. He received his A.B. in political science and M.A. in international relations from the University of Pennsylvania in 1950 and 1951.

Donald J. Mrozek, a native of New Jersey, was educated at Georgetown University and received his Ph.D. from Rutgers in 1972. Currently he is assistant professor of American military history at Kansas State University.

William L. Richter is assistant professor of political science at Kansas State University, has been an American Institute of Indian Studies Faculty Research Fellow at the Institute of Constitutional and Parliamentary Studies, New Delhi. A South Asian specialist, he received his Ph.D. from the University of Chicago in 1968 and is the author of a number of articles.

Janice J. Terry is associate professor of history at Eastern Michigan University. She received a B.A. from the College of Wooster, M.A. in Arab studies from the American University of Beirut, and a Ph.D. in modern Middle East history from the School of Oriental and African Studies, University of London. Her publications include "Israel's Policy toward the Arab States," in *The Transformation of Palestine* (1971); coeditor of *The Arab World: From Nationalism to Revolution* (1971); and an article on Egyptian nationalism.

M'Kean M. Tredway is an academic adviser in the College of Continuing Education at the American University, Washington, D.C. He is a Ph.D. candidate at the University of Denver in international relations and has served with the United States Army security forces in Turkey and Germany.